TOM CUNNINGHAM PRESENTS...

JOURNEYS TO SUCCESS

VOLUME 5

22 AMAZING INDIVIDUALS SHARE THEIR **REAL-LIFE STORIES** BASED ON **THE SUCCESS PRINCIPLES OF NAPOLEON HILL**

JOURNEYS
TO
SUCCESS

VOLUME 5

Cover Photo Credit:

Shutterstock, Inc.

Image ID:187174106

Copyright: soft_light

Woman traveler looking at Batur volcano. Indonesia.

Table of Contents

Dedication

This book and the emotionally moving stories in it are dedicated to those of you who are feeling worried, discouraged and beaten down by the challenges that life has thrown at you.

You will find kindred souls within these pages. People who have gone through defeats and disappointments of all kinds.

You will find strength and courage to carry on and press forward toward your purpose and goals. You matter to us and that is why we share our lives and stories.

Never give up. Keep your thoughts focused and positive. We are cheering you on.

Acknowledgements

Dear Reader,

This book is for you.

Our hope is to light your fire to solve people's problems to help them achieve their goals so you can achieve yours. Truthfully, we're able to share our stories of success because we stand on the shoulders of giants who blazed the trail for all of us.

Napoleon Hill and his Principles of Success have stood the test of time. Hill has shown time and time again that there is a precise methodology for success. He dedicated his life to finding and documenting these seemingly elusive principles through fascinating stories in his books.

Don't take my word for it as the numbers speak for themselves. With over 100 million copies sold, Napoleon Hill's book, Think and Grow Rich, has helped create more successful people than any other book, ever.

A book on its own is just a book. A heartfelt thanks to Don Green and the Napoleon Hill Foundation team who tirelessly ensure new generations of entrepreneurs have the privilege and benefit of experiencing Hill's success formula.

If not for the passion, care, and commitment of Tom "Too Tall" Cunningham this book would not exist. In many ways, working with twenty-two entrepreneurs in collecting their stories and sharing their insights is like herding cats. Despite the challenges, Tom's persistence, patience and kindness made all the difference.

If a picture is worth a thousand words, there are not enough words to thank Brad Szollose whose passion and talent shine through in creating the cover of this book.

Many thanks to the Journeys To Success Publisher, John Westley Clayton, for his hard work and dedication to the authors and the book series.

And last, but certainly not least, are the twenty-two individuals whose stories fill these pages. Within these pages is a treasure trove of success insights, best practices, and lessons that pay tribute to Napoleon Hill's time proven Principles of Success.

Listed in alphabetical order are my esteemed authors who took their most valuable resource, their time, and dedicated it to sharing their stories for your sole benefit. Thank you:

Anne Beaulieu, Inez Blackburn, Andrea Blackley, Chuck Bolena, Jeffrey E. Feldberg, Tony Fevola, Mike Hecktus, Spencer Iverson, Piseth Kham, Santosh Krinsky, Peter Lepinski, Dionne Malush, Lisa Manyoky, Nathan McCray, Pam McCray, Paul Morris, Doug Parker, Jim Shorkey, Charles D. Waterman, Michael Watt, Tina Aurelio, and Roger Weitzel.

My Dear Reader, the next time you face a difficult challenge and wonder if you have what it takes, always remember the wise words of Napoleon Hill who wisely said that, "What the mind can conceive and believe, it can achieve."

And if you're wondering when you can start achieving, once again, Napoleon Hill said it best with, "Your big opportunity may be right where you are now."

Wishing You All the Success,

Jeffrey E. Feldberg

www.jeffreyfeldberg.com

Foreword

By Ivan Misner, Ph. D.

*"What a different story men would have to tell
if only they would adopt a definite purpose, and
stand by that purpose until it had time to
become an all-consuming obsession."*

— Think and Grow Rich by Napoleon Hill

I love a great story. One that tugs at my heartstrings. The book you hold in your hands is a collection of great stories. An opportunity for you to learn how everyday, ordinary people just like you and me achieve incredible success in the face of difficult odds.

Each person in this book has adopted a definite purpose and stood by this definite purpose until it became an all-consuming obsession and finally a fact. Please read each story. You will be glad you did.

I am the Founder and Chief Visionary Officer of BNI, the world's largest business networking organization. Founded in 1985, BNI now has more than 7,000 chapters throughout every populated continent of the world. Last year BNI generated 7.7 million referrals resulting in over $9.3 billion U.S. dollars worth of business for its members.

Wow! That is impressive. You probably think I am bragging, right? Candidly, I am. But here's the thing: I am so proud of each one of our more than 200,000 BNI members. I am so proud of each individual BNI leader. And I am so proud of each member of our BNI staff. BNI was built upon the shoulders of all of these ladies and gentleman. Thank you, Team BNI. I am honored to "brag" about your accomplishments.

I am the guy with a vision. But as the chief visionary officer, I am just one member of Team BNI. One of my jobs is to share my vision with each person in the BNI organization.

Another one of my jobs is a shared implementation of my vision within the entire BNI organization. I take both of these jobs very seriously.

*"Perhaps you do not need all that is to be found
in the book— no one of the 500 men from
whose experiences it was written did— but you
may need one idea, plan or suggestion to start
you toward your goal. Somewhere in the book,
you will find this needed stimulus."*

— Think and Grow Rich: The Publisher's Preface,
by Napoleon Hill

Great advice! I found my needed stimulus in Chapter 10 of Think and Grow Rich "The Power of the Master Mind: The Driving Force (The Ninth Step Toward Riches). This is eleven pages of reading. Please stop now and read this chapter before proceeding. What I have to say here will make so much more sense when you do.

I used this very powerful idea on day one with BNI. The mastermind is a vital ingredient in the recipe for our BNI journey to success.

*"The 'mastermind' may be defined as:
'Coordination of knowledge and effort, in a
spirit of harmony, between two or more people,
for the attainment of a definite purpose.'"*

— Think and Grow Rich by Napoleon Hill.

This spirit is how we came together for our first meeting, in Arcadia, California, December 1984. Joining me were Carolyn Denny, a C.P.A., Lee Shimmin, an insurance agent; and Mike Ryan, a financial planner, all of whom are still involved with BNI today. Four people in our first BNI mastermind. It was a simple and as big as that!

Our definite purpose behind this first mastermind was to generate more business through referrals. We never veered from this purpose. This was the sole reason why BNI came into existence, and to this very day, BNI maintains a constant focus on this one mission: referrals! This is our all-consuming obsession within the BNI organization.

In other words, helping business professionals grow their businesses one referral at a time through word-of-mouth advertising. Helping others is inculcated throughout the entire BNI organization. This is what BNI is all about.

I want to help you and each author in this book want to help you. It is what we are all about. We believe that you can do everything that we have done and even more. We want to encourage you. This is why we are sharing our stories.

Now there is a catch. There's always a catch, right? You must follow the principles that Napoleon Hill has laid out for you in Think and Grow Rich. At least most of them. Think and Grow Rich is a formula for success. A formula for your journey to success.

Admittedly, I did not follow each principle. I did focus on desire, faith, persistence, and, of course, the mastermind. The mastermind was a game changer for the BNI organization and the reason why we are the world's largest business networking organization.

The BNI Board of Advisors is another mastermind that we created in the early days. In its many incarnations since it was formed, the board of advisors has become one of the strongest leadership tools I could possibly have. The results have been much better than I ever could have expected.

"No individual may have great power without availing himself of the 'mastermind.'"

— Think and Grow Rich by Napoleon Hill

When I established the first BNI Board of Advisors, I did not foresee just what an important tool it would be in keeping BNI operating smoothly and responding to the needs of its members and leaders. The international board of advisors and the franchise advisory board are both vital to the smooth running of BNI, but lack the caring and personal touch of those close early relationships.

To compensate for this loss of one-to-one contact, I asked BNI directors to help me appoint a smaller, more personally connected guidance council, which was eventually named "The Founder's Circle." More than 90% of this group would be elected by the directors, the rest appointed by me. Members of The Founder's Circle would be my closest advisors, people I know personally or who, by popular agreement, had made significant contributions to the growth and operation of BNI.

*"This form of cooperative alliance has been the
basis of nearly every great fortune. Your
understanding of this great truth may definitely
determine your financial status."*

— Think and Grow Rich by Napoleon Hill

When our BNI story started at our four-person meeting in Arcadia, we never dreamed it would grow as it has today. Before we started this organization, I just wanted to pay my bills. My banker was funny about the mortgage on my house. He expected me to make a payment every month. Imagine that! So, I needed to bring in more business and I felt referrals were a great way to do this. Hence, the meeting that began all of this.

Perhaps you need a shove to get you started on your journey. Or perhaps a kick to get you restarted on your journey. Maybe you just need some inspiration to keep you on your journey. Whatever your path, do not give up! No way! Never!

Again, read each person's story in this book. Find the ones that really appeal to your definite purpose. Read these particular stories over and over and over again. I promise you will be inspired.

Be sure to notice that persistence is a key ingredient in each author's journey to success. Each person in this book had their "I have no idea what I am doing" on day one. We all did — and in the midst of tons of setbacks. Setbacks are a part of all journeys to success.

Each person's journey to success was accomplished one day at a time. Desire, faith, and persistence are common themes in each story. And of course, the mastermind is essential.

I wish you the very best on your journey to success!

Thank you!

Ivan Misner, Ph.D.

Founder of BNI

Testimonials

"Inspiring. Thought provoking. Engaging. Readers are immediately drawn into the nuances of these stories that ignite passion, self-reflection and action. Journeys To Success will inspire your next best step to achieving what seemed to be the Impossible Dream."

—Joanna Cheng
Life Coach

"If you've ever felt like giving up your dream, Journeys To Success will give you that guiding light and perseverance to stay in the battle and to win the war! Heartwarming stories of success and perseverance, which are much needed during the entrepreneurial warrior's journey."

—Kalvin Mizzi
Entrepreneur
Los Angeles, CA

"Journeys to Success is chock full of hard-earned wisdom. The stories synthesize and bring to life the principles Napoleon Hill organized then pioneered all those years ago. My favorite chapter from the book is from Jeffrey Feldberg. He really takes you on his journey of building an epic company where he bares his soul during the toughest transitions and exposes the emotional hardships of temporary setback. He shares the key insights that fueled him to persist until he succeeded...and that he did. Success is not a straight road and this book may be that beacon of light you need when you feel you're off the path, when reality you're about to make your greatest discovery."

—Bruce Wang
MICROJIG Inc.
Work Safer. Work Smarter. Build Your Dreams.

"The stories in this book reinforced for me how struggle and failure are most often an integral part of success, and not defeat, as most perceive them as. Each author demonstrated how desire, fortified with persistence, and backed by faith is often the formula to achieve any goal you set out to accomplish. Journey to Success is a must read, cover to cover!

—Andrew Lazarchik
Owner/Creator, Wildcat Championship Belts
http://www.wildcatbelts.com

"Journey to Success is a must read for the world we live in that delivers a message of hope and inspiration. Twenty-one authors share their stories of overcoming adversity with passion and persistence based on the teachings of Napoleon Hill - The architect of the power of persistence and a positive mental attitude."

—Kaplan Mobray
One of the world's most dynamic and inspirational business speakers and best-selling author of The 10Ks of Personal Branding.
www.kaplanmobray.com

Introduction

If you're reading this book, I'm assuming you're searching for how to take your game to the next level. Perhaps you're frustrated from not achieving your goals and don't know where to start or what to do next. Perhaps you've just come off a huge win and want to do even better the next time around.

You may not realize it, but whether you win, lose or draw, you, me, and the authors of this book, are striving for this one "thing."

This "thing" transcends every culture and has existed since the beginning of time. People spend a lifetime chasing this "thing," only to give up. Fortunes and empires are built and lost chasing after this "thing." The precious few who obtain this "thing" are celebrated by society.

Perform an online search for this "thing" and you'll find over 1,180,000,000 references.

Curious as to what this "thing" is?

I'll give you a hint; it's a seven-letter word.

Still wondering?

Wonder no more as this "thing" is otherwise known as:

Suc-cess:

1. **The accomplishment of an aim or purpose**
2. **The attainment of popularity or profit**
3. **A person or thing that achieves desired aims or attains prosperity**

First and foremost, let me be the first to congratulate you for investing in yourself with the purchase of Journey to Success, Volume #5.

Today is a new day and your personal journey starts ... NOW!

I have great news for you. You're not alone. You, me, and the authors of this book, are fortunate to stand on the shoulders of giants who paved the way to make success quicker and more obtainable than ever before.

Now let me ask you something.

What would you say if I told you that you'd be interviewing the most successful people of our time who will reveal the principles behind their success?

Sound too good to be true?

Read on see how truth is better than fiction!

Napoleon Hill, who in my books is the ultimate success whisperer of all time, was commissioned to interview over 500 of the most successful people of his day to find the secret of their success and make it available to the general public.

The brainchild behind this initiative was Andrew Carnegie who himself was one of the most successful business magnates ever, even by today's standards.

Hill dedicated his life to this mission. Two long decades in the making, Hill identified the success principles behind the success of the business titans of his day. These success principles were transformed into a proven formula that has stood the test of time.

And the results speak for themselves.

Napoleon Hill's book, Think and Grow Rich, has sold over 100 million copies and is credited with helping to create more successful people than any other book, ever.

While the language and stories in Think and Grow Rich may seem dated, don't let this fool you for a moment. The principles and methodologies behind success are timeless.

Case in point is the twenty-two authors of this book. Despite their varied backgrounds and differences, the common theme for the writers' achievements is the application of Hill's seventeen Principles of Success.

If you're feeling discouraged from your so-called 'failures,' know that you're in great company. Hill said it best: "most great people have attained their greatest success just one step beyond their greatest failure."

Often knowing what not to do is as or more important than knowing what to do. Trust me on this one; I've learned that the hard way!

Journey to Success, Volume #5 is designed with one goal in mind – helping you to maximize and achieve your success. In telling their stories, many never told before in public, the authors are paving the way for you to leverage their experiences and prosper.

Whether you read the book cover-to-cover or read only the stories that interest you, whatever you do, get started! Success follows known principles. Apply these success principles correctly, and you're well on your way to realizing and achieving your success.

But don't think for a moment that your success journey will be easy, as it will likely be the most challenging thing you ever do. Ever.

But just as diamonds form from incredible amounts of pressure over time, your journey will help shape and prepare you for the success that awaits you.

Hill tells us, "Desire is the starting point of all achievement, not a hope, not a wish, but a keen pulsating desire which transcends everything."

And if you're wondering where or how to start, the ultimate success whisperer, Napoleon Hill, shares that "your big opportunity may be right where you are now."

As you start your journey know that you already have twenty-two raving fans cheering you on.

So what are you waiting for?

Here's to you and your success.

Jeffrey E. Feldberg

www.jeffreyfeldberg.com

CHAPTER 1

Planting the Seeds of Prophecy

By Doug "The Duke" Parker

"Happiness is, being able to dream.
Success is, making them come true!"

— Doug "The Duke" Parker

Welcome Aboard the *Train Ride* called Life...

"At birth we boarded the train and met our parents. We believed that they would always travel on our side. However, at some station our parents will step down from the train, leaving us on this journey alone.

As time goes by, other people will board the train. They will be significant, i.e. our siblings, friends, children, and even the love of your life. Many will step down and leave a permanent vacuum.

Others will go so unnoticed that we don't

realize that they vacated their seats.

This train ride will be full of dreams, joy, sorrow, fantasy, expectations, hellos, brief farewells and goodbyes of forever.

Success consists of having a good relationship with all passengers requiring that we give the best of ourselves.

The mystery to everyone is: We do not know at which station we ourselves will step down. So, we must live in the best way, love, forgive, and offer the best of who we are. It is important to do this because when the time comes for us to step down and leave our seat empty, we should leave behind beautiful memories for those who will continue to travel on the train of life.

1

I wish you a joyful journey on the train of life.

Give, without expectation, lots of love and
aloha, and you too shall reap the bountiful
harvests of Success!"

— Author Unknown

(with adaptions by – Doug "The Duke"
Parker)

"The future is only as bright as your own
horizon allows. Make certain that yours is set
on perpetual expansion."

— Doug "The Duke" Parker

It has long been said that each one of us lives in our own personal universe.

Emanating from our very being and residing within us all lies an infinite expanse of untapped wisdom. Deep within this, is the core and essence of who we truly are. The choices we make, or fail to make, throughout this journey are what fosters this sagacity and defines us as the unique individuals we truly are. The beliefs, the morals, the character and integrity that takes root and shapes our lives. Leading us down the paths of life that we find ourselves upon.

"The crystal ball always appears clear
in the rear-view mirror"

— Doug "The Duke" Parker

How often have you said to yourself, or out loud for that matter, to a friend or loved one; "I will never do that, or never go there" only to find yourself some weeks, months or years later even, in such a situation or at a place you proclaimed that you would not be?

Irony in its purest form, or is it more? Personally, through firsthand experience, I have come to the valid conclusion that it is much, much more.

You most likely have heard reference of the French word déjà vu. I'm sure that many of you have felt or experienced this sensation of being somewhere or meeting someone before.

The lesser known, opposite twin to déjà vu is "jamais vu."

In direct translation, it means "never seen." However, as with most all linguistic renditions, therein lies a much deeper, hidden meaning. In the case of jamais vu, more aptly this explanation occurs, at least in my life, more so as a phenomenon. One of having a premonition of a place, situation or scene that as something based on our present perspective, we do not ever see ourselves as a part of. Rather than this becoming ingrained as to the never/forever. In all actuality, this becomes a seed that is first planted, if you will. Taking shape in the form of some type of mental resistance only to transform, along with each one of us in our own personal journey.

Over the years, I have come to truly believe that in the moment of time when we proclaim a "forever" to this or a "never" to that to our lives we are, in a sense, triggering a subliminal "jamais vu." Whereby this thought or belief is stored as this seed, deep within our subconscious mind, awaiting its own time and place to sprout, take root and enter itself into our life in the here and now.

"If you believe in yourself and never say never,
you can achieve whatever!"

— unknown

During the course, of the half century plus that I have had the good fortune to grace the face of our beautiful planet, there have been numerous times where I have said 'never would I' or for that matter, used the word 'forever'. Most of which have always led me to the exact self-described place that I had once proclaimed I would never be or, as the case may have been, forever be.

Or, as was instance with one of my first   NSN/NSF (never say never/never say forever) moments that I can recall was, while in no uncertain terms did I think so at the time. This would become an eye-opening experience that greatly assisted in my personal growth. One that not only expanded my young horizons, it would also propel me on my way into the unforeseen voyages of life.

"No matter one's age, take pause to see the world
through a child's eyes!"

— Doug "The Duke" Parker

While not aware of this at the time, I was bestowed with the good fortune of growing up in small town USA. It was your atypical farming community in the "Heart of the Heartland," a place called Tipton, Iowa. My formative years took root in an idyllic time and place. Most of all, it was one where boys could be boys and we kids were allowed to roam free. So long as we were home in time for supper.

At the ripe old age of 15, when I knew it all and the rest of the world was, well, just plain ignorant, my parents announced that my Father had been offered, and accepted, a promotion with his company and that we were moving to a bigger town some thirty miles away.

The reaction they received from me was – "That's great Dad, congratulations and good luck, but there is no way I can leave Tipton, this is where all my friends are."

My parents went along with my stubborn (read, narrow minded) teenage steadfastness to remain in our small town. Perhaps they foresaw something I didn't, as my desire to remain in my small hometown only lasted a few short weeks into my sophomore year in high school.

"My parents are amazing people.
The older I got, the smarter they got."

— Mark Twain

I shall forever remember the Friday one early autumn evening. As I arrived home in time for supper, I walked into the kitchen to greet my Mother. Immediately my senses informed me that something was wrong, very wrong. As across her face she was wearing this, one that only a mother can give, look.

Huh oh, I said to myself, this cannot be good.

My Mother proceeded to inform me that it was no longer up for discussion and that under no uncertain terms I was starting school Monday morning in Muscatine.

But Mom, what about all my friends, I futilely countered.

You'll make new ones, she firmly said.

But Mom, I pleaded.

No ifs ands or buts, as she picked up an envelope from the counter. "Son, your mid quarter report says you are failing every single one of your classes except gym class".

"Never say never and never say forever!"

— unknown

With that, I departed my small town, school classmates and lifelong friends and blindly embarked on the next chapter of my journey.

Going from a school with a few hundred or so students, to one with over a thousand and not knowing anyone, was a bit of an adjustment to say the least.

After a few fist fights and the normal teenage, new kid in school posturing. I quickly made new friends and in all actuality, started to like school again.

It took me round about a year to realize that moving to this new school and a larger town was the best thing that had happened to me so far in my young life.

"Life provides us with an endless supply of chances, opportunities and do-overs...
Regardless of one's age."

— Doug "The Duke" Parker

During the winters of the late seventies, mother nature delivered numerous full on blizzards that swept across the Heartland in roaring fashion. Many of which snowed us in for days on end. It was during these times that I began to sense that a new horizon was in store for me after high school.

It was the summer before my senior year, a buddy and I were planning a road trip to sunny California. Two days away from departure my friend, who had just graduated, received a job offer that required him to start immediately.

The thought of cancelling never even entered my determined, yet free spirited, mind. With an unsuccessful attempt to find a replacement, I embarked all by my seventeen-year-old self on a ten state, four thousand and some odd mile journey across the great American West.

During this journey to the left coast and back, I not only discovered that I had an incurable, to this day, case of wanderlust engrained deep within me. But more importantly, while away from my humble Midwest heritage, my eyes were opened to what a big, beautiful world it truly was that existed out there.

It was literally the trip of a lifetime. Inclusive of a few of the kind, while in California, that were made famous by a certain counterculture of that part of the world that began in the late sixties.

While the vibe I got from California and her people was as good as the scenery, beaches and vast Pacific Ocean were beautiful, it was lacking something. What, I wasn't sure as of yet, but it was certainly something. I just couldn't put a finger on it.

"The Farmer and the Rancher, by genetic code,
are the most independent, entrepreneurial and
innovative of all mankind."

— Doug "The Duke" Parker

The farm economy had taken a downturn for the worse in the late seventies. Interest rates were approaching twenty percent and times were tough. This had led me to the conclusion that my childhood dream of following in the footsteps of my forefathers and becoming a full on fifth generation Iowa farmer was not going to be.

Once I returned home from my expedition to the desert like climates of the west coast my senses informed me, upon feeling the humidity of an Iowa summer, of the where and what they wanted.

A locale was calling for me, one of which was more tropical. With that, after my senior year of high school, I set my sights on relocation, to the lands of palm trees and balmy air. The Sunshine State was calling for me.

"Dreams will only take you so far. It is in those
dreams however, that one can find the
inspiration that will propel you along the
never-ending journey, in your own personal
quest of Success!"

— Doug "The Duke" Parker

While I had heard the name, I was for the most part unaware of who Napoleon Hill was and what his teachings were about. It would be some years later before I discovered that many of my own thoughts and ideals that I had developed were in fact rooted in his philosophies. The first of his many prophecies that would shape my future began to take seed in my mind's eye was the next chapter in my life that awaited me. Most everyone in my family had a formal college degree. Myself, not certain with what I wanted to do for a career at this point in my life, had no such inclination and was more inclined to take things as they came or as often was and has at times been the case since, face life head on.

"Don't wait. The time will never be just right."

— Napoleon Hill

It was during the fall of my senior year when I received a phone call from a lady with a very pleasant sounding voice, who asked me if I knew what I was going to do with my life after high school.

Without missing a beat, I replied that I was moving to Florida.

Interesting, she replied. How does a career in the airlines and the travel industry sound?

Sounds pretty cool actually, tell me more.

She continued; It just so happens that I represent a college located in Kissimmee, Florida that provides degrees in travel and tourism. Your name has been carefully selected from a list of candidates to receive one of our limited admittances to our school.

(Read, a well-crafted, sales script to lure high school seniors who were uncertain of their future plans.)

Great, count me in, was my enthusiastic reply.

A wise choice young man. One that I promise will forever change your life for the better. As she continued, she told me that an enrollment specialist will be in your area in the not, too distant future. I will have them contact you to set up an appointment with you and your parents to determine which one of our curriculums would best suite you.

A few months later, on a cold January winter's night, an attractive woman by the name of Nancy came calling and, not that I needed it, sold my parents, more so than I, on the dream of not just attending school in Florida but more importantly, of the opportunities that awaited me in the travel industry after graduation.

It was most likely the easiest sale that lady ever made.

After receiving my high school diploma in May and a fun filled summer of working and partying. Before I knew it, the Fall of 1980 rolled around and I loaded up my Volvo and was off to Florida.

Without really, having any idea what was in store for me after my graduation, one thing I was sure of was that I would not be returning home to Iowa afterwards.

Upon receiving my degree, I received three job offers. One for a hotel in Cedar Rapids, Iowa, that without a shadow of a doubt, was immediately dismissed. Another was at a hotel in St. Petersburg, Florida. The third being in a place with a rather alluring sound to it, called Coral Gables, Florida, from a company that represented hotels in the Bahamas.

One quick glance at a map and seeing how far south on the Florida peninsula this place called Coral Gables was. It was my intuition that told me that this was going to be the place for me. So off I was to the Magic City of Miami, a place I had never been, nor without knowing a single soul, to commence the next chapter in my life.

Success is not some mystical destination, but rather a never-ending adventure of living, learning and of loving. One called Life!

— Doug "The Duke" Parker

Looking back, the two ladies who sold my parents and I on the travel school, were indeed correct. They presented it not only on the benefits of attending and what a degree would do for my future, but more importantly was their timing. This helped facilitate the dream I held of my future in the tropics.

Aside from the educational aspect of learning all about the many facets of the travel industry, what stood out the most from my time there was the emphasis that they put on personnel development and the importance of dressing the part. The one that has served me best on my journey, and another of Hill's fundamentals, is how developing and maintaining a positive attitude can have the most profound effect on our inner happiness and ultimately our own success.

"To truly develop a Positive Mental Attitude. One must also foster a Creative Mental Attitude!"

— Doug "The Duke" Parker

My first position in my new career was as a reservations agent, selling vacations to the Bahamas. Mind you, I had never been to the archipelago of seven hundred or so islands before, and would be engaged in selling a product for some several months before setting foot on her shores.

It was during this experience that I developed the ability to sell something without the benefit of having seen or experienced it, one that has served me well over the course of time since.

In a few short years, with a great deal of dedication, determination, perseverance and a bit of timing and luck, I had climbed the ranks through the travel industry. By my mid-twenties, I was Vice President and General Manager of one of the largest wholesale tour operations in the Southeast United States. Overseeing a multinational staff of over fifty people. Sending several thousand passengers a month to the Caribbean and various destinations across the globe.

By the end of my third decade, I had filled the pages of two passports, traveling to over forty countries. Best of all was experiencing the people and their cultures. Several of which become a second home in a sense, as my journeys took me to their shores, numerous times.

> *"In your travels, stop and check out the local*
> *craft markets. If you find the work to be unique*
> *and interesting, stick around and get to know*
> *the people, as you'll find them to be of the same."*

— Doug "The Duke" Parker

As I look back in time at that first never say never moment, when I thought I could never leave my small Midwest town when in fact, unbeknownst to me at the time, I was planting the seed of prophecy. It was the first of many "jamais vu" moments that helped open my mind to the many colors, cultures and people of the truly wonderful world it is that we share.

> *"Though we travel the world over to find the*
> *beautiful, we must carry it with us or*
> *we find it not."*

— Ralph Waldo Emerson

My own personal journey since my earlier years of adulthood has been filled with many monumental moments of success, as well as my fair share of so called failures. But then again, if one learns something from their mistakes and failures are they truly such?

*"Success is, going from failure to failure
without loss of enthusiasm!"*

— Abraham Lincoln

In our own personal quest of success, many a soul lose sight of what is truly important in life. Napoleon Hill was no exception to this. In fact, had he heeded much of his own sage advice, perhaps his life would not have been so tumultuous. Then again, who's to say that in these times of anguish and adversity, Mr. Hill did not in fact, garner himself with this indelible insight into life that has and continues to so benefit countless millions.

"We rise by lifting others!"

— Robert Ingersol

Many a word has been written by both Hill and countless others, on Hill's imparting words of wisdom and the indelible mark that those very words have left on the populace. Allow me to speak of the trials and tribulations that one of the greatest inspirational minds that this world has ever known, endured in his own life.

Hill's most famous and arguably best work "Think and Grow Rich", a book that has sold over 100 million copies and continues to direct and inspire to this day (if you haven't yet delved into this great read, I urge you to do so at once). Unfortunately, due to a divorce settlement from his second wife, Dr. Hill reaped virtually none of the financial rewards from this work.

*"Failure is nature's plan to prepare you for
great responsibilities."*

— Napoleon Hill

Of all his anecdotes of success and motivation, none it seems, was so endearing to Hill as the birth of his second of three sons, Napoleon Blair (11/11/1912 – 8/31/1975). You see, this fellow came into this world, born without ears. Rather than lament on the doctor's prognosis that his son would neither be able to ever hear or speak, Hill took a vow that his son would lead as normal of life as possible given the circumstance.

Often met with great consternation from the various administrators of the schools that Blair attended, Hill and his first wife, Florence, did not relent. Through this conviction, was great reward. Blair turned his handicap into his own life-long mission. He provided hope and relief to people who suffered from this ailment of being deaf mutes and subsequently through his devote upbringing and as testament to his own perseverance, Napoleon Blair Hill, helped thousands transform themselves of their handicap and go on to lead fulfilling lives.

"A formal education can earn you a living.
Self-education can earn you a fortune."

— Jim Rohn

Truth, in the sense of the words, as expressed by the late Jim Rohn, (9/17/1930 – 12/5/2009) another of the Twentieth Century's great motivational and success inspiring minds. If by chance, you are not familiar with or better yet, a student of his teachings. I urge you to become one at once. You will be well rewarded.

Caveat Emptor – Don't Become a Self-Help
Junkie!

The past several years have seen the landscape become littered with an over proliferation of so called, "Self Help Gurus." Most of them claiming some sort of miracle will occur in your life if you just buy their books and invest your hard-earned money in their alleged systems.

Not to say that there aren't ones without merit and worthy of your investment, of time and money. There are, simply do your due diligence and do not buy based on emotion. The sad truth of the matter is that there are the immense proportion who are simply – "All Hat and No Cattle." An ole favorite cowboy expression of mine, meaning; (adjective) A pretentious type that is all talk and delivers no substance nor action in whatever it is that said individual begets.

"One can seek the best advice from the greatest
of advisors... However, often-times the best
advice I've found, comes from within."

— Doug "The Duke" Parker

Hi, my name is Doug and I'm a "Self-Helpaholic."

Speaking as a voice of experience, a few short years ago, I found myself caught up in the "Hamster Wheel of Self Help."

Yes, I had become a "Self-Helpaholic."

Like most all addictions one can develop in life, it began innocently enough as a mere curiosity. Before long, it had festered into a full blown addictive obsession. Watching webinar after webinar, listening to recording upon recording. Spending more and more of my precious time and money on the alleged, so called, latest and greatest.

"Everything happens for a reason in life.
Whether it seems like it at the time or not. It is
always for the best."

— anonymous

The defining moment occurred one afternoon when I had put off work once again, to listen to another interview. This one resonated differently than the countless others. The interviewee spoke on how one small powerful word could change my life for the better.

The Power Of... No!

Upon the close of the interview that day, I immediately proceeded to implement "The Power of No" into my day to day life. Breaking my habit of previous mention, honing my focus and best of all, delivering the most transformational of results.

Fortunately, unlike other dependencies that can render one helpless, penniless, homeless or in jail even. My Self-Helpaholicism is one that has opened my mind to a whole new level of conscious being. Exponentially expanding my own personal universe. The greatest blessing bestowed upon me from this not too long ago experience has been the introduction to some of the greatest minds that inhabit our universe today (Yes, that includes you).

Of all the things, we hang onto in life, so far,
the best thing I've found is... Each other!"

— Doug "The Duke" Parker

Thank you for joining me on this short chapter of my own, never ending "Journey to Success." It is my hope that, wherever you are at on your own personal expedition, that your "Seeds of Prophecy" bless you with many a bountiful harvest, as you continue to "Think and Grow Rich" and most of all, savor and enjoy every precious moment on this, the "Train Ride Called Life!"

In closing I'd like to share with you another of my favorites…

"Tomorrow is the most important thing in life.
Comes to us at midnight very clean. It's perfect
when it arrives and it puts itself into our hands.
It hopes we learned something from yesterday."

— John Wayne

Photo Credit David Joseph Portraits

Doug "The Duke" Parker | Bio

Doug "The Duke" Parker is an Actor, Author, Adventurer, Coach, Consultant, Emcee, Key Note Speaker, John Wayne Impersonator, Marketeer, Motivator, PSIA Certified Ski Instructor and a Voice Over Specialist. He is also the General Manager of the Midwest's largest marine specialty construction companies.

It is quite possible that there is no one else alive today, that has the look, stature and sound that so closely resembles that of John Wayne.

While his credits don't quite rival that of The Duke's over 170 movies just yet, Parker does have his fair share of acting and voice over accomplishments. His credits include, over one hundred fifty commercials and training videos. A half dozen or so feature films, numerous stage productions and countless voice-over gigs.

Spanning some thirty years, his Public Speaking and Emcee credits include everything from beauty pageants to large corporate conventions. Doug is no stranger to the entertainment scene.

He enjoys, an active life style in relentless pursuit of his passions which include surfing, skiing, stand up paddling, scuba diving, hot tubbing, hammocking, and a couple of successful jumps from a perfectly good aircraft.

After two dozen years in the urban jungles of South Florida, five Aloha filled years in Hawaii, capped by a stint surfing North County San Diego. Doug, while going through another of life's transitions, decided that it was time to return to the Heartland and repay the favor of a great childhood, by ensuring that his parent's "Golden Years" are just that.

Look for his next, soon to be released, books - "Called to the Big Island – The Mana Runs Deep." and "Into The Eye of The Storm".

Doug would love to hear from you and may be reached at:

563-260-2120 – 14

TheDuke@gmail.com www.TheDukeLivesOn.com

CHAPTER 2

For The True Love Of The Game

By Anne Beaulieu

In a small-town countryside elementary school, it is recess, 10:00 am. I am in first grade and I am determined to play hopscotch. Earlier, I found a skinny stick on the ground, perfect for etching proper squares in the dirt. I want them all to be perfect! If they are, then maybe the popular girls in my class will like me more. Not accepting the way I am drawing my 'crooked' lines, I blame it on the skinny stick and erase my work with an angry foot. Story of my life.

With a heavy sigh, I look over and I am met by rejecting eyes looking back at me. My loneliness consumes me, no kid my age seems to want to be my friend. I feel their contempt for me, perhaps because I come from the white ghetto, that place where second-hand clothes are bought in church basements and overbearing adults look at you as if they 'know' you will 'never' amount to anything.

I observe the pretty blonde girls with their high pony tails and fitted blue jeans; I believe I am nothing like them. From their pinched nostrils, I get that I am not welcome here any longer, so I drop my skinny stick, and start walking the chained-linked perimeter fence of the school. I wish I could escape my life. My six-year-old body already knows that I have nowhere to go.

At home, I am most often greeted by muddy pigs and glassy cows' eyes. I live at the end of a dirt road and the other day, I got blocked again by the neighbours five sons. They are a bunch of muddy teenagers who tower over my scrawny little body the same way my father and brothers do.

I am afraid of them, they drag me to their empty barn, they tell me to keep quiet, I see a row of metallic chairs. Is there a show? I don't understand. I don't want to. They make me stand in front of them, one of them pulls down my blue cotton shorts along with my white little panties. I can feel my cheeks burning red, I tell myself to keep looking at the ground. I want to cry but am too scared to cry. I want to leave but am too scared to make a move. So I escape to that familiar place within me where the burning pain fades away, where I feel almost nothing, where I think no one can ever hurt me again.

Like my father, maternal grandfather, and many others, these boy-men let me go when they are done with me. I run down the hill, naked, how did I get naked? I forget, I cannot think straight, I want to forget, I need to forget.

I reach the corner of my house, I stop. Suddenly, I am tasting salty tears on my cheeks. I quietly put back on my white panties, white t-shirt, and blue cotton shorts, in that order. I try to comb my entangled hair, but my hands are shaking. I tell myself, "Stop crying! Stop shaking! This is all your fault. Stop! Stop! Stopppppp!"

And just like that, I become cold again. I am 'tough', just like that. I stare at the old house I live in, with rats crawling inside the non-insulated walls. Anywhere seems better than this place. I wish to play hopscotch outside for a while, but I believe my squares are neither proper nor perfect. I wipe my tears and resolutely walk inside the house.

I am nine years old now and from the little I can catch from other kids my age, I seem to be the only one in my class with a mother who believes she is pregnant with Jesus Christ. She often asks me to touch her belly, she says there is a baby in there, but I see no baby at all. I do not understand why the six of us (my three brothers, two sisters, and I) are not enough for this woman with the brown glassy eyes. She scares me when she stares at the wall, eyes fixated ahead, or when she grabs me tightly by the shoulders, saying she will never go back to the mental hospital, whatever it takes.

I look at my mama and I want her so much to love me. You know, she pretends to be my friend sometimes. She says she loves me and she even pulls me into a hug and kisses my forehead, but then she lets my father touch me. Like my paternal grandmother, she keeps telling me to stop making men like him want me. Crooked squares.

What has happened to just being a kid
and playing hopscotch at recess?

Never mind my question, my father is angry again and I need to pay close attention to him. Maybe I did not pile the wood correctly. Shit! It seems I am unable to appease him no matter what I do. It is as if within him burns a frozen anger that can turn little children into dry icicles. I stay clear of him as much as I can. As soon as I notice his forearm muscles twitching or a change in his nostril breathing, I run. I run internally anywhere, but really, there is nowhere to go.

In my house, running away from a slap, punch, or kick will endear you later with a spanking or beating. Like my mother says, "I am punishing you now for all the times I have not caught you and punished you. You have nowhere to hide, do you understand?" Maybe it was then that I decided hopscotch was a stupid game with stupid rules for stupid people; I believed I would never win that game.

Sitting at the top of the stairs one night, away from and close to my father at the same time, I hear him talk to my mother. He refers to me as the "hole waiting to be filled". I coil up listening to his words, with my arms tightly wrapped around my skinny legs. I am now twelve years old and I am thinking there has to be something deeply wrong with me. What other explanation can there be as to how I can make someone else so angry? Maybe the high pony tails in first grade were right all along. Skinny stick, skinny legs, I just cannot seem to do anything right.

Ahhh, but then I score an A+ on a test and the teacher praises me for my intelligence. I am intelligent! Maybe this is the way out of my misery. I am smiling. I believe it is.

I graduate from high school at sixteen and enter university right away. By the age of twenty, I have a B.A. Translation, by twenty-two, an M.A. Economics. By my late twenties, I am a CFA (Chartered Financial Analyst). I become a cash management specialist, finance economist, mutual funds expert, options trader, Assistant Vice-President, and so much more… all by the age of twenty-six. Look at my squares now, high ponytails!

Married and pregnant with my first child, I chuckle at the graying portfolio manager in front of me, towering over my mahogany desk in his cold blue business suit. He is yelling at me for forcing him to sell at a loss the sub-AAA grade commercial paper he had allowed the purchase of in the first place. His anger leaves me cold, seemingly unaffected, for I have already seen so much worse in my life. Like me, he must learn to suck it, play by the rules, and accept that the squares sometimes do not line up for some.

You see, I have created my own game of hopscotch now and I intend to win it. Eyes fixated ahead, I am focused on writing perfect numbers inside perfect squares. By now, I have 1 husband, 1 driver, 2 maids, 3 children. 4, 5, 6, 7 become the digits pulled together as the money we make and bring home. My squares look pretty perfect to me. Many people view me as a success story. My husband and I are pulling in a truckload of money and we think we are happy.

I do not talk much about my past. I want to show the world that I truly belong, so I fight, I fight every day. I fight for my husband's approval, validation, and love. I fight to be liked by my co-workers and approved of by my boss. I fight for my perfect squares.

I am now in my early thirties and spend most of my time between Hong Kong and Shanghai. I walk with a flashy red Hermes purse on my arm and dark Gucci sunglasses on my nose. I love my beige Prada sleeveless dress; it matches what other ladies are wearing for High Tea at the Peninsula Hotel.

Through sheer will, I have reinvented my whole life. No one can tell I was ever the girl with the skinny stick etching imperfect hopscotch squares in the dirt.

Fast forward ten years. Someone rubbed an angry foot at my perfect squares. My marriage is crumbling and we fight too much! He travels too much and I spend too much time alone. I become a 'too much' mom in an attempt to prove I am not a total failure. I register my three children in ballet, violin, pottery, swimming. I keep their schedule tight so I have little time to think for myself. At night, I go to bed exhausted. I feel more alone than ever. Crying into my pillow, I ask myself, "Who will ever be there for me?" I am not realizing yet that I have an emotional hole in my heart that no money, no person, or thing can ever fill. My squares, perfect or not, are empty.

I sink into a dark depression and file for divorce. I am 40 years old. On an already skinny frame, I lose another 25 pounds in less than 3 months. Getting up is too hard and I often puke in the shower. I only have to drop a spoon on the floor and start uncontrollably sobbing. I stop picking up the mail or answering the phone. I am frail, falling apart, and I am scared shitless to lose the kids.

Over the next few years, I somehow gradually start picking up the pieces and realign my squares. I put the lost weight back on. I reduce my daily coffee intake from seven cups to three. On one beautiful spring day, I decide to attend a business seminar led by Dov Baron.

I watch him standing on stage.

"Who are you hurting by playing small?" He asks.

I do not like what I am feeling. Something in me is uncomfortably stirring, something long forgotten, something that is howling in pain.

I manage the nerve to ask Dov if he will mentor me. "What do you want most in your life?" He asks during our first session together.

"I wish to have a deep loving relationship with me." I answer.

He looks at me with piercing blue eyes.

"Are you clear?"

"I am."

He smiles and asks, "Who are you without your intelligence?"

I do not understand the question; I am asked to keep pondering it and come back to see him the following week.

Five months later, I decide to apply to the Authentic Speaker Academy for Leadership (ASAL) led by Dov. I want to become an authentic speaker.

First boot camp, second day, early morning, Dov asks me to talk in front of the class about a painful story from my childhood. I agonize immediately. What is the conveniently right thing to share?

I carefully choose to tell about the time my father tried to break a solid pine chair on my back for saying no to him. I was seven. I tell the class I wondered how many bones will break and if I will survive this blow. In my head, that anecdote was far better than telling them how I saw my father kill my kittens by smashing their heads onto a flat rock in front of me or that time when he carved a whip out of a winter tire to beat us with.

When I finish talking, I look blankly at my coaches and fellow classmates. Many seem horrified. I retreat deeply into myself. I want to cry, I want to leave, but somehow I know this is the safest place I have ever been in my entire life, so I stay.

Dov walks up to me. His eyes are the bluest I have ever seen. They are big, wide, and piercing. In his eyes, I see a lot of softness and also what I think is pain. I am puzzled, why the pain? I think I must have displeased him. I knew I should have told a more 'normal' story! I am sad, I believe more than ever I cannot do anything right.

He plants both feet firmly on the ground in front of me, and he asks me the weirdest question ever:

"What is the lie?"

I do not get it, what does he mean by that? I start panicking, I am now feeling like a self-loathing piece of shit. I want to leave, I want to stay, and I want to know what the hell he means by 'What is the lie?'.

He is relentless, he keeps asking me, "What is the lie?", over and over for days. I am tired, I am not hungry anymore. I am highly anxious by day and I have severe nightmares at night. I keep crying, I am looking more and more like a ghost. He never gives up on me.

I want him to tell me the answer to his question, but he says I need to figure it out for myself. He keeps me spinning and spinning inside my head until everything begins to swim and something in me finally cracks open. In that moment, I see for the very first time that I was not truly feeling, I just thought I had been feeling all along. That was the lie!

20

I had been living a lie!

Here I am, believing I had been feeling all my life when, in fact, I was reacting to life from my head! I was shut down! This is why the people in that classroom seemed horrified. I had been preaching for years that I was a deeply feeling human being when, in fact, I had very little compassion for me or the child inside of me. Oh my God!

> *Just like in the movie The Matrix, Morpheus*
> *had given me two pills*
> *to choose from and I had just swallowed my*
> *truth.*

So much started to make sense. Having spent decades trying to please others, living vicariously through my children, using money and my brain as a shield, I did not know who I truly was. I did not know my own heart!

This meant that who I am had been deeply buried under all the feelings and emotions I had shut down as a child to survive my crazy environment. I was as unconscious as one can be.

My ego-mind could not accept this truth about myself. If I accepted my truth, this meant I accepted having lived 45 years of my life highly unconscious. It was too much for me. All my rage came out in a tsunami of shit.

Memories violently awoke! Memories of being sexually abused, emotionally tormented, physically beaten. Days and nights, I cried. I cried out of rage, anger, sadness, sorrow, despair, and hopelessness.

I knew I did not have me because I did not know the real me.

In my mind, I believed I was massively screwed up and everyone should stay away from me. I, who had spent decades building the perfect image, was now reuniting with this deeply wounded child within who thought she was a worthless piece of shit.

Dov often says,

"The truth hurts before it sets us free."

A repeat from the past, I lost 20 pounds in less than 3 months. Frail again, I re-live the devastation in my life. The nasty divorce, the toxic relationships with the men that followed, my lack of a genuine loving relationship with my own children and one with myself.

I had nothing, nothing real, because I did not have me. I did not truly love me for I had so little compassion for me.

It is often said,

"Once we know we cannot unknow."

I could not unknow. I burned all my bridges, threw all my relationships to the ground. In my self-consuming rage, I was lucid enough to know that if I did not have me or a loving relationship with me, then my whole life was a joke, an illusion, a tragic tragedy. I was done with this shit.

I wanted the real deal with me.

Every week, I sat on my mentor's couch. In his wisdom and kindness, Dov started modelling what a healthy relationship with the self looks like.

"What do you need right now?" He asked.

I looked at him, shy, eyes on the ground. No one had never really asked me what I needed before.

"I need a glass of water," I answered nervously.

"Then give yourself a glass of water."

By giving myself what I needed, I started slowly healing the little girl inside of me. She had been crying for my love and attention for decades. I am pleased to say that **the child within has genuinely become my number one priority.**

Like in all magical stories, on a beautiful autumn day, about nine months after having made that first crack into my thick ego walls, compassion for myself was birthed and began trickling in.

I was taking a walk and I saw a yellow leaf dancing in the wind in front of me. I gazed at it, smiling in awe. It was so beautiful in its simplicity. It was living, it was dying. It was breathing, it was falling, it was life!

I burst into tears, this leaf is just like me. As I walked into my mentor's office that week, he could see the light starting to shine in my eyes. He smiled and simply said,

"Now the true work can begin."

I started forgiving myself for what I do not know.
What I do not know I do not know.
The same is true for others.

I started forgiving my father, maybe he had a mother who did not love him and this is why he did not know how to love me.

I started forgiving my mother, maybe she had been molested by her father too and this is why she did not know how to stop others from doing the same to me.

I started seeing myself in the homeless' eyes, maybe like me, they knew they might not have a home in their heart too.

In this space of forgiveness and not knowing, I went looking in my heart for the little skinny legs who once upon a time held a skinny wooden stick in her hand.

I want to play hopscotch with her, for the true love of the game.

"Now what?" I asked Dov.

"You have burned your whole life, you got your wish," Dov answered. "You have a choice. You can rebuild the same shit into your life or you can do something different."

Sitting in front of him, I did not know what to do with my life. I had officially been putting my life coaching career on hold for the last 1.5 years. I had stopped coaching because I believed it was wrong for me to coach anyone if I did not have a genuine, loving, caring relationship with myself first.

I am crystal clear. If I coached anyone in a wounded state, I would just be healing myself through them. No, I had done enough damage already.

"What do you love to do?" Dov asked me.

"I don't know, I love to write. When I was a kid, I told myself stories until I fell asleep."

"Then write, become a storyteller."

Still not knowing if I had what it took to make it as a storyteller, I picked up my skinny stick and started drawing imperfect lines. I started sharing my story.

Strangers on Facebook started befriending me. At first, they were trickling by 5 or 10 online friendship requests a day. Soon, they were 25 to 50 a day. Where did all these people come from? What did they want from me? Didn't they know I was screwed up? Maybe they did, maybe this is what attracted them to me.

Maybe people just see themselves in me.

Over time, thousands of people have come and are now forming a loving and supporting community with me.

This is new for me, being loved for no reason.

In my life, one of the hardest realizations I have had to face is the following:

If I do not know who I truly am,
then I do not know what love is, how to love,
and how to be loved.

I had very weak emotional boundaries and weak emotional boundaries are loveless for the self (therefore for others) as they lack compassion for within.

To truly know Love,

One has to have a deep relationship with their self.

One has to commit to knowing their self from the inside out.

On this discovery journey, I feel I am just taking my first steps.

"Why me? Why so much pain?" I asked Dov one day.

"So you can be a guiding light for others like you," he kindly answered.

I nodded gravely. I was now 45 years old and

I had finally found my life purpose.

I started a blog, a simple blog, with no real marketing promotion anywhere. Within 8 months, it had over 25,000 visitors. In my storytelling journey, I share my hopes and dreams, my moments of despair and my joys of clarity. I have since then become an internationally accredited Emotional Intelligence Coach and have proudly graduated as an Authentic Speaker.

I am learning to feel the true love of the game.

On a beautiful morning in October 2015, I woke up and looked at my dog. He suddenly seemed bigger, a lot bigger. I thought I was having a problem with my vision. I decided I needed some fresh air.

I stepped outside and saw a lamp post. It looked as if it was closer to me, like a popped up image in a children's book. Everything around me seemed vibrant with colors. Tears going down my face, all I could say was,

"Thank you, thank you, thank you."

More weeks went by and I started hearing what I now affectionately call the music inside the notes.

It is an incredible feeling to be vibrating notes
of love
and feel the world vibrating the same notes
within us.

I am now feeling the flowers, trees, grass, and... people! I am hearing children's laughter even though there might not be any children around. For those of you familiar with what is called the dark night of the soul,

I have emerged on the other side.
I have stopped consistently being in survival
mode.
I am now learning to embody the love
vibration.
I am Love
Also known as 'The Lady Who Smiles at
Flowers'.

Let's face it. We all face defeat at some point in our life.

"Every adversity, every failure, and every
unpleasant experience
carries with it the seed of an equivalent benefit
which may prove to be a blessing in disguise."

— Napoleon Hill

I have been asked many times if I would change anything in my life if I could go back in time. My answer is the same every time: 'No!'. Everything that has ever happened to me has made me who I am today and I love who I am deeply.

> *I now understand*
> *My sorrow carves my joy.*
> *Forgiveness and inner peace are the born*
> *children of compassion for the self.*

Personal development work is lovingly holding two little skinny legs gently in our heart.

Today I trace perfectly imperfect squares and I smile. I am an adult in the school of life and I am here to learn as well as to teach. My squares no longer need to match and numbers are just that, numbers. What matters most to me is my internal happiness.

> *I get that I am the only person in my life*
> *who spends every minute of every day with me.*
> *I am the only one who can make me truly*
> *happy.*

So, hold my hand, walk inside with me.

Let's play hopscotch together,

For the true love of the game!

On this loving note, did you know the game of hopscotch is played around the world? Fascinating, isn't it?

Anne Beaulieu | Bio

Anne Beaulieu is an international speaker, empowering coach, and thought leader in the field of Emotional Intelligence and the Founder of Walking Inside Resources Inc. As an accomplished author and community builder, Anne is a powerful catalyst for positive change and embodies successful life strategies that keep empowering men and women across the globe every day. She has become a transformative influencer on social media by sharing openly her personal struggles and daily insights in order to give voice, uplift, and inspire anyone who has ever felt responsible for everyone and everything in their life. In Anne's own words: "I empower people to become the leader of their own life, the leader of their thoughts, feelings, and decisions." Anne can be reached at anne@walkinginside.com, www.walkinginside.com or by phone at 778-888-4507

CHAPTER 3

Determined Decision

By Peter Lepinski

As an Executive & Business Coach I get to work with a lot of high performing executives and business owners. One common trait of those who are successful is that they do two things. I relate well to those two things.

When I was a young boy I was not what you might call the picture of health. I had severe asthma and was often hospitalized starting on and off from the Fall through to Spring with Winter being the severest of the seasons and summer being the best. My asthma was so severe that I came close to dying a number of times, but thankfully, the ambulance service were able to get me to a hospital before that happened. I missed a lot of school and I failed grade 7 because in that school year I was hospitalized on and off for more than six and a half months. It was during that year that I started thinking my life would not amount to much of anything other than chronic asthma limiting me in what I could do. Then in the Spring of that year, I got really mad and made a decision. That one decision made a significant difference in my life.

I was in the hospital looking out a window at some kids about my age playing down on the street yards below, knowing that I was going to fail the year in school and that I would have to repeat it next year. I would say I was emotionally at the bottom of the barrel. I sat there watching those kids for quite some time and as I watched, a change started happening. I longed to be out with my friends playing and the more I thought about it the more determined I became to not be sick the rest of my life. It was during that time, watching those kids, that I made a decision that I would never, ever again spend a day in hospital for this miserable illness and that this illness was not going to control my life. Since that Spring I have only been in a hospital for a knee operation and that was for only 5 hours and 45 minutes. Going into the hospital, my two goals were to get my knee operated on and get the hell out of the hospital. As a note, I walked out without crutches as well being the determined person that I am.

It was that Determined Decision that started me on my road to health. I started developing a clear vision about how that would look in my life, how my life would play out going forward. I spent a lot of time thinking and planning my next steps and then setting very clear goals. After all, I had nothing but time on my hands while I remained in the hospital. I then started the learning process. I asked incessant questions about Asthma to my Doctors and other people I knew who currently had or previously suffered from Asthma. One of the things I found out was a belief that you could outgrow Asthma. I am not even sure if that is the case but at that time I believed it was possible to change my health and life.

Having that strong belief, and a vison of what the future could be, with the help of my parents and doctors we embarked on a journey that became successful and I achieved my goal. A few years later I joined the military after twice being refused because of my previous history with Asthma. I could go on more about this story but I only use it as the prelude to what I really want to talk about.

In order to be successful you have to be determined to achieve your vision. I meet many people that talk to their vision of what they want but fail in it being so much a part of them that little else matters. Once you have a vison and make a determined decision to achieve it, your whole existence and purpose works towards achieving that vision.

When I decided to become a Business and Executive Coach I decided to join ActionCOACH. There are many positive reasons I decided to join them and I won't get into that here, but I will tell you about one of the many thing I learnt. I learnt a formula that I bounce around in my head constantly and I want to thank Brad Sugars for showing me this formula. It goes like this:

$$\text{Dreams} \times \text{Goals} \times \text{Learning} \times \text{Plan} \times \text{Action} = \text{Success}$$

When I saw that formula up on the screen, I immediately connected it to what happened to me in the hospital. It all starts with making a Determined

Decision to go in a very specific direction. (When I use this, I subconsciously change Dreams to Vision)

Napoleon Hill in his book Think and Grow Rich says "You are the master of your destiny. You can influence, direct and control your own environment. You can make your life what you want it to be." This is true all the time. We all have access to many resources and support systems. But nothing will start until you make that Determined Decision to create a change from where you are today.

When I work with people, or am hanging out with friends they often say about my goal; "Well that's fine but if the vison is unclear the goal is just really a to do rather than leading to a Determined Decision which results in the Vision or Dream.

There is one more important and powerful idea about achieving your vision that I learnt along the way as well, and that is that you must have a WHY. Your vison will only be as powerful as your WHY. My WHY when in hospital was to never lose another day of my life to asthma and to live every day the way I wanted. It's the WHY that keeps that determined decision going. Your WHY has to be absolute and you need to keep it top of mind at all times. It's what will drive you to take the necessary actions to achieve your dreams or vison.

Once you have made a Determined Decision and have a clear Vison or Dream you want to achieve and you possess a strong WHY then you have to set clear goals that will lead to your vision. I know most people know that goals have to be S.M.A.R.T. (Specific, Measurable, Achievable, Realistic and Timely), and that is very true. I often find that people set goals that are vague and not measurable or they are simply To-Do lists.

Say for example you want to increase your personal wealth and establish a passive income. You may decide that you will do this by purchasing or investing in businesses or rental income properties. A goal that you may use for that is:

"I will start 2 businesses in the next 18 months". That is Specific, Measurable, Attainable, Realistic and has a Time Frame. To achieve your vision, you have to focus on your goals. In other words, focus on the input and the output will come. I see too many people focusing on the outcomes and get frustrated, when if they simply focused on the inputs they would achieve their desired results.

Now that you have your goals set, what do you need to learn. You may need to learn details about the type of business you have in mind to start up. You may need to learn how to become more of a CEO rather than just a business owner. You may need to learn how to hire good managers. You may need to learn who are the potential customers and is there any other competition and if so what are their strengths and weaknesses. The list can go on and on. Failing to learn can often lead to frustration and disaster.

The next phase is then to get to the tactical portion of achieving your Dream or Vision. The detailed Plan. This is the To-Do List, or rather the To-Achieve List. This is where you detail the activities that need to take place to achieve your goals. This should be as comprehensive as possible, detailing who will be responsible for the activity and when the activity is to be completed. Next is the actual execution of the activities. Only then can you hope to be able to achieve the success you want.

In my case with my Asthma I unknowingly followed this process and that is why it smacked me in the jaw the moment I saw it up on the screen. It put a process to the way I went about achieving my Vison of staying out of the hospital. Now this model sits at the back of my mind and as I look to achieve my Visons and Dreams I use this process as I go forward in my life.

A few years ago while I was at a 90 Day Planning workshop I was holding for my clients and other interested Business Owners and Executives I was thinking about how out of balance most business owners or Executives work and how they accomplish all the things necessary to achieve their results. I came up with this model.

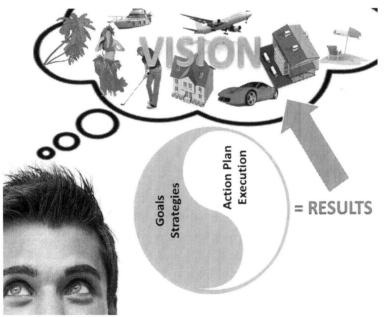

First and foremost, you need to make a Determined Decision and have a burning desire to achieve your Vision. The next steps are to set clear S.M.A.R.T. goals, and develop the strategies to use to achieve your Goals.

Strategies are often misunderstood. Let's for example say that the Business Owner or Executive wants to increase overall revenue in their business or departments. Often I hear; "I will do more marketing". Marketing in itself is not a strategy. Executing a flyer campaign, door knocking, advertising on television, etc. are marketing strategies.

Now you have your Vision, and Goals and have decided on your strategies to achieve them. Now comes what I call the Great Divide. The great divide is between the Goals and Strategies and the Action Plan & Execution of the plan.

Think about this: How many people do you know that go to their business or company and turn on the lights and just start doing stuff? I know many and at times I have even done it myself. Walk in, turn on the lights, grab a coffee and just start doing stuff. A good indicator that you are doing stuff is at the end of the day you say to yourself that is was a busy day but I really didn't accomplish a lot. That thought is a sure sign you are doing stuff. Lots of activity but very little productivity.

Then there are those that may have a to-do list and execute the STUFF on the list thinking they have been productive. No, you just got the to-do list stuff done.

Many of my clients are in either part. Some are excellent at the Vison part of the business and if you are the Business Owner or an Executive that's definitely where you need to be. I always say the Owners and the CEO are responsible for the Vision of where the business or organization is going. Those Business Owners and Executives are usually running good companies and they engage people like me to help them move their organizations to a higher level.

The second group I meet are the ones that are good at the Goals and Strategy piece of the Great Divide. They can set goals and develop strategies and even the Action Plans, but lack the ability to ensure accountable Execution. This group often lacks passion and quite often are frustrated because of lack of results. The reason for that is that they are just working, not working for something that they want. Simply wanting a lot of money is not a Vision. It's the WHY that matters. Why do you want a lot of money? What can you specifically envision doing with the money? Details friends Details.

When you put all of that together you get harmony, and your business or life is in balance which delivers the Results that achieve the Vison.

There is one more part to all of this. I mentioned that you first need to make a Determined Decision about what you really want and have a clear understanding of WHY you want it. That's the driving force. The next part that comes into play is the discipline to do the work and keep it in place.

Take for example a person who wants to lose weight. They set goals for dieting and exercising and then lack the Self Discipline that will get them there.

Better yet, making a Determined Decision to live a different lifestyle will be more impactful. The Vision could be to lose 50 pounds in a year and maintain that weight. By setting clear goals (i.e. 1lb a week) developing Strategies and Action Plans will assist greatly in the actual Execution that is required to achieve the Results you are looking for. But this can go the way of the Dodo Bird if you do not have the discipline to make that happen.

Once I made that Determined Decision years ago, I unknowingly used these principles to achieve that Vision of not being hospitalized and instead to be out living in the world and playing with my friends. There was one other part that I did during my journey, and that was to get other people involved. I told everyone who would listen, and those who probably didn't want to listen, about what I wanted to have happen. I told them with a Determined Resolve that I was not going to ever go back into the hospital for Asthma. What happened was that I got people on my side. Not only may parents, friends and Doctors, but many other people who I came into contact with including the best athlete in the school and a person who became a great mentor to me in my early years. It was with getting the help of a village of people to my cause that helped me achieve my Vison.

When I made that DETERMINED DECISION some 40 plus years ago it absolutely consumed me. Every action I took and every decision I made was with that Vison in mind of staying out of the hospital. I would get on the bus once a week for 3 years to go and get an allergy shot. I hated needles but I was determined to get out of the poor health cycle I was previously in. I started running everywhere, even if it was just a few steps. I would run rather than walk. I played sports all the time and hung out with the jocks in school.

There were many other things I did to put my mind in the place it needed to be and to get my body in a healthy state. It all started with a DETERMINED DECISION to change my life.

Peter Lepinski | Bio

Peter Lepinski was born and raised in Regina Saskatchewan. After a life-changing episode, Peter describes in his chapter of this book, as a teenager he joined the Army Cadets and then at the age of 16 joined one of the Militia Units. Shortly after High School, Peter joined the Canadian Armed Forces and became a professional soldier. At that time Peter served almost 3 years and decided to leave the military to further his education.

Peter had married by then and moved back to Regina where he worked a full time job and attended classes at night, returning to the Canadian Armed Forces after University.

During his reenlistment service, Peter honed his leadership and organizational skills in the Canadian Armed Forces, serving with and leading NATO member troops in areas around the globe. As a veteran, Peter entered the corporate business world and achieved significant financial results and operational effectiveness for the business organizations he worked for. In his corporate roles Peter has filled various management and leadership positions and he has been responsible for up 220 million dollars of company business. Additionally, during the mid-90's, Peter owned his first small business.

In 2009, Peter became a Certified Business Coach and opened an office in Grande Prairie, Alberta bringing business coaching to the Grande Prairie market. In 2012, Peter also became a Certified Executive Coach. Currently he is the owner and senior partner in Business Innovation Group Inc., working with business owners and leaders in growing their businesses and lives. In addition to running his business, Peter is a published best-selling author, he does public speaking engagements, seminars, workshops and is an active volunteer member in the community, currently holding the position of Club President for the Rotary Club of Grande Prairie After Five Club.

Presently, Peter has been nominated to serve on the Canadian Forces Liaison Council, (CFLC) whose mission is to support reservists in Canada – especially to have job protection when they deploy.

Peter can be reached at 780-538-4699 or peter@bigbizgrowth.com

CHAPTER 4

The Unyielding Power
of a Positive Mental Attitude

By Lisa Manyoky

"Whatever the mind can conceive and believe,
it can achieve."

— Napoleon Hill

When I was a kid, I was quiet—maybe even shy. I did not like being quiet, but at that time in my life, I was uncomfortable. I had short, poker-straight hair that always looked as if it had been trimmed with nail clippers. I wore un-stylish white cotton socks to school because I was allergic to polyester. I wore sensible shoes, thanks to my mom's high regard for responsible footwear. I also had the kind of classroom smarts that earned me the nickname "The Brain."

I would much rather have had long, flowing hair that I could curl and braid. I would have preferred wearing burgundy, nylon knee socks with trendy footwear like the other girls. And I would have chosen popularity with boys over straight A's, flawless penmanship and precision with markers.

I tried to work around my "deficits." I let my hair grow long and used enough Dippity-Do to fill an oil drum, but it would still never hold a curl. I defied my allergy and wore polyester socks until the itch became unbearable. Mom eventually gave me a little wiggle room when it came to shoes, but she never let me wear clogs! All the while, my grades remained off-the-charts good, handwriting flawless, and artwork excellent.

My mother assured me that I would appreciate my "gifts" some day, including the results of wearing sensible shoes, but I was not too interested in her vision for my future. I just wanted to fit in. So, I became the consummate observer of people—a bit of a backgrounder—secretly pining for what I did not have and watching others to learn how to get it.

Then came soccer, which gave me an unexpected nudge up the social ladder of acceptance. Until the early 1970's, soccer had been available locally only to boys. Now there was a league for girls. For whatever reason, my father—who was not always happy in our home—decided to head up a team and insisted I join. I did, and I loved it. I was good at it, too. How fortunate that when it was time to play soccer in gym class at school, I scored goal after goal. To this day, I remember the look of shock on the faces of my classmates, who regarded me only as the smart girl with blow-the-curve grades. They wanted ME on their team. Kicking a ball in a net changed their perspective, and mine, too. I got a taste of feeling included, and I liked it.

"Happiness is found in doing, not merely possessing."

— Napoleon Hill

So I kept playing soccer. And then I played softball. And then I ran track to keep in shape for soccer and softball. I excelled as an athlete. I got confident. I made peace with my intelligence and managed to cope with polyester and uncooperative hair. I became known for my artistic ability. I transformed into a social butterfly with a knack for reading people, especially when they were feeling "uncomfortable." That sensation was all too familiar, so I was quick to pass along compliments, acknowledge others for something meaningful to them, or invite them to come closer when I saw them recede into the background. This became a way of being that is still my way of being.

By the time I was a sophomore in high school, I had great social momentum, until I came home from school one day to my mom's announcement that my father had unceremoniously packed his bags and left. This was a crushing blow, and yet not a total surprise. We knew he was unhappy, but divorce was uncommon back then. I was embarrassed. The isolation that came from feeling "different" reared its ugly head again.

To add insult to injury, my father was the president of a school bus company that had belonged to my mother's family. Since NJ was a no-fault divorce state, all my parents' assets—including the business—would be split 50/50. My mother had the option to claim her father's company OR our house, its contents, her car and $200,000. She was bold. She knew that if my father were in control of the business, then he would also be in control of our money. Leaving herself vulnerable to his authority was a risky and unpleasant proposition.

So, on September 28, 1981, my mom called for a meeting of the board of directors, which included her father, my father and the corporate attorney. Just before that meeting, however, my grandfather sold my mother his share of stock, making her the controlling owner. After the transaction was complete, she and the lawyer went to the bank to revoke my father's banking privileges. They reconvened at the office, where my mother promptly fired my father. Yes, my mother fired my father!

To make matters worse, we had to leave our home and give up everything in it but our personal effects. Worse yet, my father used the $200,000 of his settlement to open his own school bus company in the same township, making my mother his competitor, vying for the same work.

This is about the time I recognized a new sensation: a ferocious intolerance of unkindness. I did not like the spiteful decisions my father was making. The law entitled him to half of what we owned, but as far as I was concerned, it did not grant him the right to be reckless with his family. As his frustrations mounted, he lashed out. He hired a sheriff to photograph and inventory every item under our roof—and I mean everything. He put our house up for sale. He took my mother to court regularly. He loaded conversations with tricky double entendres—obvious only to those he intended to hurt. Eventually, I tired of his behavior and the vigilance required to speak with him, so we stopped talking altogether.

My mom, on the other hand, was remarkable. She was a 42-year-old housewife who became a full-time school bus company owner overnight, with peripheral business experience. She was gutsy but nervous, so she appealed to the employees, admitted how little she knew, and promised that if they helped her, then she would do her best. All but one employee stayed. They were loyal to my mother, and she upheld her promise to them in return. She cultivated a respected reputation in her industry and succeeded.

"Faith removes limitations!"

— Napoleon Hill

My mom beat daunting odds. She secured a mortgage despite her 20+ years as a wife and stay-at-home mother. She figured out how to simultaneously manage a household, raise three kids and run a business she had to learn fast. She served dinner on paper plates with plastic utensils at a card table with lawn chairs on plywood flooring for a long time because my father kept most of our belongings. Even so, we had some of our best laughs at that table.

Through my mother, I learned the might of a positive mindset and the beauty of reciprocity. My mom showed me that despite gut-wrenching fear, refusal to succumb to its muscle would deliver the resources needed to accomplish her goals. She taught me courage, tenacity and grit. She showed me that you could lead with kind authority, that generosity paid huge dividends by default, that defying the odds offered rich rewards, and that faith really did move mountains.

Although my lifestyle growing up was dramatically different from that of my friends—and most assuredly not one I would have chosen—it turned out better than OK. My mother made it so. She rose to the call of challenge, even during times when she was afraid. I remember her saying many, many times: "Everything will work out. It always does." It was not lip service either. She believed it, and her faith in a good outcome let me believe there would be one, too. There always was.

> *"A quitter never wins and a winner never quits."*
>
> — Napoleon Hill

For the most part, life moved along nicely. Looking back, there is no doubt that my unconventional upbringing, the influence of a legacy of entrepreneurs, and my mother's strength shaped who I would become. I became unafraid of taking risks and was willing to defy norms, and wrongful authority, and the odds.

Even though I had the grades to pursue medicine or law, I went to college for art, but a "starving artist" I would not be! I insisted on pursuing a career that would not only give me the ability to earn a good living but would also offer me the freedom to work from home when I became a mother—my greatest aspiration. The introduction of the Macintosh computer made design a profession that was attractive to me, and it was something I could do from home. Voilà!

Upon graduation, I landed a job as a designer at an advertising agency in Princeton, NJ. Although my employers treated me well, I knew after only six months that I was built to be independent. I left to launch my own design consulting business with high hopes, determination to succeed and zero clients.

At 24 years old, I was on my own in a number of ways, many days with a pit in my stomach but still committed to my goal of running my own business. Thankfully, clients came seemingly out of nowhere. People I needed to propel me toward new opportunities "showed up" with impeccable timing. Business ramped up fast and never slowed down. When I met my husband and became a mother, it gave me the freedom I sought to be a hands-on mom.

*"Set your mind on a definite goal and observe
how quickly
the world stands aside to let you pass."*

— Napoleon Hill—

As hoped, motherhood went superbly well. Oppositely, marriage did not. On the morning of March 26, 2006, my then husband of almost 13 years took our kids to school, came home, announced that he had a "light bulb moment" the day before, realized that I was not the woman of his dreams, and was leaving. For an instant, I thought he meant for work; he meant for good. He then packed up his shaving kit, threw a few belongings into a garbage bag, put his house key on our dining room table, and left. He had already emptied our home of all his other belongings. He saw an attorney only days later and sued for divorce within a month. His terms were demanding and his timeline aggressive.

I was devastated. I felt stupid. I had promised myself that I would never marry a man who would do to his wife and children what my father did to his. Now it seemed as if history was repeating itself—with a vengeance. Sadly, my husband did not act alone. He collaborated with (and ultimately married) my close friend of almost 30 years.

Two people I loved blindsided me and my children. I knew how my kids felt because I had lived an almost identical experience myself. I also knew I had to help them believe that life would be wonderful even though their father chose to live elsewhere.

Being deserted by a parent can halt emotional growth in its tracks, unless someone steps in to fill the gaps the absent parent creates. My mom taught me how to accomplish this feat when I was a kid, but her lessons eluded me when I found myself in her position decades later. I was too raw with betrayal and grief. I cried plenty as I struggled to manage my emotions and, at the same time, insulate my kids from my fears, meet a demanding schedule of business deadlines, run a household alone, keep up with expenses minus my husband's income, pay alimony, organize a congested calendar of kids' activities, and deal with the merciless process of divorce litigation.

I felt like life was pinball, and I was the ball. I was overwhelmed by overwhelm. Thank goodness for my mother-in-law's unforgiving but loving reality check one summer evening, only months after my husband left. Usually mild-mannered, she scolded: "Lisa, your mood determines the mood of the household. Those kids will follow your lead. They need you to be happy. Get happy."

In short, my mother-in-law told me to spend less time licking my wounds and more time figuring out how to preserve my kids' morale and restore joy to our home. I could not believe my ears! I had the right to be upset! I defended that right and accused her of not understanding how I felt. Surprisingly she agreed, but went on to say that it did not matter. She insisted that I get a grip, stand my ground where I could, fight to protect my livelihood and…get happy.

With a singular comment, my mother-in-law shut down one circuit and tripped several others. My ferocious intolerance of unkindness kicked in. My mother's permission to defy lit up. My business wheels started spinning in new directions. The lessons of a lifetime merged into purpose. And Mama Lion roared!

"If you are ready for the secret, you already possess one half of it, therefore, you will readily recognize the other half the moment it reaches your mind."

— Napoleon Hill

With new perspective, I put my business head in charge of my personal life. I sensed that litigation would be brutal. The upcoming months would require energy, smarts, humor and lots of support.

I became a quick study in family law. I recognized the limitations of a legal process that was structured to be expedient, not fair. I also discovered how ill-prepared the court was to determine a reasonable divorce settlement between two self-employed people whose ethics, business models, career choices and professional performance standards were worlds apart. I had to negotiate my own deal to minimize fallout. That required extraordinary willpower when emotions were charged, stressors oppressive and stakes high. It demanded learning to live with a less-than-ideal agreement that would last for the next fifteen years. Even so, with eyes wide open, I assumed the lion's share of custodial and fiscal responsibility for my three kids who were seven, ten and eleven at the time. I also made sure that the deal I made could not be revisited or changed every three years, which NJ divorce law permitted. My lawyer warned that a non-modifiable decree was risky—it would deny me access to any benefits my husband might gain after divorce. I dug in my heels and proceeded with my plan anyway. I believed that my lifetime of high performance and sound ethics would deliver me what I needed to take care of my children. More importantly, I did not want my husband to ever be able to ride the coattails of my diligence again. It was a big pill to swallow, but I gulped. I have never regretted my decision.

My resolve was firm and ongoing, yet I felt alone and lost many times in the months that followed. Thankfully, those times never lasted long. Throughout my entire divorce ordeal, my mother and my in-laws remained my champions and allies. The rest of my family reached out with cheer frequently. Friends arrived at my side when I was tired and stayed until I caught my breath. Longtime colleagues lent a compassionate ear day or night. Clients were patient when I needed extra time for deliverables. My martial arts pals pushed me to exercise my body to keep my mind sharp. I earned my first degree black belt the same year my husband left and my second degree belt a few years later. I became proficient in kumdo (swords). I lost familiar sources of income through no fault of my own but found others to replace them. I saw a marriage counselor alone to help cope with my losses and to ensure that I was doing right by my kids as they coped with theirs. I mastered the art of keeping my cool during stressful dialogues. I appreciated my gifts, which gave me the ability to find my way during dark days. I found my people, and my people found me.

When I think about how my life has unfolded so far, its path makes a credible case for every one of Napoleon Hill's 17 Principles of Success. Like many, I endured unwelcome hardships, but…

"Every adversity, every failure, every heartache carries with it the seed of an equal or greater benefit."

— Napoleon Hill

My marital lifequake became the pivotal catalyst for important change. Once the dust settled after the divorce—which was over and done with in 10 grueling months—I began to feel a relentless, intuitive push for a career shift. I sensed that my collection of professional skills and life lessons were part of a bigger career picture. I could not see that picture clearly, but there was no mistaking that change was essential and prescribed. I had a big problem, though. My design career was a known quantity that provided the income I needed to raise three active kids. I could not shut down business, find a new "thing," cross my fingers and hope for the best. So I decided to explore new opportunities while continuing to run my design business, which was exhausting.

At first, I thought I would write a book about coping with life while managing a contentious divorce. However, the further behind me my divorce became, the more I wanted to leave it there. So I kept searching.

I became certified in life coaching, but it did not feel quite right. I got trained in relationship coaching for singles, but it was more personally beneficial than professionally. I became authorized to administer DiSC® personality assessments, but it felt like a small part of the big picture. I hosted a radio show for singles, which was a great adventure but not the professional home I sought. Then, I took a graduate coaching course called "The Neuroscience of Success" with Dr. David Krueger from Houston. I was fascinated by the topic and immersed myself in learning about the neuroscience of mindset and its effect on performance, relationships and communication. I became licensed by Dr. Krueger in his specialty-certified coaching system, which blends neuroscience, psychology and quantum physics with coaching. Most recently, I pursued certification by Dr. Judith Glaser from New York in Conversational Intelligence®, which is based on the neuroscience of conversation, connecting and building trust. Ah, yes!

> *"Persistence is to character of man as carbon is to steel."*
>
> — Napoleon Hill

At this point, the stars aligned and angels sang. I figured out how to integrate my personally and professionally developed understanding of people, communication, words, brainpower, behavior, aesthetics and energy—with kindness as a rudder—into a career focus. I found a singular purpose in their collective impact and developed "The Presence Equation: Look good. Sound good. Be good. Do good.

This integration felt right. It drew from my expertise in branding and design as well as a huge personal inventory of empathy, a hunger to spare others from the isolation of feeling invisible, and the ability to articulate my lessons for them with a bright spirit and a unique command of words.

I remember how lousy it felt to not have the impact I sought when I entered a room, and I know how good it feels now that I do. The Presence Equation is my way of helping others develop presence if they do not have it, refine it if it is weak, or repair it if it is not working at all. It is a powerful system of discovery, exercises and coaching that helps people understand and manage what they put out there—whether visible or not—so they can achieve personal and professional goals more efficiently.

Looking back, I am not sure I would have chosen some of the challenges that came my way, if given the option to bypass them. However, I would not trade in the results for the world. Life has worked out not in spite of these difficulties, but because of them!

You see, those "backgrounders" I treated kindly remembered. They told me so, and many are close friends to this day. Our friendships remind me of the long-lasting power of noticing someone and extending a gesture of kindness.

My hair is short, but I found my cut. I outgrew my polyester allergy, too. And, for what it's worth, I live down the street from a shoe store. The brothers who own the business are the sons of the man who sold my mother sensible shoes. My feet are in great shape. The store inventory now appeals to the sensible shoe owner as well as the trendsetter. I am still a customer.

I have been paid handsomely over the years for my handwriting, and I made a career out of art.

My intelligence was a gift after all. My degree in design from Rochester Institute of Technology gave me an unparalleled foundation for combining creative skills with technology. I attribute my fast success to these early studies.

I achieved my greatest aspiration and became the mother I dreamed of being. I was spared a discontented spouse and raised three amazing kids mostly on my own. They are happy, currently in college or college-bound, and flourishing.

My father's penchant for tricky dialogue taught me the power of words—spoken or written. To date, my command of words is a driver of business. I insist on speaking the truth with tact—always—and teaching others how to do the same. (By the way, my father was diagnosed with leukemia when he was 49 years old. After a lengthy estrangement, I resumed a relationship with him and ushered him through to his death at 50. I got answers to my questions and made peace with him before he died.)

Throughout divorce litigation, I lived the importance of deftly managing spoken and written expression and negotiating with poise in the face of unfavorable conditions. I remember the bitter taste of adversarial communication and learned how to neutralize it fast. I also recall how miserable it felt to wake up every day to involvement with people who were not my people and how to cope until I was able to extract them from my life. These memories continue to generate feelings that fuel my business initiatives.

My in-laws became part of my family head count. Their unflagging dedication to me and my children made tough times more bearable and good times better. Every child should have grandparents like these two.

My mother is 77 years young and feisty. She runs her School Bus Company to this day. She is my hero who loved deeply and gave me the permission to defy, that which did not serve me, even when defiance meant hardship. She assured me that "everything would work out." It did.

Life WAS like pinball. I WAS the ball. But I had control of the flippers after all. The gross injustices that threatened to consume me lost their power when I decided they could not have mine.

Had I known of Napoleon Hill as the years unfolded, I would have been comforted by his principles. I inadvertently followed them without knowing they existed.

Hats off to you, Napoleon. You laid the groundwork for the deliberate pursuit of a rich life. I, as a woman who is devoted to your beliefs, vouch for their integrity, merit and effectiveness. Thank you.

"Life delivers if you let it. It delivers faster if you believe wholly that it will."

— LISA MANYOKY

Lisa Manyoky | Bio

Lisa Manyoky is a firecracker of a personality who is the developer of "The Presence Equation: Look good. Sound good. Be good. Do good." Lisa is known for her acute understanding of the visible and invisible information exchange between people that constitutes presence. She has made it her mission to help others develop, refine or repair theirs. Her energetic focus on the domino effect of presence draws from a lengthy career in graphic design, a series of personal challenges, the grit it took to raise three kids mostly on her own, and a longtime immersion in the neuroscience of mindset and communication. She has integrated a suite of disciplines and an altruistic approach into a service that helps others identify what makes them tick; set goals; recognize and make good use of their own natural assets; close the gaps between desire, intention and perception; and find their rightful place in their world and THE world.

Lisa is also the proud mother of three kids who keep her tire treads worn and her heart full. She is a loyal friend to many, a champion of underdogs, the "words maestro," and a bright spot in every room.

Lisa can be reached at lisa@ThePresenceEquation.com.

CHAPTER 5

C.H.A.N.G.E. Can Change Your Life

By Andrea Blackley

The summer of 1999 came to a celebratory end with the receipt of my Marketing degree from Xavier University in New Orleans, Louisiana. At the age of 9, I had a strong desire to become an OB/Gyn., just like Dr. Heathcliff Huxtable from the Cosby Show. Growing up in a single parent home, I was constantly inspired by the illusion of that lifestyle. I figured that becoming a doctor would help that dream to come true. I eventually discovered that my dislike of biology in high school would become an even greater irritation once I got to college. As a Freshman at Xavier, the lectures, tests, study sessions, etc., screamed BORING to me, so I did what seemed to be a popular collegial occurrence, I changed my major to something where I could be more social and study less. After two semesters of being "tortured" by forcing myself to do what I had no passion for, I spent the remaining six semesters, including three sessions of summer school, earning my Marketing degree. Finally, it was time for the REAL world.

My induction into the world of responsibility came in my first professional career, as a branch manager trainee with Enterprise Rent-a-Car. Primarily, this was a fun venture and I saw myself being promoted to a manager one day. I was enthusiastic about driving the company's cars, especially the new ones. I loved the challenge of having the highest sales for the Damage Waiver because it was always a healthy competition amongst other trainees and sometimes came with bonuses and privileges. Additionally, having my own medical insurance made me feel like a "big girl," and I was feeling that I was on the right path towards a secure adulthood. After about a year, I realized that I wanted to do more than just rent cars. I was not clear on what exactly that I wanted to do, but I was vividly unblemished about what I did not want to do any longer. Once the emotional connection was severed between the employer and I, it was time to call it "quits." As an eccentric soul, I did not turn in a two-week notice, I just left; it was the end. Next move!

Interestingly enough, the next chapter of my life was as a bill collector. HA! Yes of course I had collectors calling me too, so naturally I was pretty good at squeezing that dollar out of consumers' hands, on 30, 60, and 90 day late accounts, because I felt some sort of compassion since I was also being pursued by collectors. Once again, after about 13 months of this mundane routine, I felt no growth. I felt stuck and dumbed down, so I gave my two-week notice with Foley's corporate offices in downtown Houston, and decided to become a teacher. I had been running from the educational field, because that's what the majority of my family was doing, and of course I wanted to be different. Destiny, however, had her turn, and the 3rd grade classroom would become my next career, with the Houston Independent School District, in August of 2001.

I never thought that I would be called Ms. Blackley on a daily basis, by 7, 8 and 9 year olds, but it happened. I cannot say that I loved it, but I was elated to have weekends off and finishing work by 3:30 pm. Teaching, nevertheless, caused me to grow. So much so that I earned Teacher of the Year fir 2003-2004, in my first year teaching the Gifted and Talented students. Although it was an incredibly humbling honor, I was yet to be fulfilled. Additionally, I was five years out of college, 3 years into teaching, and things were not adding up for me financially. I had gone to college and earned a degree, but where was the big money? There was no desire to go back to school and get another degree, because the loans for the 1st degree were already creating nightmares. There had to be a better way. That was the thought that was penetrating every fiber of my being...there HAD to be a better way! After becoming teacher of the year, what is next? That accolade did not increase my pay, but it did add to my credibility. Credibility was not paying any bills however, and I needed more income and to be more fulfilled.

On June 9, 2005, I was blessed to become the mother of a beautiful son, Nicholas Colin King. Although his father and I were together, we were not married. By choice, I became a single mother of this beautiful new life. My mind was constantly thinking about how I was supposed to take care of my son AND myself, when I was already struggling to take care of just me? As a parent or guardian, the responsibilities that come with parenting are not only astronomical; they are often times unexpectedly expensive. I was only familiar with single-parenthood because of my upbringing; however, I did not see myself as a single parent. Fantastically enough, I have always been naturally resourceful. By default, I became an entrepreneur, selling handbags and jewelry, tapping into my undiscovered entrepreneurial side. My mom used to always tell me that I would never be broke because I relentlessly found ways to bring in money when absolutely necessary. I had yet to understand my innate ability to simply think differently.

It was April 22, 2008...I had just been hired for my 2nd job with Nordstrom in the Houston Galleria, while wrapping up my 7th year teaching. As a single mother of a now 2-year young boy I asked God, "HOW am I supposed to teach for 5 days a week, work a part-time gig for 4 days a week, and be a mother to my young son?". To me that meant NO TIME OFF...EVER! At the same time I knew that I had to do something. The answer I received to my HOW, was to JUST DO IT! It was just like the loud voice that I heard in the parking garage of Nordstrom on a Sunday after church, while I was alone that clearly said, "Get a job at Nordstrom!" Luckily no one saw me having a very brief conversation with "the voice", that I knew to be God, because I then began to challenge that instruction. "What do you mean?" I said, receiving a very stern silence in return. I had no other choice, considering this was definitely a divine assignment, but to listen and act. I will save you from the details of every step of me getting the job, but I would be remiss if I didn't mention a few of them. The application process online was like applying for a secret service position for the President. Considering I was doing this while in the classroom, I had to manage my time to get it done, including a personality test. Amused by the requirements, I remember saying, "Sheesh, this is just for a retail position...they need all of this?" I followed through and upon the submission of the application, within about 3 hours; I received a response for an interview. That blew my mind, because I figured it would take some time to evaluate the personality exam, amongst everything else. The interview was set for the following Wednesday at 11 am. I agreed before even asking my principal. I was completely honest with her when I asked for the time off for the interview. All I will say is that when things are meant to be, and divinely orchestrated, nothing will get in the way. Dr. Patricia Allen had my class covered and the rest is HERstory. Although I had no idea at the time, this would be a life-altering occurrence. April 22, 2008, was absolutely the beginning to the next phase of my life.

For many years, recess for my students was also recess for my imagination. I would often find myself daydreaming about what I could be doing to better spend my time. As the cars drove by, I wondered who was in them and where they were going, and why they weren't at work. I never wanted holidays and summer breaks to end because those were my only doses of freedom. However, once I added Nordstrom to the equation, there weren't any more free days. There were only 7 days of non-stop, high volume and high impact human engagement...a mixed equation of teaching, learning, and sales. Talk about an overload, but for some reason I was excited about it. I believe that a partial cause of the excitement was due to the fact that it was the total opposite of teaching 8 and 9 year olds how to develop higher standards for themselves. Also, I am a fashionista, and I looked at this as an opportunity to be creative in my wardrobe, while simultaneously being artistic with my clients' jewelry and watch selections. It was similar to shopping for me, with their money, and then allowing them to borrow what was really mine. I know, it sounds weird, but it worked for me. I was intrigued by building a clientele and being able to aid women who effortlessly spent hundreds and thousands of dollars, based on my opinions and suggestions. It was a fun assignment but subconsciously the experiences were planting seeds of wanting more for myself. The innocence, at that time, was that I had no idea what the subconscious mind was and I was unaware of the power that it had to initiate creation. The mystery of operating in a positive unknown, can open up new worlds to those who are in position. It's rather sensational!

One Friday during the mid-afternoon, a professionally dressed, rather handsome gentleman walked through the store, strolling past my department in a brisk manner. He was looking in the direction of my co-workers and I, but didn't make any contact. Then suddenly, he disappeared. A fellow associate, who was much younger than I was, was so captivated by his presence that she wouldn't stop talking about him. She repeatedly asked with passion, "Where is he?". I must say that it was somewhat amusing, because I was totally disinterested in the situation, but she kept bringing it up by asking her question. Some time went by, I am not sure how long it was, and I was working in my assigned jewelry bay with my head down doing some inventory. Suddenly I heard, "Hi, my name is David!" Those 5 words on June 13, 2008, yes, Friday the 13th, were the catalyst of a day where I actually felt my life change, and I had no idea what was in store.

The conversation between David "I Believe" Imonitie and myself was the initial stimulus that allowed for my new growth to take root. He introduced himself skillfully and began to investigate what Andrea Blackley was all about. Undoubtedly, I wanted to give the perception of being more than a sales rep, so I mentioned a travel business that I had invested in, and shamefully had done absolutely nothing with it. What are the chances of him being a part of the exact same business? He would never know whether I was active or not, right? WRONG! He was affiliated with the very same company and began to ask me all of these questions that had me looking like a deer in headlights. "Uhhhh," seemed to be the best answer that I could give him, as he soon realized that I was putting on an unnecessary front. Fortunately, that did not deter him from asking for my information so that we could keep in touch. I exhaled, but concurrently, I was somewhat embarrassed by not knowing what I was talking about when it came to that particular business. On my way home that evening, I reached out to him, because I was curious. I wanted to know if I had my hands on something that could literally change my life, and was he the one to accelerate that change. That conversation led to a meeting 7 days later, where I was officially introduced to the industry of Network Marketing. He also shared something called personal self-development with me and told me that a commitment to it can give you a brand new pair of eyes. Of course, I was clueless to what that really meant, but I would soon find out that it was now time to see things from an altered perspective and go to places mentally first, and then learn how to turn my imagination into my reality.

All of my life, reading was like a disease that I did not want to catch. I didn't like books. I always fell asleep reading. If I had any books, they had never been read. Bookstores were a waste of space to me. In school, elementary through to college, I always found a way around reading; yet, I still received nothing less than a "B," in a class that required it. Even becoming an educator did not encourage me to change my outlook on the book life. All I knew was that I would rather do just about anything else but read. That was my unapologetic truth, until David familiarized me with audio books. YES, I can LISTEN to the words and not have to read them? Now I could do that. Nonetheless, an additional challenge presented itself when I was only used to listening to music in my car, not someone talking to me. Considering the fact that I consider myself an excellent student and follower I began to listen to these words of growth, mental stimulation, and prosperity, and gradually, things in my life began to change. My mind launched new ways of thinking. Beliefs that I had grown up with were now being challenged and disputed. The conversations that were now of interest to me were void of meaningless chatter and full of huge visions and possibilities. On April 22, 2009, an exact year after being hired by Nordstrom, David and I made a transition to another company that impressively had a strategic partnership with The Napoleon Hill Foundation. It was the beginning of September 2009, in Montego Bay, Jamaica, where the partnership was announced and I was able to purchase my very first copy of Think and Grow Rich, in audio and a hardcover. By this time I had graduated from just listening to audiobooks and had come to love being submerged in a book, because now I had to see the words that would change my life.

I was captivated by the words, "Truly, 'thoughts are things,' and powerful things at that, when they are mixed with definiteness of purpose, persistence, and a burning desire, for their translation into riches, or other material objects." Thoughts are things, …what did that really mean? I was still a novice to this mind stuff, but I loved the way that it made me stretch my thinking. Definiteness of purpose…did I have that? I already had an unconscious familiarity with persistence, because when I wanted something I didn't stop until I got it. And a burning desire…what was it that I truly wanted to become, and was I willing to go through the burn to get there? Yes, indeed, Napoleon Hill had now opened a can of wisdom that left me yearning for more. I wanted to apply these readings to see if and how they really worked. I did not read the book in its entirety because it was so profound and thought provoking. I discovered ways of choosing what stimulated me at that particular time and was elated about the fact that I could skip chapters, and it was ok to do so. I did however; spend a considerably great amount of time on this "definiteness of purpose" thing. I wanted to be convicted in my drive towards a greatness that I had no clue of what it would entail to accomplish. But I knew that I wanted it and I was willing to do the work that was necessary to get it.

By the end of September 2009, I was a full-time entrepreneur living on my own terms and taking full responsibility for the freedom that I wanted to live every single day of my life. Approximately 2 weeks after the Jamaica trip, my desire to free myself was so strong that I made the decision to quit teaching permanently. Nordstrom had been a part of my past since December 2008, so my persistence seemed to be yielding promising results. My faith had been fully activated and there was no stopping my imagination. I wanted to become a 6 figure earner with my then company and I was inundated with the thought of it, allowing my actions to be aligned with my desire, and using the process of self-suggestion. I was learning how to control my thinking by seeing myself where I wanted to be. Affirming the possessions of my burning desires allowed me to feel the manifestations and within 12 months of consistent practice I was a documented 6-figure earner with that company. Who knew that meeting David as a stranger on a superstitiously unlucky day, would lead me to such an accomplishment. My thoughts actually manifested, because of principles that were practiced.

I believe that success begins when you make a decision to change any unwanted circumstances, whether they are past or present. Our futures are contingent upon the choices we make to believe, activate faith, and execute. Achieving a level of accomplishment that at one time was considered a dream had now turned into my reality, and I was confident about doing even more. It is often said by thought leaders that once you stretch your thinking you will never return to thinking of mediocrity. For the next 3 years I was what you would consider "new money." I upgraded all the parts of my life that I had always imagined. The materialistic aspect of success had become somewhat of an obsession, and I can honestly say that despite all the success principles I had learned throughout the process of elevation, I somehow allowed fear to work its way back into my life. By the end of 2013, I had moved from Houston to Tampa. Here is where my lesson of humility began.

I ended up losing pretty much everything that I had worked so hard for. Situations that I had been training people about, like recovering from repossession, foreclosure, depression, doubt, fear, and unbelief, were now my reality. I was completely devastated about the situation that I was in. I had no clue as to why I was experiencing these things personally, after being what I thought was a guide to helping so many people achieve the beauty of happiness. The incredible book, Outwitting the Devil had been gifted to me a couple of years prior, and now I was understanding how Napoleon Hill became fearful of his future, because of a series of events that he witnessed, that planted those seeds of regression. Only because there is not enough time to go through every detail of what happened from October 2013 to December of 2014, please understand that I could no longer speak about losing yourself and anything that was attached, in theory. I knew better in regards to my thinking, words, images, emotions, and how together they can and will create a certain state of being. Despite knowing that I was lost and seemingly helpless, it was an absolute fight to get back into personal self-development because I felt unworthy due to my mistakes but I found a way. I had to consciously force myself to believe again, one day at a time. Remembering how I was able to manifest my prior creations of happiness and financial strength, I then relied on the law of attraction to get me back on my feet. I knew that my thoughts were to become things. After taking the courageous step of partnering with my current company, Total Life Changes on December 28, 2014, I was able to create a multiple 6-figure income within only 12 short months. My life had been given another dose of grace, and the past was now a series of powerful lessons.

Once we decide to believe that all things are possible to those who choose to believe, then anything becomes possible. Practicing taking control of our thought process is a mandatory necessity to anyone who has a burning desire to create greatness; not just for self-gain, but for world impact. Today, significance and living out my definiteness of purpose is why my heart beats. Having given the gift of Think and Grow Rich to so many people along this journey, I am clear that thinking and growing will always initiate change. Choose Happiness And Never Give Excuses…it is an ineffable way to live.

Andrea Blackley| Bio

Andrea Blackley is nothing short of GANGSTA…, which is a perfect description of how she chooses to live her life, and a snapshot of her energetic personality. She is without boundaries, limitations, doubt, and unbelief. Andrea is an unwavering candidate in the belief that THOUGHTS ARE THINGS!

Having had a single-parent upbringing with her mom, Andrea discovered the meaning of strength at an early age. Through the common and seemingly expected and unexpected struggles that many single mothers experience, Andrea decided at a primary age, that she would only live in and entertain high expectations. When she unexpectedly became a single-mother at 28, her desires went into overdrive. Andrea was a 3rd grade school teacher for 8 years, and chose entrepreneurship organically. Being controlled is not in her DNA, and she will humbly remind anyone of that. Since 2008, the industry of Network marketing has allowed Andrea to dream big…as it is only through this industry that she was introduced to the principles of Napoleon Hill. When she understood that you could THINK and GROW RICH, she decided to believe that it was only a matter of time before it was her time to prove that believing works!

Andrea can be reached at 832.790.5461 or amillionaireb@gmail.com

CHAPTER 6

Summoned To Love By Grief

By Tina Aurelio

Finding love and forgiveness after the death of my son Michael.

It has been two years since my eighteen-year-old son Michael, passed away from a drug overdose. In that time, I have made a conscious decision to heal and move forward from the "hellish" state that his death sent me spiraling down into. In writing this, I am forced to look back and go deeper into my feelings, which I am finding to be an immensely painful task. I am remembering so many years of laughing, crying, loving, hurting, joy and pain. The last four years of Michael's life my emotions were a full out battle between fear and love.

Looking back at it now it has been a journey of awakening with all the privileges of love, faith, miracles and God.

On one hand looking back and realizing where I am today, it's a miracle that I am still breathing. My son Michael was my baby; when he passed on I left with him. My whole world was shattered and, along with a broken heart I no longer had a place in this world. On the other hand, in his short life, Michael was and remains my greatest teacher. For me, Michael became "Michael the Great Awakener". He showed me the beauty of his existence in heaven, and made me see the same beauty that has always been here on earth. For that I am eternally grateful. In search of your heaven Michael, I have found my own.

This story is dedicated in memory of my son, Michael Anthony
(June 10th, 1996 – March 11th, 2015)

My precious Michael, my heart, thank you for your endless love…you transformed death into life and made it something beautiful. You have shared your love with me and others and you are guiding and helping me and others all over the world. I am so very proud of you! No words could ever describe my love for you. I miss you, I miss the hugs and kisses, I miss our "date nights". I miss telling you to be good and be careful when you were leaving for school or going out with your friends. I still have some tough days with grief, but I am happy for you, I really am. Michael, I never want this to go unsaid. There are no words to express how much you mean to me. The day you were born, God sent me a blessing- and that was you. For this I thank Him every day. You are the true definition of a son, in every way. It is because of you that my life has meaning. Always remember that I know how much you love me and how much you care, I can tell by the relationship that we share. Whether we are together or apart, please do not ever forget- You will always have a piece of my heart!

I love you, forever my heart, Momma.

After years of Michael's battle with drug addiction, it was early on a Wednesday morning, March 11, 2015, when I got the phone call that Michael was in the hospital and had overdosed. In a dream like trance I had made my way over to the hospital to find him in a coma. A few hours later I stared in disbelief as the monitor that Michael was hooked up to flat lined and my beautiful son was taken from my life.
Michael Anthony Falcone - June 10, 1996 – March 11, 2015

From the moment that I learned I was pregnant with Michael, I began to visualize his future. I imagined what he would look like and feel like in my arms. I visualized playing with him at the park, teaching him how to ride a bike, celebrating his birthday, his first day of school, his ups and downs, growing up, getting married, and having children of his own. I created a beautiful new existence in my mind and it forever included Michael. When Michael passed, my beautiful world that Michael had so much helped to create was shattered. I was left broken, disoriented, and struggling to cling to any piece of that world that could have been with Michael in it.

It was early Wednesday morning, I believed I was dreaming when Michael's life flat lined on the monitor. It was not real! This was not what I had chosen for my beautiful boy with a golden heart. I remember the nurse calling Michael's time of death. I felt my heart split into pieces and I could only think; *I am not going to make it.* My heart was torn and I wanted only one thing. To be with my beautiful son. Nowhere else would ever be tolerable.

Nothing can fill the gap when we are away from those we love, and it would be wrong to try. It would be easy, wouldn't it, to somehow close down the valves of love so we couldn't be hurt this much again? For a while I felt numbness, I was lost, I couldn't get my bearings, I felt like I didn't belong. But without the love of God and my family and friends, I would not have made it through this time of grieving.

Love calls to love. I was summoned to my grief by love, and I am healed by love. I believe I will not be healed, if I do not participate, if I do not answer to the love of others by my love for them. Yes, it takes risk and courage to love again. It is my courage that affirms the love I share with Michael.

If there is one thing I know that I can share with others who may be going through their own grief it is how changeable my moods can be. One moment I am relatively calm, in control, keeping my grief at bay. The next moment, I am overwhelmed, my equilibrium is shattered. Anything can send me off – a fragrance, the words of a song, an article in the newspaper that reminds me of my Michael. The first sign of spring and my son is not here to share it. Even Mother's Day sent me reeling in vortex of sadness, pain and suffering.

I sometimes wonder about my sanity. When will my moods be more measured so I am not always in danger of being swept away, of falling through the trapdoor of despair? My life has been shattered by loss, I realize that it will take time for the pieces to come together again. I am patient and loving with myself, honouring the moods, the pain, the good or bad of my grieving. I trust, I am on my way to being healed.

I have started picking up the pieces, and the strength to rebuild my life. It is strangely reassuring – this suggestion that the pain of that empty space will always be with me. Because while I do want to feel better; I do not want to ever forget my son.

I believe my ability to love and care for the world is not limited. It does not mean that taking on a new love means replacing an old one. Time does not expand, but love does. What was once loved and cherished is not replaceable. But in allowing myself to love again I am starting to feel whole again.

I want you to know that we do not get over the loss of a loved one. I know that once Michael passed on out of this physical world and into the world of the spiritual, I realize that I cannot experience him as I once knew. But I can always experience him in my life by keeping his memory alive in my mind and in my heart. I realize that *Michael is a spiritual being, not limited to physical properties.* He is with me and around me more than ever before. Knowing that makes life seem possible once again. I write letters to him often. I want to share with you, my very first letter to him.

My Letter to Heaven:

Precious Michael: I miss you! I have had to spend some time without you on our physical plane and I have thought long and hard, where to go, and what to do with all the anger, pain, suffering and sorrow. To be honest with you, I got exhausted with all these emotions running through me day and night. I prayed for strength and tried to understand and asked why my darling son with a golden heart had to leave.

This is what I understand: You and I, had many discussions on our dreams and life. It really made me sad to think that you were not able to fulfill them; and more importantly, I would not have any part in your life. I apologize for thinking this way. My understanding is that you are to fulfill much more now in your eternal life, and I was selfish to think otherwise.

I am forever grateful for loving me as much as you did and I know your love for me now is eternal and everlasting. Your passing is my new life; I am grateful and I thank you for your gift. My new life has you in it every step of the way, I know in my heart you are right next to me.

I remember, reading a quote in your journal "**God has painted the sun in my eye lids, and when I close my eyes, I always have a sunny day.**" *I see that too now, when I close my eyes I see "sunny" you.*

My life without out you will never be the same. I promise, I will do my very best to carry through everything we talked about. I will take the risk of believing and see where it leads me. I will not be intimidated by the opinions of others on how I should be feeling. I know you are with me always as I am with you. My faith is found in my unconditional love for you, and not in the degree of my grieving. Most importantly I will not be afraid. As you said: "**When you are afraid…you are not living!**"

I wanted you to know that in search of your heaven, I have found my own.

I love you, Mom XO

I will always be Michael's mom. When Michael grew into a young man, he made choices that I did not approve of. The last four years of Michael's life where tough and hard to endure. But I never stopped loving him. He showed me to accept him and love him just as he was. We never stop being parents even though our children choose a different life path. For my whole life, I will love Michael and all his heart and think about him every day.

> *Falling in love with you Michael was always easy. Our short time together was always filled with love, laughter, joy, anger and tears. It is when you want to be together despite it all, I discovered my Eternal Love for you!*
> *—Momma.*

Michael was born on Monday, June 10, 1996. He greeted his parents and the world with a peaceful smile. Instead of cries of protest at the bright lights and all the faces looking down at him, he seemed content of his surroundings. I had a very easy pregnancy with Michael, no morning sickness, and he never kept me up at night. He joyfully grew in my womb without making a fuss.

Michael loved it when his big brother, Rudy, would have conversations with him while he was in utero. He would poke out one of his limbs to let us know he was listening. It was all about love for Rudy when he was communicating with his little brother while I was carrying him. All was enchanting and a mystery to Rudy until I brought Michael home. I will never forget the look on Rudy's face. He usually gave me the same look when I served him vegetables. He looked at Michael then looked at me and said, "Oh, okay great, now bring him back!"

I referred to Michael as a "cherub". My term of endearment for him was "cotton ball". He would only cry when he needed to be fed and changed, and amused himself by marveling at his surroundings. Self-sufficient always, he insisted on managing everything on his own.

His love for life and nature was beyond measure. He took care of everyone and everything without being asked. Michael had a "golden heart." He was a kind, gentle, fun loving, happy-go-lucky child. He was well liked by everyone who came in contact with him. No question about it.

It was no surprise when Michael started junior kindergarten that he went to school joyfully each day. No complaints, no kicking and screaming. I often wondered how blessed of a mom I was. It was unbelievable how this child would never cause any trouble or complain about anything.

Each day when I picked Michael and Rudy up from school, we would do something fun. A beautiful memory comes back when I helped Michael put together a giant puzzle of "Sully" from the Disney movie "Monsters". This puzzle was "life-size." Watching and participating with him it was so magical. He expressed perfection when he placed the pieces together and when he carefully glued the puzzle together and placed it right above his bed.

Life was just easy with Michael; it was just that way. As he grew older, Michael demonstrated unconditional love for children. He loved to tell stories, play with them, but his favourite was to read to them. He never lost his patience. Come to think of it, Michael never lost his patience with anyone. A pillar of strength and a great listener he was everyone's go-to guy. He had all the answers and solutions for all his friends. He was always available to extend his help to anyone. He was everyone's number one fan.

A sports aficionado, Michael played hockey and soccer, and skate boarded with his brothers, Rudy and Cole. He had memorized all the sports statistics for our Toronto Blue Jays, and our Toronto Maple Leafs and our basketball team, the Raptors.

Michael turned into a great fisherman. He felt at home being out in nature. During his spare time in his later teens, Michael could be found at one of the many rivers in the areas surrounding Toronto, fishing for salmon and trout. A catch-and-release sports fisherman, Michael took lots of pictures of some of the "whoppers" that he caught. He loved camping and roughing it. I remember clearly when we took him camping for the first time; he instinctively knew what to do. From setting up our tents, collecting wood and building a fire, and catching frogs and other critters. He was a chameleon that way, adapting quickly to every surrounding and every new place.

A lover of all animals, Michael would bring home every single stray cat that would cross his path. He would have this long explanation as to why we should keep it. It broke my heart every time I had to say "No, sorry honey, it someone else's cat!"; if you could have only seen the look in his eyes. Each time my heart would explode.

Michael fell in love with Art and Music. He loved to draw. He had books of artwork that he put himself into from a very young age. If you were looking for Michael in the vicinity of our home and needed to have a conversation with him, I would always have to ask to remove his headphones. He would have music blaring at all times. He really did not have a preference of Artists or Music, he just listened to everything; believe or not, even Country Music!

Michael also loved shopping! He loved his Ralph Lauren "Polo", from hats, to clothes, to shoes and cologne. To that he added every other make of hat and shoe which he neatly lined on shelves and the floor in his room but somehow could not find it in himself to make the bed.

Michael was my personal shopping companion. He would shop with me always. He would patiently wait for me while I would try clothes on. He was very honest and would make suggestions. "What son does that?" I remember about 5 years ago on boxing day he spotted a coat that was very furry and bear-like. He insisted that I should try it on. He thought it was perfect for me. I did try it on, and yes, I truly looked like a mama bear. He could tell that I was not crazy about it, but he loved it. In a matter of seconds, he builds up his case on all the reasons he believed that I should buy the coat. What is a mother to do when she is being flattered by her son? And yes, in the end, I bought the coat. I occasionally still wear it and recall the conversation with such passion on Michael's part.

When Michael was six years old, I separated from Michael's dad, after seventeen years of marriage. It was a brutal custody battle. Michael and I were separated for a full year before we reunited again. When I got Michael back it was on part-time basis. Michael was heartbroken. I have always felt that the divorce affected Michael deeply. I believe that children do not have a way of accepting and living the reality that has been dealt by their parents. I also believe that it impacted Michael to the point of escaping his emotions towards his family life.

When Michael started High School, everything changed. He became quieter at home, withdrawn from our family. He no longer joined in family gatherings. He always had other plans. He had nothing much to say most of the time. "Shoulders shrugging" was his way of communicating. Everyone was telling me it was just a phase, but as time passed it became apparent to me that something else was going on, a mother always knows. His behaviour was the first change I noticed. He used to care so much and then he never cared at all. He also became demanding and rude when he did not get his way.

It became difficult to get him to get up and be present to his life. For example, getting up for school was devastating. I dreaded when the clock went off at 7:00 a.m. We would argue every morning, after all the fighting he would finally get up. He would get mouthy and belligerent each time. He had no patience and his aggression became worse as time passed. Another change was that he could not commit or keep appointments. He always stood me up or kept me waiting forever.

I also noticed that he would tell me where to pick him up and then he would phone me and tell me it would be somewhere else. And then come up with an amazing story (fiction) as to what happened. It was so exhausting just to listen to him sometimes. I just wanted to say to him, "I don't want to know, honey." or "you are ok, and it is good enough for me."

I would get calls from his Principal, advising me that Michael did not show up to 1st period. I was so naïve and I would always say to him, "It's not possible, I just dropped him off!". I also noticed he was asking for a lot of money, all the time. Excuses galore for what he had to do with it. Lying now became second nature. I recall calling him on the lies, and he could not have cared less.

Michael had no luck with his cell phones. I always found this strange; he would come home and say he lost his phone every 3 to 4 months. His iPods were another item that just seemed to disappear that we replaced often.

Our life together changed from a mutual loving respect to yelling matches, slamming doors, silence, and lies, and in the end Michael would shut me out. Sometime I would give in to him, just to have some decent time with my son. I held on to the lies, and I convinced myself that he was telling me the truth.

I spent hours, days, and years standing by the sidelines, with hope that he would return to me again, as I once knew him. Michael became my obsession and my addiction. I spent days in my own web of lies and denial. I protected him. I wanted no one to know, I gave in to him. I believed him when he lied. I justified it when he stole. I could not lose him. No matter who he was and who he had become he was my son and I loved him.

The death of my son is a pain so deep that it cannot be expressed into words, and everyone experiences it in their own way. I was faced with emotions that I believed would never exist in my being. I felt like I was drowning. I felt I was paralyzed, nothing felt real. Everything became jaded. What is happening to me? I would wonder. Did I care? No! I just wanted to run, be alone, and the possibility of dying was always there. I decided to talk to other parents who have also lost a child. It was helpful, because they share a similar pain experience, but even between grieving parents the mourning process can vary greatly. It is not uncommon for grieving parents to distance themselves from old friends or family members; I know this was true for me.

The death of a child is life changing. I am not the same person that I was before Michael's death. Early in my grief journey I was disoriented because the sense of how my life with Michael would play out had been destroyed. As I picked up the pieces of my broken life, I discovered new strengths and build a new set of beliefs to live by. I found myself driven by a conviction that I must make the most of the time I have, because I realized that life is too short.

My grief will never cease to exist, but at some point the grief will not consume my life as wholly as it did in the beginning. I started setting new habits, rituals, and traditions to remember the joy that Michael brought into our life, this has helped me in keeping Michael's memory alive.

The death of my son has given me the opportunity to return to love and faith in God. The belief in the afterlife has eased my mind in knowing that Michael and I are, and always be, sharing Eternal Love.

My life without my son will never be the same. *I will take the risk of believing* and see where it leads me. I will not be intimidated by the opinions of others on how I should be feeling. I know Michael is with me always as I am with him. My faith is found in my unconditional love for Michael, and not in the degree of my grieving. Most importantly I will not be afraid. As Michael said, *"When you are afraid...you are not living!"*

Every day our kids have to make choices that we, as parents, never even dreamed about when we were kids. Peer pressure is a powerful thing, and many times, our kids will reluctantly go along with the crowd and do things that they are not comfortable with and know are harmful in order to gain acceptance.

The pressure to belong and fit in is widespread an unrelenting. Yet despite this we have come into this life to experience freedom. From an early age, schools, our families and cultural influences push us to follow certain behaviours, norms and rules. For some of us, the feeling of belonging is comforting and provides a sense of identity, friendship and connection to others. But sometimes the expectations of others can also create inner turmoil, tension and confusion.

This behaviour repeated itself with Michael and over time it manifested itself in a full-blown drug addiction and ultimately, his death. As parents, how can we tell if our children are abusing substances? This was a question I asked my self 24 hours a day. *Do I want to know? Maybe it's just a phase? He's experimenting...*and so on. Unfortunately, too many parents really don't want to know the answer, I certainly did not, because this is one subject that was too scary, frustrating and guilt-laden to deal with.

As it is very difficult for me to address some of these symptoms, I realize that I am addressing the Michael I did not know, the symptoms of his disease. And for all of you parents experiencing this or have experienced it, please know that you are not alone. I thought I was. I did not want anyone to find out, the shame of it all. The last four years of Michael's life were relentless; there were times I did not know if he was going to make it. I only know, that God does not give you more then you can handle.

These are some of the signs Michael demonstrated. There are many more out there, I am only listing what I have experienced. I encourage you to look further if you are experiencing this disease as a parent.

My loving Michael turned mean, angry and aggressive. This happened with the onset of puberty for Michael, but it is much worse when there is substance abuse going on. No matter what I said or did, I could just not win! I was afraid or reluctant to confront my child due to violent outbursts or reactions from him when I attempted to inquire about any part of his life. Just remember, when a kid is backed into a corner, he may have discovered that the best defense is an offense. Many teens, particularly boys, find that by coming back with loud yelling, they can be very intimidating to their mothers. I am proof of this act. I feared my own son. Suspect drug use if your child has lately become very irritable, unpleasant, or is bullying other family members, if he is very easy to provoke, starts to use a lot of profanity, seems tired, worn out, sleeps most of the day away and is apathetic a lot of the time, or develops a nagging cough, has constants sniffles, runny nose, or nosebleeds.

His appearance went down the tubes. Michael was always a sharp dressed young man. Only the best brand of clothing hung in his closet. I started wondering why he did not care about his appearance anymore. He wore track pants that were too baggy on him, and t-shirts with negative or drug sayings on them. These kinds of clothes may attract other kids who use drugs, and cause kids who are not into that scene to shy away from your child.

Michael stopped looking after his personal hygiene, and did not care about his looks any longer. His clothes smelled like marijuana, his hair was not washed and stringy. He used profanity to get me off his back when I pointed it out to him. His favourite saying to me was, "What the fuck, Mom, relax!" He wore dark sunglasses all the time. His eyes where red and he was never out of Visine eye drops. And most of all, it was heart breaking to stand there on the sidelines and watch him lose his passion and zest for life.

Michael never ever admitted who some of his friends were who abused drugs. He kept this a "secret" along with protecting his cell phone. He would always have me drop him off to a friend's house that I knew. His whereabouts after that would remain a mystery. **If you really think that drug-using friends are considerate enough not to do drugs in front of your child or that your child is just sitting around watching them use while not using himself, think again.** If your child is actually resisting taking the drugs, you can be sure he is being goaded and coaxed into using along with the friends. Misery loves company, and it's no fun to get high by yourself. Kids who are not using do not pick users as friends. It is also no fun to sit around and watch other people get "stupid" on you. So you can bet that if your child's friends are using drugs, then he/she is using with them.

I remember a Saturday morning Michael coming out of the shower and walked out of the bathroom with just a towel wrapped around his waist. I took a double take, I could not believe my eyes. I could count his ribs and his shoulder joints and collarbone were pronating out of skin. I questioned what was going on and he assured me that he was watching his weight. I really believed him, because as a young boy he was overweight and had issues with his weight throughout his childhood and early adolescence. So I immediately backed off the subject. But I went on about the fact that he had gone to far and he should start eating and just make better choices with food. For Michael, it was a cover up for the abuse of methamphetamines, which speed up the system and took away his appetite, thereby causing drastic changes in his weight.

Michael came home and cleaned out the pantry. This was also a sign that Michael had just been out smoking pot, which is notorious for causing "the munchies." I would find countless boxes of cookies, chips and crackers underneath his bed when I searched his room.

This behavior was accompanied by red eyes, slurred speech, nasty temper, uncontrollable laughing or exceptional drowsiness, I was sure that Michael had been up to something. Also, he did not smell pretty. Pot smell is very prominent; it gets everywhere including his hair and clothes. Parents and care givers please keep in mind that **the marijuana our kids get hold of today is many times stronger than the pot that was available when many of today's parents were kids,** and it is far more harmful. It is now often laced with other drugs. Marijuana can cause permanent short-term memory loss, particularly in younger kids whose brains are still developing. Marijuana is in no way a "harmless drug" as many of its proponents would like us to believe. In my son Michael's case it was the Gateway Drug that lead him to his death.

No one sets out to become an addict. What our children are searching for is the escape from dulling the pain that often comes with the ups and downs of everyday life. Every day this world announces illusionary and deafening ways to find bliss and yes, this includes our children and drugs.

Michael's sole preoccupation was getting a hold of enough money to fund his habit and he soon started stealing to fund his lifestyle. Money, jewelry, Play Station, Xbox, all went missing from our home. Every three to four months or so, he would say that he lost his cell phone. It was only later that we realized these things had been sold for drugs.

After all the signs and symptoms of my son's addiction. I still could not face the reality that was in front of me. I just wanted to keep my head under the covers and when I emerged everything would be back to normal and Michael and I could resume our loving relationship.

Michael's death left me with a trail of emotional upheaval, numbness and despair. When Michael died I thought I lost my life. I didn't know where to turn for answers. After all, I was raised Catholic. This belief limited me and made it difficult for me to ask questions. Nevertheless, my mind could not rest. The only thoughts I would have constantly were: *Where are you Michael? Are you safe? Are you alone? Are you homesick? Why did you leave me?* I had to find my son!

During all my despair and deep grief and my broken heart, Michael did his best to leave signs for me to let me know that he did not leave me and he is with me always.

I would hear *"I am not dead mom!"* I finally fell asleep for a few hours before the planning of his funeral, and I asked him, *Please Michael, where are you?* In my dream state, Michael appears in a Golden Meadow with his soccer ball, his six-year-old self. He is dressed in his white t-shirt and black shorts, having fun kicking the ball around. He kicks the ball to me and says: *"Run mommy, run, faster, get the ball, mommy!"* Till this day, I hear him laughing so joyfully while he was playing with me in that Golden Meadow.

While planning his funeral, I felt like I was cut off from my feelings. I was observing this woman (me) going through the motions. I saw her pain and suffering but I was not connected to her. I had lost my identity.

I specifically remember walking through the funeral home trying to choose a casket. I would hear: *"Mommy, I love this one…it has a lot of personality and great lines."* I was standing right in front of the one I was marveling. Me: How can you love a casket? The only thought I had was: Once you are in it, I can never hold you again. Michael's reply to me was: *"I am holding you right now."*

With all the pain and suffering, I dismissed all the never-ending love from him, because I thought: *This is not real, Michael you are coming home right?*

Right after his funeral, Michael's attempts to get my attention were endless. He would move my jewelry around, from the dresser to the bed. He used the same bracelet all the time. The first time it happened, I just assumed that I had lost the bracelet. He kept on doing it until I paid attention. Other times I would be driving and I would feel his presence guiding me to this or that radio station, every time hearing songs with the same theme of messages of love and forgiveness. The first song he chose for me was *"I Bet my Life"*, from Imagine Dragons. Here are a few of the verses from that beautiful song:

*I know I took the path that you would never
want for me
I know I let you down, didn't I?
So many sleepless nights where you were
waiting up on me
Well I'm just a slave unto the night
Now remember when I told you that's the last
you'll see of me
Remember when I broke you down to tears
I know I took the path that you would never
want for me
I gave you hell through all the years
I've been around the world and never in my
wildest dreams
Would I come running home to you
I've told a million lies but now I tell a single
truth
There's you in everything I do*

Michael loves music. I believe it comes with his Artist abilities to express his feelings through music and art, but unfortunately he kept this expression to himself.

After his death I would walk out in the mornings and find a white rose or red rose by my car door. I would hear Michael when I was getting dressed, especially if he liked what I was wearing, I can hear his sweet voice saying *"you look beautiful mom!"* I would question these acts of love with Michael all the time. Am I going crazy? What is happening to me? The divine part of me would assure me that this was real, Michael confirmed what I saw and heard was real: *"Trust this mom!"* *"There is life after death, I am not dead!"*.

Michael's passing left a trail of various states of emotional upheaval, from the upheaval though came a great wonderful gift. A spiritual awakening that becomes stronger and richer every day. A week before Michael's death, his life was the worst I had ever seen. I prayed constantly for him, for me and for our family. As far as I was concerned, I was walking this path and life lesson alone. But I was certain that I had enough faith in God that He would not leave me. Then, Michael disappeared from home two days before his passing, and I was left in "hell". I retreated to my office, shut the door and I fell on my knees and I asked God the following: *"Please Father of Heaven and Earth, help Michael, he is yours to do what is your will. Please think of Michael first, I place him in your loving heart and caring hands, please make him happy and healthy, and please return Michael to me whole, happy, healthy and safe. Amen."* And He did!

God's Will was done. He answered my prayer, but I was not pleased with God. I was sent in a state of shock and pain filled with grief and I felt punished, to say the very least. WHY WOULD A LOVING GOD be so cruel as to take Michael away from me?

I trusted God; I refused to understand why God would do this to me, why Michael would do this to me. What I failed to understand was that He did, indeed, return Michael to me just as I asked, not in a physical state, but in a Holy state.

For many of us parents, the loss of our child also means another change. "Who am I without my child?" I felt incapable of living life without my Michael. I remember holding back my emotions and I did not want to express how I felt about Michael's death, but each day the overwhelming wave got worse like a snowball rolling down hill, picking up more snow, more momentum and speed as it rolls down. The first few months of my grief I often recall as the "robotic phase". I was numb, the significant role I had with Michael was gone.

We all have different belief systems, different levels of spiritual understanding, and once again we are faced with a choice; we can either grow stronger or be controlled by our circumstances and be paralyzed with fear. I personally chose to grow stronger. One of the first steps I took in my healing journey is to live the life that Michael would be proud of. I can continue to teach my child how to handle life situations in a positive way. I decided that I would turn this tragedy into service and create a positive outcome.

No matter how a child dies, whether from a freak accident, an overdose of drugs, or a terminal illness, the first sense he or she has when leaving the body is one of freedom. Think of it as taking off a heavy overcoat in the heat of a hot summer day. All the pain, torment and suffering are gone. The suffering, powerlessness, helplessness they once felt on earth quickly fades away. Instead, the spirit feels incredible joyfulness and an overwhelming sense of peace.

Michael's passing is an ending of one part of my life, but also the beginning of another. Once I was able to accept what happened to Michael, forgive myself and forgive Michael, I became someone who could help heal the world.

Acceptance and forgiveness allow us to start a new chapter in our lives and clear our space for new opportunities to reach us. Michael has given me a gift – and a new life purpose. It is up to me to fulfill my soul's purpose and mission in life.

One of the most challenging tests of love is our ability to let go. In the physical realm, we think love as being close to one another, holding hands, talking, looking into one another's eyes, sharing activities and cuddling. The call to experience a higher form of love often comes in the most difficult ways. When there is a committed love bond between two people on a soul level, the connection is extremely strong. This bond transcends the veil and goes beyond death of the human body.

Michael's death is the Great Awakener. When Michael passed over to Heaven, part of me went with him. Even when I know in my heart and in communicating with him every day that he is safe in Heaven among our family and friends, I still miss him. Grieving is a process that like death, shook me to the core. Compassion, understanding, and supportive family and friends help me through the difficult and lonely days and nights. But it is still not easy. When Michael passed on I experienced an emptiness that nothing seems to fill. I can truly say, that when Michael passed on; his death made it's way into my life. I am forever changed.

My deceased child does not want me to feel sad. He has on many occasions insisted that I move on with my life in the best possible way. The loss of Michael caused me to feel unbearable guilt, blame, doubt, fear, and anguish. No words are enough, no hugs and kisses are enough; nothing seems enough to console me. Grieving parents are different from others who are grieving. All expectations for a normal life are shattered for us. It has been the most painful experience imaginable for me and there is no quick fix. It takes time, love and effort to move forward. Patience above all, is essential.

Although there is no set way for someone to grieve, I have learned that there are healthy ways to go through the process. One of the most valuable insights I can share is to remind you to attempt, as best as you can, to place yourself in a state of mindfulness. It is important not only to be aware of yourself as a spiritual, energetic being, but also to live that way every single day.

Healthy grief means dealing with emotions, unhealthy grief means masking or numbing emotions. I have found through Journal Writing and Letter Writing, and Meditation with Michael has helped me better understand life after death. I talk to Michael through meditation, prayer and automatic writing and in return it opens up my senses to receive messages in return from Michael.

Although I am grieving Michael's passing over, I realized that it is important to be aware that I am still and forever will be a source of love to him. When Michael's death arrived, he seemed forever gone. But he is not. Yet communicating and connecting with Michael, not only helps me, but also supports him in many ways.

Michael's gift to me, and what makes me happy, and where I most succeed, is in the love that engages my spirit. I have accepted that I am right where I am meant to be, doing exactly at this time what I am meant to do right in this moment.

I believe Love will conquer all. Once we get to the realization of loving ourselves and breathing that love into every single experience of every single day then you start to make a big progression at that point. There are no strings attached to love. Love does not hold back. As we are made in the likeness of God and God is Love, then we must strive to express our love in everyone and in everything we do, say and are. There is no separation in the Love of God.

Love yourself unconditionally. Take time for you. Understand you. Honour whatever emotion comes up, it is okay, to love even those unwanted thoughts and emotions, that is what the moment is asking you to do. We are made of God's loving energy. Recognize it; enjoy it; and forgive yourself. Our loved ones are not in pain anymore…they are freed.

Michael's Blog: Our Journey of Love and Faith – Conversations with my son Michael in Heaven. www.tinamichael777@wordpress.com

Tina Aurelio| Bio

Tina Aurelio is a highly motivated "wellnesspreneur", life coach, and motivational speaker, dedicated to empowering individuals. Tina educates on a holistic approach to designing an optimal lifestyle. She demonstrates focus to a life of vitality and connected purpose. Today, she combines her knowledge and experience about the physical, emotional and spiritual body to help individuals connect to the core vitality that spurs truly remarkable lives.

Tina has over 14 years of experience in working with students and individuals in teaching and coaching. Dedicated to serving and assisting and educating individuals to become strong, healthy and well in all areas of their lives, including their happiness and wellbeing. With Tina's unique approach to addressing life, health and wellness concerns, her clients and students often see drastic improvement with their quality of life.

Tina's life purpose is about inspiring, teaching and coaching individuals to achieve their best life. Tina draws on the lessons she's learned from her experiences to motivate people fulfill their potential.

I believe in implementing effective guidelines to create success and enable people to live life on their terms, healthy in mind, body and spirit. – Tina Aurelio.

To learn more about Tina Aurelio – www.holisticbodyworx.ca and www.forzadonna.com.

CHAPTER 7

Perseverance Through Adversity

By Chuck Bolena, M.Ed.

"Adversity introduces a man to himself"

— Albert Einstein

Created during a weekend camping trip came the idea for a week-long adventure riding from DC to Pittsburgh, with all we needed to complete the trip carried in small, single-wheeled trailers hauled behind our bicycles. These trailers would be powered by myself and Larry, the other alpha male willing to take on what seemed impossible for two middle-aged men, and our spouses. Although we had shared similar, short-term trips, this would be different. We planned to unite our love of camping and love of biking into an epic journey that would surely test our willpower, perseverance, and physical endurance. That weekend, around the campfire, a dream took form and a bucket list item moved from an idea to a desire that the four of us wrapped our minds and excitement around. Planning began, as theory became a reality and a new adventure was born.

This trip was planned using two trail systems that connect as one. The Great Allegheny Passage (GAP) is an incredible trail that uses old defunct railroad corridors running from Pittsburgh, Pennsylvania to Cumberland, Maryland. This trail winds its way through many small towns, country farm fields, and back wooded hills and valleys; many of the sights are breathtaking! After 150 miles it connects to the old C&O Canal Towpath in Cumberland, which has its own uniqueness and beauty, and continues another 185 miles into Washington, DC for a total of 335 miles (539 km); perfect for hikers, bikers, walkers, and joggers. The majority of the GAP consists of crushed limestone making the ride very smooth. The C&O, on the other hand, is not as groomed, making the ride much rougher. Most of it is dirt, allowing for a lot of rocks, ruts, and roots, which became a humorous verbal caution by the lead rider calling out safety hazards encountered on the trail. Occasionally you will hit a section of trail that is asphalt or cement, which is a rider's blessing. There are picnic areas along the trails, as well as remote campsites for use, and you are guaranteed to see wildlife on the trail; anything from deer, turkey, quail, or chipmunks, to the occasional rattlesnake or black bear.

My wife, Darlene, and I have been riding bikes for over six years, mostly on different sections of this trail, and we have been tent camping almost as long. Our little 'Adventure Club,' which includes several other couples we travel with, has had some incredible experiences over the years. Together we had completed this bike trip from Pittsburgh to DC three years earlier so doing it again, in reverse, created little anxiety or concern for me of our ability to complete the ride. However, different preparation and training would be necessary as we chose to do it without support this time; little did I know what lay ahead.

Thursday evening, the day before our departure, we were prepared. The pickup truck is sitting in my driveway loaded and ready to roll the next morning. We have two bicycles in the back of the bed strapped in with all our gear and two bicycles on a bike rack attached to the back of the truck. Our preparation to get to this point was just over two and a half months, and I feel we did very well. We practiced riding various distances and hills. Larry and I practiced riding with the trailers we would use to tow all our gear. We planned our Friday morning departure time to start our drive to DC (6:00 am) and mapped out how to find mile marker 0 (the start of the C&O Towpath). We knew how far we needed to travel each day to get to our chosen campsite, and knew our average speed (9-10 miles per hour) which told us how long we would be riding on the trail each day. We had a hotel reservation scheduled on Monday at a Marriott in Cumberland – there was a reason for this, as you will soon see! We had our meals and water for the first three days packed, as options on the trail were limited. We also had clean clothes packed in the truck for our big finish in Pittsburgh as we planned on celebrating at the Cheesecake Factory for dinner! We had this! We were ready! We were excited!

Friday morning, 5:50 AM – Darlene and I were out the door, driving in the dark to pick up Larry and Cheryl. They were our biking companions for the next seven days. They jumped in and the chatter and jokes about what we just got ourselves into started filling the truck as we made our way to pick up George and Vicki. George owns the truck and is our ride to DC, and his wife, Vicki, was along for the ride. When we arrived at George's house, we all scrambled out of the truck for a last minute bathroom break before we set off for our four hour drive to DC. As I walked towards the truck with George, he asked an innocent question, "where's my bike rack?" As I looked at the back of the truck, I saw nothing. Then it dawned on me – no bike rack means no bikes! I screamed to Darlene, "Where's our bikes?" I was in shock! I instantly knew they had fallen off; I just did not know where.

We jumped into the truck and started backtracking to find the missing bikes. It was still dark out, and our fear was they would not be seen and run over, possibly causing an accident and surely being destroyed. My mind kept thinking I blew it! I am the one who put the rack on the truck, but not being familiar with it, I obviously did it wrong. I ruined the trip, and we haven't even started! The drive felt like forever, but we eventually came across a heap of metal on the side of the road only a few miles away. Relieved that we found them, we were now faced with the reality of the damage that took place and wondered if they were salvageable.

In my head, I still thought we were done. Finished! We separated everything, installed the rack on the truck and put both bikes back on; then I began to assess the damage. Four bent rims, bent handle bars on Darlene's bike, torn seats and road rash on grips, pedals, mirrors, etc. My front wheel was bent beyond use, but I had a replacement back home. I was not able to straighten the other three rims, so I loosened the brake pads to keep them from grabbing. We picked up the spare wheel at my house and were on our way!

After stopping for lunch, we arrived at the location of mile marker zero in DC around 1:00 pm. We made it! We unloaded the truck and geared up! We rode our bikes over to the mile marker to get pictures and prepare for the start of our journey. When I made the first turn, my trailer behind my bike buckled and locked up my rear wheel. Now what? The weight in the trailer was unstable when turning at slow speeds; we knew this was a possible issue, but this is the first time it caused damage. I had to take everything off my bike, disassemble the back wheel and straighten the axle back into shape. This was concerning. I removed several bottles of water from my trailer in hopes of lessening the weight to fix the problem; it did not. We pressed on and started our ride, quickly realizing these trailers were more problematic for both Larry and me then we anticipated. We had difficulty steering on the rough terrain of the C&O and the weight of the trailers pushed our bikes, challenging our efforts to ride safely, especially on the narrow passageways 10 feet above the canals. Less than a mile down the trail, still in the heart of Washington, I came off a section of cement and the impact jammed my derailleur (my rear gear changer) into my spokes, tearing one right out of my rim and locking up my back wheel. I was frustrated, angry, and concerned that this trip is never going to happen! This is not the image I saw when I was preparing for this trip!

As much as I was losing patience, I quickly located a bike shop within a few blocks of us. My wife and I got there, got fixed up and back on the trail with Larry and Cheryl in just over an hour. I made a phone call to George, who did not get very far in the DC traffic, and asked that he find a two-wheeled trailer to replace my single-wheeled demon-cart. We lost a significant amount of time, and the idea of getting to our first campsite 30 miles away seemed impossible. We got back on the trail and struggled to make it 10 miles outside of town; found a section of trail accessible by vehicle, and coordinated with

George to meet us to swap out trailers. When I pulled into the parking lot, my trailer buckled and jammed my derailleur again. As we waited for George and Vicki, I made an effort to repair my bike and Darlene prepared dinner for the group – Ramen Noodles and bottled water. Yum! (We actually grew to like this meal as we ate it for lunch or dinner most days.) It is now around 6:30 pm, soon to get dark, and George and Vicki arrived with a new two-wheeled trailer for me to use. Things started looking up. To test the adjustments I made on my rear wheel and gear system, I rode around the parking lot shifting through the gears, and it happened! My derailleur completely ripped off my bike rendering it useless! I'm done! I'm finished! I am without a bike, and this trip is over! It was like I got punched in the stomach and could not breathe.

I think this is where I was mentally finished. My wife spoke up and told me to call a bike shop and try and get it fixed. Reluctantly, I pulled out my phone and searched for another bike shop nearby. When I called, the shop manager told me he probably did not have the parts and that he was getting ready to close the shop at 7:00 pm. Again, my wife speaks up and tells me to buy a new bike! What? She tells me to ask if I purchased a new bike, would he stay open for me? I asked, and he said he would. We decided that I would go with George and Vicki to get a new bike and the others would keep riding on the trail towards a designated campsite a few miles further where we would meet up later. I loaded my broken bike, body, and gear into the truck, and we were at the bike shop by 7:00 pm. I looked over the selection of available bikes; test drove a couple for fit and decided on one that I would buy to replace mine. As the shop manager made a few adjustments to my new bike, I found one that would fit Darlene perfectly. With a few efforts to get the best deal, I walked out of the bike shop with two brand new bikes to replace the ones that fell from the truck that morning. Now dark, we loaded up the bikes and soon met up with the others at the campsite. George and Vicki loaded up the two damaged bikes, bid us farewell, and headed home. Encouraged by the relief of riding new bikes and working with a two-wheeled trailer that offered more stability, I'm now faced with figuring out how we make up the 15 miles lost so we can arrive in Cumberland by Monday. Cumberland is where we have reservations at the Marriott and is the midway point of our trip. Making it there by Monday gives us enough time to complete our journey by Friday in Pittsburgh.

We were in bed before 9:00 pm and for some reason, as my head hit my small travel pillow that night, feeling exhausted, dirty, sweaty, and sore all over, I thought about all the concepts and principles I have learned over the years regarding success and failure. I especially thought about the need for a positive mental attitude. Although I experienced failure time and again, and I physically (and mentally) felt defeated more than once this day, my mind maintained the pulse of positivity allowing me to see through the adversity and focus on the desired goal. I fell asleep fast and slept sound that night; we all did.

The next day we woke early with energy and excitement to begin a new day. It did not take long, but we quickly found ourselves joking and laughing over the agony and chaos experienced just hours earlier. There was no way we could have predicted such a day, yet we managed to overcome it, and I believe it was due to the condition of our minds more than the preparation for our trip.

We did arrive in Cumberland on Monday and enjoyed our stay at the Marriott. The hot tub and pool were just what we needed for our torn, tattered bodies – I told you there was a reason for this reservation! The remaining days of our adventure were tremendous, pleasurable and frequently disrupted by moments of turmoil and more setbacks. Crazy things like being stung by a bee while riding, bending another rim and breaking another spoke, Cheryl experiencing severe back spasms due to an accidental fall before the ride, and Larry's single-wheeled demon-cart creating enough havoc to his bike to require Gorilla Tape and rope just to keep it together! We arrived in Pittsburgh on Friday as planned and enjoyed an incredible meal at the Cheesecake Factory. We laughed, shared memories, and joked about who had it the worst.

We did it! We had a desire. We turned that desire into a goal, built plans around it, implemented it, adapted, modified and sought expert counsel when needed. We struggled much, and laughed and supported each other even more. We grew from this experience, challenged our limits, and now realize that we are capable of doing way more than we ever thought possible.

Wayne Dyer wrote, "The state of your life is nothing more than a reflection of the state of your mind." How would you have handled such calamity if you were on this bike trip? How have you handled hardship in the past? How do you manage adversity today in your everyday life? My goal in sharing this story with you is to demonstrate the power of thought. To show you how 'what you think' can make or break you in life. I had every reason to quit during this trip, especially on the first day. Each obstacle I endured challenged me more and more, and I had to decide each and every time what my choice was going to be. I had to decide how I was going to handle adversity. It was not easy, and the biggest battle I faced was the one in my mind!

The secret often sought out in the well-known Napoleon Hill book, Think and Grow Rich, is simply this; "you must take possession of your own mind and direct it towards ends of your own choice." You can find Mr. Hill sharing this compelling statement in a short video clip found on YouTube (https://youtu.be/yfTgahE7WjI). Control your thoughts and control your actions! That is the secret. This simple understanding is the key to your success, or your failure, depending on how you choose to use it – it does not discriminate.

In my profession, I help individuals and teams change the way they think so they can achieve the results they truly want. This process is not easy, as any change is uncomfortable. However, the benefits are tremendous, and the results are proof that the effort is worthwhile. Change takes place in the mind, your mind, and is the only way for you to experience long-lasting improvements in any area of your life – health, wealth, love, happiness, or spirit.

I am going to leave you with two resources you can use to improve your results starting today.

First, read The Common Denominator of Success by Albert E.N. Gray. Successful people are driven by the desire for pleasing results; unsuccessful people are driven by the desire for pleasing methods. You have to be committed to your goals. If you have this mindset, you will pursue pleasing results, regardless of the adversities faced.

Secondly, I want you to study the diagram at the end of this chapter. This is The Creative Cycle and is something that we use in our coaching program to provide a clear roadmap on how to achieve any goal you want. Do not let the simplicity of this diagram fool you. It makes no difference if you are starting a business, trying to lose weight, improving your marriage, or riding from DC to Pittsburgh on a bicycle, the process for improving and getting the desired results is the same! This image did play out in my head many times throughout the trip, along with a quote by Og Mandino which I would repeatedly say, "I will persist until I succeed." This diagram, and Og Mandino's words, pushed me through several difficult experiences in this trip and was extremely valuable to my success.

Here's how it works:

1. What do you really want? And, where do you really want to go? What are your desires? If you are not sure, grab a pen and notepad, find a quiet area, and start writing. Brainstorm everything that comes to mind on what you want out of life without thought to how you will accomplish the goal or limiting yourself based on your perceived reality or restrictions. Freely dream! Once done, read over your list and prioritize the things that excite you the most and that you want to go after first.

2. What is your 'why?' What are your motives for pursuing this goal? Knowing your 'why' provides clarity and purpose, and reinforces the value and the commitment you will put forth to achieve your goals. Without this, it may simply remain a dream or a 'someday' wish.

3. Create an Action Plan. Write down, step-by-step, exactly what you need to do to achieve your goals. Seek expert counsel from those who have gone before you. Research books and online information, everything and anything relating to what you are trying to accomplish. Be specific, clear, and place a time frame on your plan to reinforce accountability. The key is, you must write it down!

4. Take Action. Even if you don't feel ready, start now! Remember, change is challenging and often avoided. Most failure happens in this phase because many wait until everything is thought out 100%. Complete readiness never comes. Think of something you are great at: maybe juggling, riding a bike, investing, or speaking a second language. How good were you on day one? Were you an expert or were you scared and horrible at it? Did you want to quit? Sure! But you didn't and look at you now! Don't let the fear of failure keep you from becoming the expert you are capable of becoming, just know failure is often part of the experience of success. Just do it! You will get better!

5. Analyze your results. Become a scientist, not critical and judgmental towards yourself or your efforts but objectively review your results and determine if your plan is working. If it is, follow the diagram and keep taking action – 100% execution. Stay in the lower portion of The Creative Cycle and do, do, do. If your plan is not working, go back to your action plan, reevaluate, seek expert counsel, modify your plan, and get back into action.

6. This diagram is a closed loop system. If you stay in The Creative Cycle, you cannot help but to improve and succeed. If you stop taking action, or stop analyzing your results objectively, or stop seeking expert counsel, you will not succeed. You must stay disciplined and focused.

7. This brings me to the two arrows on either side of the process: Willpower and Persistence. These two traits are a must, especially when adversity presents itself. There are other traits that you must develop to consistently achieve success in your life: integrity, courage, desire, faith, accountability, and adaptability, to name a few. Humility may be a key ingredient when doing an honest self-assessment to determine where you're lacking and begin the process of improving yourself each and every day. Here's where 'taking possession of your own mind and directing it towards ends of your own choice' comes into play. As you become better, so do your results!

Now it is your turn. What is your next big adventure? How will you persevere during adversity? Take this information and begin to create the image of what you really want. Write it down, commit to it, and take action!

The Creative Cycle
Building the image of EXACTLY what you want!

#1 What do you really[3] want? Where do you really[3] want to go?

#2 What is your WHY? Your Advantages? Is it a Worthy Goal?

Seek Expert Counsel

#3 What do you intend to give? Create a definite Action Plan

Willpower

Is your Plan working?

No Modify

Yes 100% Execution

#4 Analyze Your results

RESULTS

Take Action! Don't procrastinate! Act Now!

Persistence

Results from Thinking – All Rights Reserved

Chuck Bolena| Bio

Chuck has a long history of success, both in the US Air Force as a Nuclear Launch Officer, Instructor, and Evaluator, as well as in the pharmaceutical and medical device sales industry. He holds a Master's Degree in Counseling and Personal Development and uses his skills, training, and personal experiences to nurture his passion for helping others overcome life's challenges, and it shows! Chuck was a client of Jim Shorkey early on, and after achieving tremendous success in his professional life from the experience, he has partnered with Jim full time to help deliver Jim's Blueprint for Success to others seeking to create massive gains in their life. If you want to learn more about how Chuck can help you go after what you want in life, or would like to receive a complimentary discovery coaching session to uncover your true desires, he can be reached at chuck.bolena@resultsfromthinking.com

CHAPTER 8

Greatness Lies Within

By Pam McCray

Bankruptcy, Repossession, Lay-offs, Living paycheck to paycheck, in the midst of the financial ups, there were also these moments of financial downs. The journey to success is never a straight path. It is a journey that many don't travel; it is a road that unfortunately many never take the time to embark upon and sadly it is one that many quit. It's a journey in which there will be some times of abundance, and there will be some times of failure and struggle, but when we realize that it is a process that we were designed to endure and embrace, change begins to happen and a shift starts to take place in our lives.

Taking it back to where it all began, I grew up one of those network-marketing babies with parents who believed in the industry of network marketing. From a very young age, I can remember being in the atmosphere. With parents who were in the industry, I grew up knowing and understanding the concept. Through the companies that they were a part of many, which are household names that lead the industry today, it was simply a part of our life. Cartons and boxes of products, being a product of the products, were very common in our household. Our parents taught us the power of transferring buying habits at an early age. My mom was an educator, in addition to pursuing a host of other activities. This industry allowed her as that educator to not spend her summers working and instead we spent our summers on many vacations around the world. My father was a bonafide entrepreneur, owning both a barbershop and liquor store, so I honestly believe that I was born with the desire to chart my own destiny.

I grew up in Paterson, NJ as that shy and very timid kid. I was that girl that had the buckteeth, glasses, bunny-tail instead of a ponytail hair do, and that caused me to have little confidence and low self-esteem in myself. Let's just say I was not Ms. Popular. As life began to move forward, braces, contacts and the power to change began a transition in my life! In 1987, I found my soul mate, the love of my life, my husband Nathan McCray, on a senior class trip to Disney

World. Yes, we met in Frontier Land and spent our time having fun in Tomorrow Land, not realizing that Tomorrow Land would be our future together. Nate was from Florida, and it's amazing how our lives have come full circle. From Ft. Hood, Texas to Charlotte, North Carolina to Atlanta, Georgia to now presently living in beautiful Weston, Florida. Only now our lifestyle is worlds different from what it was when we first set upon our journey.

In 1991, we arrived in Charlotte NC with our first-born Briana in tow. With Nate right out of the military, we were excited to start our new life in a city with such great possibility. Nate used his military roots and training to secure a job, in which in years to come he was blessed with the opportunity as an engineer in telecommunications. For the first ten years of our marriage, I also worked outside the home in the finance and accounting field. Once our son Christian was born, our decision for me to become a stay at home mom and concentrate on our growing family was our priority. We knew it was a sacrifice to choose to become a one income household, but it was a sacrifice we were willing to make in order to make sure that our children understood the value of time together. It would also afford me the opportunity to work on our dream full-time, as Nate could only do it part-time while having a career. As that engineer, Nate began to travel a lot for many contracting opportunities. Opportunities that provided us with more income and freedom than we had ever imagined, yet there was that sacrifice of him rarely being home. We viewed it as a short-term sacrifice for a long-term gain. Nate traveling all the time was one of my motivations for continuing to press on in the industry of network marketing because we always knew that there was money to be made and it was an industry that offered freedom and we always dreamed of this becoming our reality. There were many ups and downs, but we rode the waves. It meant the world to me to be able to stay at home with our children, and I poured my whole heart and soul into it. Homeschooling our oldest daughter for many years alongside with my mom was one of my greatest accomplishments. It was the best feeling to no longer have to tell our children that I could not be somewhere or do something with them because I had a schedule to work in which I did not control. I loved being in control of my day!

With the birth of Christian, I continued to look for ways to create additional income in our household. In 2002, I made a decision to obtain my North Carolina Real Estate and Brokers license and was ready to become the agent of the year! Armed with some business cards and determination I was well on my way to a lucrative career in real estate, or so I thought. I did close several deals a year, not as many as I would have liked, but in 2008 the market shifted. During the time of pursuing real estate and many years prior, we tried opportunity after opportunity in the network marketing industry. Many I quit before we even got started. During those times, I did not understand how important it is to practice the principles of the industry and to truly grow and develop into the person that I would want to attract in our business. Therefore, failing in every business was a common denominator. During our times of failing in all of those opportunities, I always had the drive to do something, but I was on the journey of actually figuring out what my purpose was in life, beyond being a wife, mother, and daughter. In the midst of real estate and many network marketing opportunities, I was able to find something I got excellent at to bring in extra income…eBay! I was thankful to have a husband that just allowed me to be me. I learned the art of eBay, making money online without leaving home. Not realizing that this one day would be the very way that I could help our family in times of struggle.

Getting married at the young age of 19 to my amazing husband of now 27-years, meant that personally, I had a lot of room for growth. I consider one of my greatest accomplishments in life was finding the perfect person to spend my life with at an early age in which this union birthed our four beautiful children. Later came Zahria and Jaden. In the midst of the love and excitement of wanting to be that perfect mother, wife and also a primary caregiver to my elderly parents as they grew older, I realized one day that I forgot who I was. Not even forgot, but how about I realized that I never took the time to recognize who I was. Who was I created to be? What was my purpose? I knew that God had so much more for me to do personally, yet I allowed fear to stop me. Fear of the unknown, fear of public speaking, fear of failing, fear of meeting new people, fear of rejection, fear truly held me bound. I can say that fear is crippling and if we allow fear to take control of our lives, it will be the very thing that keeps us from reaching our God-given destiny. As a result of the fear that existed within, my purpose was also hidden within. I am thankful because God had given me a husband who always believed in me before I ever began to believe in myself. His belief in me caused me to keep going, inspired me to keep growing and helped me to face the very things that I feared. Nate was committed to helping me find my real life purpose. Two of the most important days in one's life is the day that we were born and the day that we discover why, which is our purpose. One of the greatest principles of success that Napoleon Hill shares in his book *Think and Grow Rich* that changed my life is knowing your Definiteness of Purpose. When one makes up their mind and then goes after it, this is when the actual journey of achievement and success begins. I knew that I had a passion and a feeling of fulfillment in helping others, but I did not know the avenues or the vehicles that I would be given to fulfill the purpose that God had given me in my life. I knew that something existed on the inside of me and I set out on a journey to discover me. A Mommy On A Mission was birthed as my mission to become a "Mompreneur Extraordinaire" was launched.

I began to develop a positive mental attitude, a P.M.A. I believe that this is one of the greatest principles of achieving success. Without belief, without positivity, without getting yourself into a zone to truly know that it is possible, one can never become all that God has created them to be. I began to shift my mindset, from looking at the negative, the circumstances, to finding the good in every situation. It was not easy at first, but I learned that looking at the negative brought about more negative. My husband Nate played a huge part in this always saying to me "Baby, Improvise, Adapt, and Overcome." In the beginning, I thought he was crazy, but then I began to realize for my health to be affected by stress, that it just was not worth it. I began to visualize and speak the things that I wanted to see in my life and happen in my life. When I made a decision, and the keyword was I had to make a decision, the way that I looked at life began to change. There were many times of struggle in our life, and so during those times I intentionally had to shift from focusing on the fight to instead putting emphasis on the success that I wanted to see. During the times in which the work was inconsistent, contracts ending and even before and on our way to that 6-Figure income, there were many occasions of improvising, adapting and overcoming. Filing bankruptcy a few times was a Band-Aid for us. Getting ourselves in debt over our heads became familiar for us. Hiding from bill collectors, payday loans, repossession, this was all common for us at one point in our lives. Can you imagine having to experience your husband, who has worked so hard and sacrificed to provide for your family, having to sell our last vehicle? Not just sell it, but to have to walk home because we didn't even have money for a taxi. After that, renting cars for over 2 years became common for us. At the time, we did not understand, but we are thankful for our journey today. Nate and I laugh to this day at how when we got married in 1989, that collectively we barely had two nickels to rub together, and therefore the foundation of our relationship is and has always been love. A strong foundation has allowed our relationship to stand the test of time. It was our life, but we knew that it was not our final destination. We always believed that one day we would find financial freedom. A fundamental principle to success is belief and faith that is applied. The greatest personal development book that was ever written, The Bible, says "Faith without works is dead," so applying faith is to take action. I began to realize that adversity and defeat were all a part of my process to become the person that I would need to become to have the success that I desired to have. I began to understand that in due season the very things that I pictured, the very things that I wanted, would one-day manifest if I remained focused and controlled my attention to our common goal which was to live the life that we knew our family deserved.

In the midst of my journey, In 2008, I became a part of an organization in a company with a young lady by the name of Stormy Wellington, who at that time was blowing up the Atlanta market with reshaping garments and billboards on buses. I was determined to meet her. One thing that I understood early on was that showing up is 80% of success and I was the one that showed up even when others began to quit and fall off. At that time, I did not understand the principle of success by going the extra mile and rendering service, but I began to serve not realizing that it would get her attention. She started a weight loss challenge and needed someone to facilitate the workouts (go figure something that I share all the time that I don't like to do, but I do like the results that I get). I was newly certified as a Zumba Instructor so why not! I had no idea what I was doing, but to the women involved I was the expert, who was too funny, but we got our goals achieved. For 30 days I drove twice a week for over an hour in Atlanta traffic and my mission was accomplished, Coach Stormy knew who I was! As time went on our business relationship grew into a friendship and sisterhood.

There were a few more network marketing and Internet marketing ventures that would come and go. They were all a part of my process to help me to be the leader that I am today as I continue to strive to be better at it every day. In 2014, we launched another business with Coach Stormy and another friend and business partner, industry leader Demond Coleman. We did something we had never done before, applying our faith and our belief. We realized that insanity was doing the same thing over and over again and expecting something different to happen, so we decided it was time to do something different. We visited Stormy for her birthday celebration in February in Miami and what was scheduled to be a 5-day vacation, turned into a 5-week mission. A mission that truly raised my belief to an all-time high in this industry. We created a mastermind alliance, in which we had a common goal, and we locked arms. During this season, I was stretched beyond all stretching, and the very things that I feared were the very things that I had to do. That 5-week stay, with all of us being financially challenged at the time, created a unified bond among us. We had sections of her house that we claimed as our office...words, images, and emotions became, even more, a part of our lifestyle. As we paced around her pool, as we jumped on a single trampoline one at a time because we could not afford a bigger one, the affirmations that we speak today were birthed. I'm Happy, I'm Healthy, I'm Humble, I'm Wealthy, I'm Strong, 6-figures a month! We began to speak it, we began to see it, we began to feel it, we began to believe it. In our minds it was already done. Our creative vision allowed us to see beyond where we were at that present moment and to see where we knew we were going. Every area of life that we are experiencing success in today is the reality of a dream that was visioned a long time ago. All of us have dreams, but way too many of us die with those dreams inside of us, and for us, we knew that was not an option, and that is why I never gave up.

That opportunity came and went just as quickly as it came. For the first time though, Nate and I saw success in this industry, making 5k our first month, but it did not last. Great company and product, but the cost of the product and the demand for the product, having only one product, helped us to quickly know that people buy what they want, not what they need. During the time of that launch, Nate and I made a decision that the Miami area would be our home before the new school year would start for our children. We didn't know how it would happen, but we were confident that it would happen. With contracts for Nate here and there and the times of surviving off of our 401k savings, we put a plan into action so that in August we would move. In August 2014, we did just that. We left Atlanta with the hope of new beginnings. We blessed family and friends with items from our home, the momentums that we wanted to keep, we put in storage, and we all left with one suitcase. What did not fit did not come as we embarked on what we called "The McCray Family Adventure." We had a plan but did not realize everything that God would allow us to go through and to grow through.

In November 2014, Corporate America failed our family again at a time in which it could not be more inconvenient. Living in a new place, in which we had not only moved our family, but I had also flown back to Atlanta to get my parents because I could not leave them behind. My mom at this time had Alzheimer's that had set in and I knew that God had chosen me to make sure they were taken care of. Not only were we in a foreign land, a new city, but it was the holidays! We had painted such a grand new life for our children, what would we do now? By January 2015, we found ourselves homeless looking for a hotel until we could figure out our next move. Our friend Stormy opened up her home to our family, and we found ourselves all under one roof again. This time with our three children, sleeping on air mattresses. The house was full, but at the core of it all was love and a strong desire to win. Many people were coming by her house during the day and evenings, and we found ourselves hiding our children in the garage, not wanting others to know that we had no place to go.

Broke and broken in the industry of network marketing, in the midst of it all, I said yes one more time to Total Life Changes when Coach Stormy said yes. Did I believe? Not really, I was beginning to lose hope, but I made a decision to borrow her belief one more time and create another mastermind alliance. I believe that a person's next level in life is dependent upon who they are connected to, walking with, and surrounded by. I told her no at first, but thank God for wisdom. She called me two weeks later to let me know she was pulling the trigger and I made a decision to say yes. At that time, she shared with me that her sister was down 21 pounds in 2 weeks and another friend had lost 17 pounds. I had this tea in my purse and did not drink it until I heard the results. I began to drink our flagship detox tea called the Laso Tea, not knowing that one cup of tea would turn into restoration, freedom and changing thousands of lives. The awakening for me was when I had the opportunity to attend a women's empowerment event in Danville, Virginia in which at that time I shared my 8-pound weight loss story that I had achieved in 6 days. I then experienced this little pack of tea multiplying to $400 in retail commission money in 20-minutes, and I knew that I had something different in my hands. Nate recognized my passion towards building this and although he was not in the forefront in the beginning stages, we would not have had the success that the company yielded in the months to come had he not been right by my side. The mom that our children knew could no longer do all the things that they were accustomed to doing and Nate stepped right in so that our children would not be affected.

I worked and worked and worked and change began to happen! I bought into a vision that was bigger than myself. Lose 5 lbs. in 5 days and make 50k before Christmas by putting 50,000 new team members into our movement. Did I believe I would make 50k by Christmas? No, but I knew Coach Stormy would, and I figured if I could just get a fraction of it, it would bring change to our lives. As a team, we crushed the goal by enrolling 57,000 new business partners thus birthing our 1000 Families movement. In less than 60 days, in an industry that we had failed in for over 20-years, I was able to earn 22k. Yes! Suddenly it happened! As we got the monkey off of our back, I quickly began to realize that this was not about me or us, but about the lives that I could help to change, the lives that I could impact. In doing that, the lives of those that said yes began to change. Our team began to grow. In taking the focus off of us and now putting emphasis on the phenomenal team of people that we had always pictured having, many success stories began to happen. In an industry where we could never achieve any level of leadership, in 5-months time, we were National leaders. God began to shift everything in our lives. In 7 months we were able to become 250k Ring Earners and restoration began to happen. It was at that point that Nate said that if one can put 1000 to flight, two can put 10,000 to flight and together we began to build the business. In less than 5 months, we more than doubled our income becoming 500k Ring Earners. As many lives continued to change, we became the first million dollar earners under the leadership of our coach, in 17 months. I was truly able to turn my weight loss goals into 7-Figures in 17 months after losing 20 pounds in my first 31 days! Keeping God first, family, and then business, teamwork, having phenomenal leadership and implementing the 17 Principles of Success by Napoleon Hill to create growth have been the cornerstone of our success. We are thankful for our CEO, and Founder of TLC, Mr. Jack Fallon and our visionaries who paved the way, our coach and for our team. Without our team first believing in us, none of this in this industry would be achieved. Together Everyone Achieves More! It is possible to live the life that you dream of. Once we realize that we are equipped with everything that we need on the inside of us to win, recognize our purpose, take action, stay focused and realize that we are "Created For Greatness" then that is when the greatness will arise from within and exude on the outside. Created for greatness, yes my God, "I am Created for Greatness!"

Pam McCray| Bio

Pam McCray is a mother of 4 beautiful children, wife to an amazing husband of 27 years, and a daughter first. She recently added the title of grandma. As an entrepreneur for over 20 years, she always believed that the Industry of Network Marketing would one day afford her family freedom. With God first, family and then business, she has always had the desire to be in control of her day and her schedule to have the time freedom that both she and her husband Nate wanted her to have with their children and their family. It was Pam's drive, motivation, and her husband's belief in her that has resulted in the entrepreneur and leader that she is today. Not knowing her God-given purpose, she set out on a journey to find out why she was created.

After failing for 20 years in the industry of network marketing, she is the true epitome of what never giving up, belief, and personal growth can do. One yes to a company called Total Life Changes less than 2 years ago has enabled her family to go from living paycheck to paycheck to now having money in the bank. She and her husband Nate are National leaders. Her weight loss goal turned into 7-Figures in 17 months. She loves helping others and has engaged in a vision to help change the lives of 1000 Families. She believes that everything you need to be successful exists on the inside and that you are "Created For Greatness!"

Pam can be contacted by email: joinpamtoday@gmail.com

Phone: 678-355-8729

Website: www.7FiguresIn17Months.com

Followed on IG: @pammccray1

FB: www.facebook.com/pam.mickensmccray

CHAPTER 9

A Ph.D. in Business Experience Exceeds All Else

By Michael Watt

"The women in my office are petty and uneducated," Grace whined. "They hate me because I'm young and they're not, I'm educated and they're not and, well, I'm pretty and they're not."

The young woman was right. They did hate her, but not for the reasons she cited. Their ire stemmed from the unjustifiable airs of superiority she felt she earned because she went to college.

"Graduating from college doesn't necessarily make you smarter than those who don't go," I explained. "If anything, the more you know the more you realize you don't know."

"Huh?"

"I've worked for a lot of men and women in my day," I said. "Most of them were successful, others not so much. But the smartest, most successful business owners I knew never went to college."

"How did they learn to run a business without a college degree?"

I laughed. "They learned what they needed to know, as they needed to know it. What they couldn't figure out for themselves they hired the right person to figure out for them. But they always made a point of knowing a little bit about everything so whomever they hired couldn't pull a fast one on them."

"What do you mean?" Grace asked.

"Well," I said, "one of them – Jack – was so busy he needed to hire a right-hand man, someone to run things while he was generating more business. So Jack, who was in construction, met with dozens of men. One highly-recommended candidate was cockier than he had a right to be. He kept telling Jack how 'stupid' his current boss was.

"At first Jack thought, 'why would I hire someone who's going to bad mouth me behind my back?' But a little voice told Jack to let the interviewee keep talking.

"'How so,' Jack asked.

"The candidate spent the next hour telling Jack the myriad ways he – the candidate – was ripping his boss off because his boss was 'clueless,' in the candidate's eyes. Jack was so enthralled he asked the candidate to come back for a second interview, knowing the candidate would see this as the two of them hitting it off. Sure enough, the next time they met the candidate regaled Jack with more ways he and the crew were "outsmarting" their employer.

"'I had no intention of hiring the guy,' Jack told me later. Jack wrote down all the ways the candidate showed him how a construction crew can steal time and resources from the contractor they're supposedly working for. Jack told me what he learned from these interviews probably saved him hundreds of thousands of dollars over the years he was in business.

"'I shudder to think what I would have lost if I hadn't listened to that little voice in my head, telling me to let the guy talk,' Jack said to me later."

"Was Jack your first boss?" Grace asked.

"No. That honor when to Gene, an Old Soul if ever there was one. He hired me to wash dishes in his catering hall when I was 14," I said. "I learned a ton from him, too, probably more than I should have at that age. Commercial kitchens are not for the young or faint of heart."

"Like what?" Grace asked.

"A few things," I said. "For starters, Gene always worked from a list. Nothing fancy – sometimes it was on the back of an envelope. But he was always doing something productive, even if he was just sitting there, thinking up new ways to drum up business. He was also organized. I remember one day he asked me to find something in a filing cabinet. As I looked, I came across a yellowed invoice for a funeral – his father's, back at the turn of the 20th century.

"Lots of people make lists and are organized, but never get anywhere in life," Grace said. "What drove Gene to succeed?"

"His birthmark," I said.

"His birthmark?" Grace asked.

"Gene had a hideous birthmark along the side of his nose. Then, just under his left nostril, the birthmark formed a ball that would hang over his lip and jiggle when he got angry. You never wanted to see that birthmark bounce."

"Why didn't he get it fixed? And how could that lead to his success?" Grace asked.

"When Gene was born in the early 1900s the surgical techniques to fix such things did not exist and even if they did, his family could hardly afford the bare essentials in life, much less extensive plastic surgery. So as a kid Gene vowed to make enough money to pay for such an operation once it was possible so he wouldn't have to tolerate the taunts of his mean-spirited classmates or the stares from strangers.

"Ironically, by the time the doctors figured out how to fix his face he could easily afford the procedure but he opted not to have it. His birthmark and, yes, the jiggly ball hanging over his lip, had become an integral part of who he was."

"So overcoming adversity served him well," Grace said. "What else?"

"Gene knew his numbers, and never wasted anything," I said.

"This was back in the 1970s when inflation was rampant," I added. "Gene would buy whole sides of beef and then bring in his butcher friends to slice them into smaller cuts of beef – prime rib, roast beef and the like. They'd wrap the cuts and store them in a freezer. As the price of beef went up, he could – and would – charge more for the dinners he served. Once his crew was done carving the sides of beef, they'd grind the fat so it could be used in the fryer and – once the frying oil had to be changed – he sold the old oil to the grease collectors. Nothing went to waste."

"He most have done well in the catering and restaurant business," Grace said.

"He did, up to a certain point," I said. "Gene never changed. Red meats like prime rib and roast beef fell out of favor in the mid-1970s and by the time Gene realized the wedding reception industry and brides' preferences had changed, it was too late. He had to sell his catering business and the restaurant that went with it.

"So I learned from Gene to stay current with trends," I said. "And he's not the only one. In the late 1990s I worked for Danny, a man who never went to college but ran a company, Inticipate, with four partners. I asked him one day why the company was called Inticipate."

"'In the early 1990s,' Danny explained, 'I Installed phones in cars – this was before cell phones became so prevalent - and then would upsell the installation by convincing the customer to have his car windows tinted while we were installing the phone. It worked like a charm, until I woke up one New Year's morning and realized the proliferation of cell phones had rendered my installation service irrelevant and, to add insult to injury, the state had outlawed window tinting. I promised myself that my next company would always keep an eye on what was coming down the road, envisioning the future, if you will.'"

"What else did Danny teach you," Grace asked.

"Plenty. Like Gene, Danny knew cash was king and you had to make sure you kept it flowing, like the heart pumps blood through the body," I said.

"Take the case of the conference room table," I went on. "For the first two years I worked at Inticipate Danny and his partners would often work through the night, taking the occasional nap on the one piece of furniture that could accommodate a body: the company conference room table. Many of us expressed consternation at the thought of working where one of the partner's had been sleeping a few hours prior.

"Ew," Grace said.

"Well, yeah," I said. "But when the tech bubble burst in 2002, Danny gathered all the employees in the conference room to give them a pep talk about Inticipate's future. He walked us through what to expect in the months ahead, that things would be tight but Inticipate would muddle through.

He closed with this bit of news: 'One of our bigger customers is going out of business,' he said. 'They can't pay us what they owe so they're giving us their beautiful conference room furniture. You won't have to work at this table any more,' he said. "Oh, and by the way, one of the reasons why they're going out of business - and we're not - is because we didn't waste money on conference room furniture.'"

"Here's what else I learned from Danny: mindset," I said to Grace.

"What do you mean?" she asked.

"Even though things were getting tight during the early 2000s, one of the partners I mentioned earlier used to pay somebody to detail his fancy sports car in the parking lot outside of the office, in plain sight of the employees. The partner was single and had been very successful prior to launching Inticipate. His car was his one indulgence and his passion.

"Still, seeing a partner getting his car detailed as the company was reducing its workforce angered many of the staffers and, to be honest, struck me as insensitive. I thought I would do Danny a favor and bring this to his attention. Once I did I knew right away I wasn't going to get the answer I expected.

"'I appreciate your concern,' he said, 'but my partner earned that car and the right to have it detailed every week by taking risks and working hard. So instead of bitching about what he's doing your co-workers should ask themselves, 'What can I do to be more productive? What risks can I take so I can reap the reward of a nice car and having it detailed whenever I want?'

"Danny was right. His partner earned the right to have the car and to have it detailed. He had no reason to keep it under wraps, nor would doing so benefit the workers in any way – other than to confirm that things were tight."

"They don't teach that in college," Grace said, picking up on the theme of these anecdotes.

"Right," I said. "You know what else they don't teach? Persistence."

"Persistence?" Grace asked.

"Yes. Heed the words of Harvey Mackay, who wrote "How to Swim with the Sharks without Being Eaten Alive:" 'I've known entrepreneurs who were not great salespeople, or didn't know how to code, or were not particularly charismatic leaders. But I don't know of any entrepreneurs who have achieved any level of success without persistence and determination."

"Let me guess," Grace said. "Jack, Gene and Danny were persistent and determined."

"Of course," I said. "You have to faith in yourself and your product or service because if you don't, who will? Without faith there is no persistence."

"How else does persistence pay off?" Grace asked.

"Great question. I'll give you an example. Jack, the construction contractor, had faith in himself and in God. When times were tough he would pray for guidance and direction. He was a devout Catholic but it doesn't matter who your God is, you just have to believe in that Higher Power guiding your life."

"I'll bet that faith was tested," Grace said.

"And you'd win that bet," I said. "During one particularly brutal recession Jack's construction work had all but dried up. He was down to his final few dollars when his neighbor offered to invest in his company."

"So his prayers were answered?" Grace asked.

"On the contrary," I said. "Jack knew if he took his neighbor's money she would make his life miserable. So he dug deep down into his resolve and figured out a way to keep the doors open without having to bring in an unwanted outside partner. He got through the crisis and thanked God every day thereafter for seeing him through."

"Which reminds me," I said to Grace. "As different as each of these men were, the one common trait they shared was their gratitude for what they had, even when they had little."

I chuckled.

"What so funny," Grace asked.

"I was just remembering one November, working at Inticipate," I said. "My co-workers and I were trying to convince Danny to let us have the Friday after Thanksgiving off so we could enjoy a four-day weekend. We had been putting in a lot of hours and thought we had earned it.

"Danny thought for a moment and said, 'I think we should celebrate how thankful we are for having jobs by showing up for work on Thursday AND Friday. How's that?'"

"We all worked that Friday."

"That's sounds more like a Grinch than a grateful boss," Grace said.

"Being in charge can never be about winning a popularity contest," I replied. "That said, each of these men had an innate ability to make people feel special, to make them want to go above and beyond their primary responsibilities. I have never seen a successful business owner not have that ability. You can manage and measure all you want, but if you can make people look forward to coming to work and meeting the challenges of the day then you're halfway there."

"I want to look forward to coming to work," Grace said. "How can I make the other women in the office be nice to me so I can focus on meeting challenges. I'm not their boss."

"That's a tough one, Grace," I said. "I suggest you embrace the philosophy of another man who never went to college – the Dalai Lama. 'Whenever possible, be kind,' he said, adding: 'It is always possible.'"

Michael Watt | Bio

Michael Watt, aka "Mr. Long Island," has made it his personal mission to ensure his native Long Island's vitality by advocating for the small businesses comprise the region's economic backbone and the Young Professionals who represent its future.

In addition to serving as Community Manager for LaunchPad Westbury – Long Island's sixth entrepreneurial incubator flying the LaunchPad flag, he is the Executive Director and Founder of The LIincs Organization, an association for young professionals on Long Island. He co-founded 516 Magazine, which highlighted Long Island's entertainment, recreation and leisure opportunities; launched LongIsland.com, a regional search engine, and ran the Long Island Partnership, an umbrella organization representing Long Island's dozens of economic develop agencies. The Long Island Business News published his op-ed pieces every other week from 2010 through 2015 and he has been published several times in Newsday's Op-Ed Section. He has won several writing awards from the New York State Press Association as well as the Long Island Press Association.

By tapping into his writing, public relations and marketing skills he has created an extensive network of public and private sectors connections. He can be reached at 631-678-6193 or michaelwatt@longislandinc.com.

CHAPTER 10

Give Birth To Your Joy

By Charles Duncan Waterman

On a sunny Spring afternoon, I was having lunch with Alex, a new friend of mine in the community of Newmarket, Ontario. Alex is a very intense, yet insightful man, who is always ready to provide an explanation to the ways of the world and the meaning of life.

After driving around town for a few minutes, we decided on a Caribbean meal of Jerk Chicken and Rice at Sunrise Caribbean Restaurant. The owner Pat was very pleasant and engaging so we felt quite at home.

During my conversation with Alex, he said, "Charles, we are pregnant"! Of course, I was thrilled, and congratulated him and his wife. But then he said, "No, you and I. Us. We are pregnant". It got even better....

"We're having Twins", he said. "You are carrying one and I, the other one... That's right, we, both of us are pregnant... As a matter of fact, so are all the people here in this restaurant. We are ALL Pregnant... How do you like that?" It's time to Give Birth.

That was a powerful statement and it got me really thinking. We are all pregnant, with something, with Spirits. For some of us, it might be things of the world and works of the flesh. We might be pregnant with the Spirit of inadequacies, anger, hate, depression, anxiety, resentment and fear; others, pregnant with pride, jealousy, dishonesty, arrogance and ignorance. The Bible speaks of these things in Galatians 5:19; things such as adultery, fornication, uncleanliness, and many other sinful acts. Alternatively, the fruits of the Spirit are outlined in verses 22 which make references to love, joy, peace, longsuffering, gentleness, goodness, faith, meekness and temperance.

We are already pregnant from birth, pregnant with joy, excitement, hope and unconditional love. We have not yet learned how to be cynical, suspicious, or fearful of others. Sadly, as we develop, many of these spirits creep into our lives.

Only you and God know which one of these Spirits are growing inside of you. If we live in the Spirit, let us also walk in the Spirit. If we have a Spirit of Joy, let us live our lives joyfully. Rejoicing in the Lord always. Rejoicing in the Hope of the Glory of God.

We Rejoice because we have peace with God through our Lord Jesus Christ and, as we are reminded in the Book of Proverbs, the Spirit of Wisdom is living in us. We are given the promise that the Lord possessed me in the beginning of his way, before his works of old. Before the mountains were settled, before the hills were brought forth. When God prepared the heavens, I was there. When He created the clouds, the sea, the foundations of the earth. Then, I was by Him as one brought up by Him, I was daily His delight. Rejoicing Always before Him. Rejoicing in the habitable part of His earth. Doesn't this promise make you excited? Doesn't it make you feel like a little child, hanging out with his dad? Learning how to ride a bike, or playing ball with him? Do you remember that feeling? Isn't that a great reason to rejoice?

In Philippians 4:4 Paul tells us to "Rejoice In The Lord Always".

Rejoice Always.

It is not always that easy though. Not always easy to be happy when things are just not working out. Times like these cause us to resort to the comfortable state of worry or panic.

Knowing that the Spirit of Joy lives within all of us from our birth must be the place we go to. This is our core. It has never left us.

So many times in life I've had to dig deep within to find that Joy. Most recently was the period of Fall 2009 to the Spring of 2010.

I had been in the seventeenth year of my second marriage. Our first child, a son, was a winter baby, who was born on one of the heaviest snowfalls of 1992. Our daughter came just fifteen months later in the spring of 1994. For many years, we had the perfect "million" dollar family. We attended church regularly; the kids attended Sunday school and were acolytes. I sang in the choir, and worked within walking distance from home. My ex-wife worked for a variety of companies, which in most cases required her to travel considerably. The presence of either parent was always there to tuck the kids in bed, read the story and say prayers.

Life appeared to be moving along smoothly until the decision was made for me to fulfill my dream of starting my own business. I had been in business for most of my adult life and was hungry to get back to the retail clothing trade that I loved.

My father was a tailor who always said that it was better to own a small business than to have a big job. Being an employee was always my last resort to employment. I was never truly happy or contented in that role, so I had to give birth to the entrepreneurial passion, which I had been pregnant with for all this time.

My dream required me to move out of the city for the summer months of 2004. This period was emotionally challenging for us as a family because my focus was now on making a success of a seasonal retail venture in the beach community of Wasaga Beach, Ontario. The kids were not encouraged by their mother to visit during their summer holiday, for fear of them being negatively influenced by the wild, teen, beach life of Wasaga.

Ironically, it was not Wasaga that should have been feared, but rather the life within the home without my presence. This absence, or "abandonment, leaving me holding the bag" as it was referred to by their mother, I believe was one of the greatest challenges of my life. The kids were at the ages of twelve and ten, now highly impressionable. Sometimes it felt like I was out of sight and out of mind in their eyes.

My methods of raising them were based on my own Caribbean upbringing of respect of God, others and self. These values have worked for my siblings and I, so I was confident that my family would be on the path to success as those before me had been. Unfortunately, with my absence, the balance, which existed before, was now tipped in favour of a more unstructured way of life and behaviours.

On my return to full time parenting in the Fall of 2004, there was quite a bit of relearning to do for both kids and parents. My return was met with difficulty in restoring authority and discipline in the home, providing an atmosphere of struggle between me against the kids and their mom. This position has not changed to this day.

The summer business venture lasted for three years until November 30th, 2007 when a fire razed through the commercial mall where my store was located, destroying most of the buildings, including my store. No one was harmed as the season had been over. The decision was made not to return and rebuild. My family referred to it as a sign to get out of Wasaga. I did.

Feeling defeated, angry, miserable and certainly with a spirit of fear, I trusted God to restore my confidence and my family dynamics. I was led to consolidate my debt and filed for bankruptcy.

Confidence returned sooner than the smooth sailing on the home front. The children were now young, intelligent, independent adults, and I had missed their growth internally and externally. Elements of their behaviour were not to my approval, so instilling discipline and appropriate conduct was met with strong resistance from all partiers. Their attitude towards me was not what

I had raised them to become, so the climate in the home was strained. This made for a hostile environment, as neither of us was willing to assume our various roles.

My ex-wife and I differed strongly on raising the kids and as I was absent, they were leaning towards her familiar methods of upbringing. I felt as though I was going to the right, she was going to the left and the kids were going up the middle into the oncoming traffic. The lack of respect shown to both parents by the children was not appreciated or tolerated by me. This resulted in heated arguments, loud confrontational encounters and an overall toxic environment for all, especially young children.

The wheels fell off the bus one day as I came home to the strong smell of smoke coming out of my daughter's bedroom. There was no one in the house. I had repeatedly asked that cigarettes not be brought or used in the home, but clearly, my opinion bore no weight.

This was the day when this activity would be stopped. I removed the door from its hinges and took it to the basement leaving the room open in plain view.

My son came home to find the door gone and angrily demanded its return. My daughter arrived shortly after to discover the privilege of privacy now revoked. An expletive filled bomb dropped and a call made to mom who was out of town. When I was summoned to the phone, I made it clear that the door would not be returned until the commitment was made of a behavioural shift-taking place. This prompted my daughter to pack a suitcase and leave the house, wheeling it up the street and out of sight.

Upon her mother's return, we had a conversation of our future and it was stated that she wanted a divorce. This did not come as a surprise to me as our marital relationship had died several years ago. She moved out of the master bedroom and slept on the family room couch for the next eight months, leaving me alone in the third-floor master suite.

These were some of the deepest darkest moments of my life. During this period, my relationship with God grew even stronger. I spent hours reading my Bible and staying in fellowship with Him. I asked Him to watch over the minds of my children and soften the heart of their mom towards God. I would repeat the verse of Psalm 23:4 " Yea, though I walk through the valley of the shadow of death, I will fear no evil: for thou art with me; thy rod and thy staff they comfort me".

I knew that God had not forsaken me, or my family. I prayed daily that He would protect my children from themselves and the world. He has.

That was my reason to Rejoice.

Sometimes I would play the music of Kirk Franklin, over and over. My favourite song was "Looking for you". Music provided an escape.

It was during this time that I understood the concept of giving birth. I realized that I had always been impregnated with the spirit of Joy, and now was the time to give birth.

From birth, I was being prepared for a time such as this. From birth, it was clear that I would always have to find the joy within me.

I had been down this road of pain several times before.

I was born in the tropical paradise of Barbados to a family resigned to accepting that they would probably not have a son. They had had six girls already, so when I was brought home to this brood, it was a celebration of epic proportion. My father's prayers for a son were answered and God blessed him with a successor. My dad understood that success without a successor is failure. He made it his life's purpose to pour his knowledge of music, literature, science, politics and law into me. He created the environment to teach without even realizing that he was teaching. Therefore, the lessons I learned and the habits I adopted were both constructive and destructive. The habit of procrastination has been running through my veins from a young age. This is one of my traits, which I'm still struggling with. The habit of self-sufficiency however, has also been in me and this habit has provoked me to find creative ways of existence all my life.

I was now the only boy in a family of girls and therefore I had to make the choice to be a boy or a girl. My sisters took great pleasure in dressing me in their clothes and braiding my hair with ribbons. For many years, I was their living doll. This attention did give me a sense of privilege, as it also taught me how to relate to the different personality types of my sisters.

Before I ever knew or heard of Napoleon Hill, I had developed a winning personality as a result of my ability to create alliances with my sisters individually.

The security of family gave me the confidence to move mountains. I could do anything. And I did.

My world came crashing down one September morning in 1963, shortly after my fifth birthday, and my first day of school.

My three-year-old sister and I were anxiously awaiting the arrival of my mom who had gone to the hospital to give birth to yet another girl.

As we were playing outside, the morning silence was shattered by the piercing screams of my aunt with the news that neither mom nor our new sibling would be coming back home. My mom, not yet forty years old, had died giving birth to my baby sister and they were now both dead.

The eldest of my sisters was about sixteen years old and she was the first to receive the details of what had happened. She reached a vocal pitch, which I never knew possible. Hearing her in this agonizing pain instinctively produced my feeling of compassion for her. This was my first true experience of what pain sounded like, what death sounded like.

Our home was covered with the cloud of mourning for the following week.

In those days, the casket containing the body of the dead was brought into their home for the last time, before being taken to the church and burial ground.

Our mother was brought home in a black Cadillac hearse, and placed in our modest living room. Family, friends and neighbours came to view her lying in the coffin.

Although I cannot remember her face, my memory of that day is still very clear and vivid in my mind. The casket was a dark, polished mahogany with brass handles and a glass window displaying my mom's pursed lips and closed eyes. The casket sat on a silver collapsible trolley with black wheels. My father and his friends stood waiting to lift my mom into the hearse. My sisters, my dad and I were then led into a black sedan, which seemed to stretch the width of our wooden chattel house. As we drove off, I could see the emblem on the front grill of the hearse which I later came to know as 'Cadillac".

Until this day, I associate Cadillac with death and solemn memories.

We drove for what seemed to be eternity until we reached St. Georges Parish Church. After service, inside, we proceeded to the gravesite at the back of the church. By this time the rain had started and the light was fading. The gut wrenching wailing of my mom's sisters, her friends and her daughters was intoxicating. My dad picked me up and took me under a palm tree for shelter from the rain, and to console me.

We arrived back home to the smell of flowers and death. The feeling of emptiness consumed me, and this hollow space in my stomach kept me trapped in the arms of despair and sorrow.

I laid in our wooden chaise lounge and cried uncontrollably for hours and hours. This was the closest I had even been to my own death. The pain was endless. There was no end in sight.

My broken-hearted father sat beside me and calmly told me that it did not matter how much I cried, no matter how long or how hard, nothing will ever bring her back.

Nothing!

Nothing!

These words brought a sense of finality to me. They also brought the sense of acceptance to the fact that I no longer had a mother.

As I laid in silent recovery of the trauma, I felt a peace come over me and at that moment I made up my mind that nothing or no one would ever bring me to this degree of pain again.

Nothing!

No one!

Period.

It was then that I believe the Spirit of God took hold of me. The Comforter came and dwelt within my being from that moment. That sense of peace and calm took over my entire being there and then.

With the decision to control and protect my joy at all times and at all cost, I made the decision to live for the moment. Whether there was food or clothes, I never worried, because I always knew the result would be the same. Death would come eventually. Life was short, and there were no guarantees for tomorrow. Nothing was for certain. Life surely was not.

This attitude towards life prepared me for what would follow. I had recently completed high school at St. George's Secondary and was working at Cave Shepherd department store in the city of Bridgetown. I would spend the weekends with my aunt and cousins in the beach community of the Garrison.

My life was great, I was eighteen years old, I was making money, I lived in the city, I had cool friends, I attended parties and explored life.

I was getting ready for work at my aunt's home on Monday morning, December 13th, 1976, when death called again. The call came to us that death had called my dad. Dad had been out for his morning walk, and was heading back home when he collapsed in the street. He had just turned sixty.

At my dad's funeral, I made another life changing decision.

I had lost my mother at five years old and now my father at eighteen. I had to leave this country. It was now my sole purpose to find a way to leave the country of Barbados. There were too many reminders of sadness, grief, and death there. Everyone and everything reminded me of death. I had to get out of this pit.

I moved permanently to my aunt and her family's home close to the beach. The popular, tourist filled beach of Accra on the south coast of Barbados, became my office. Here I would conduct daily interviews with tourists from around the world, with the goal of deciding which country I would choose to live in.

England was a non-starter because of its race riots in Brixton and other negative news.

The USA was never appealing, as the news we received growing up were that of multiple killings in New York City, Brooklyn and The Bronx. I learned the word "assassination" from the US news when reports of John F Kennedy, Robert Kennedy, Martin Luther King and Malcolm X were assassinated.

Canada was always the country of choice for me. The many Canadians I met on the beaches of Barbados confirmed the decision to make Canada my new home when the time came to emigrate.

So, on January 18th, 1982 I arrived in Toronto, Canada in search of the joy, which God had promised.

I found joy in many things and in many people here. More importantly, I found joy in the close relationship, which I established with my God. God had brought me out of the darkness of pain and sorrow, and into His marvelous light. He taught me to trust Him and have faith in Him.

My grandmother always said to me, "Charles, The Lord is going to open a door for you".

The Lord has been opening doors for me every day of my life. As I grow older I pay close attention to doors, which are presented to me and I ask God to let me know whether or not they are from Him.

God opened a door for me recently when I was asked to contribute my voice to the 17 Biblical Principles of Success audio program. This is a series of inspirational interviews on how to put the power of the Bible to work in your life.

My long-time friend, Phil R Taylor gathered a group of fifty-one spiritual, business and community leaders together and we created the seventeen-cd series. We provide thought-provoking discussions on these principles found in the Bible.

The 17 Biblical Principles of Success are:

1. **Trust In God**
2. **Humility**
3. **Confess and Repentance**
4. **Integrity**
5. **Courage**
6. **Fellowship**
7. **Kindness**
8. **Goodness**
9. **Thankfulness**
10. **Joy**

11. Self-Control
12. Wisdom
13. Faithfulness
14. Prayer and Meditation
15. Perseverance
16. Giving
17. Love.

When Phil asked me to participate in this project and speak on a topic, the principle of Joy was the obvious choice.

The spirit of Joy has filled my entire being since I surrendered my life to God and allowed Him to open the doors of my life. When I choose to walk through the doors He has opened for me, the road is smooth and the path is straight. The Joy is everlasting, and it is by His grace that I enjoy it day after day.

I fully understand and appreciate the Joy within, because of the pain I endured. Joy becomes the reward for our pain.

God has displayed His love for me time and time again. In my darkest moments of grief at my parents' deaths, or my happiest moments with the birth of my children, God has been my strength and my salvation.

This unending love is unspeakable and indescribable. You know it when you have received it. I think of Isaiah 61:10 which speaks of us rejoicing and being joyful because God has given us all we need by clothing us with his salvation, and covering us with His robe of righteousness. This is an amazing reason to rejoice. One can literally feel God's arms holding us close to Him.

This feeling is brought to life when, as a bridegroom, we are waiting at the alter for our bride to walk up the aisle toward us. The anticipation. That promise of great times ahead. When we get that feeling of knowing someone loves us so much that they are willing to spend their lives with us. That feeling gives us the confidence to do all things. The same is true when we feel God's love for us. This is the reason we have this Joy. The knowledge of His love ignites the flame of joy in us and the fire burns uncontrollably through us.

This joy now becomes power, strength, a net of love which we cannot hide and which catches the attention and souls of those around us.

When you are conscious of the joy inside of you, it is impossible to contain it. People notice you. They feel your energy and are drawn to your engaging manner. You become non-threatening even in tense situations, and can diffuse explosive circumstances calmly and peacefully. In most cases, winning favour with the parties involved. God gives us the ability to season our words with grace when we encounter different personalities in our daily lives.

In order to create a pleasing personality, it was important for me to first seek God, and establish a relationship with Him by studying, meditating and memorizing verses of His word, the Bible. With these words in my heart, I am able to identify and avoid situations, which are not of God. These words protect me from myself, because I know the outcome when I am not using His words to guide my life. These words provide the roadmap for my life and, as a result, this comfort brings clarity, peace and joy to my life.

The joy of knowing I don't have to earn God's love or His grace brings me the greatest joy. Joy becomes a by-product of God's love. This knowledge causes me to want to please Him even more. To humbly ask for His forgiveness when I fall short and commit sin. I repent and work on leading a life of which God will be proud.

Studying the 17 Biblical Principles of Success has really helped me to define the stages, and identify the areas of my life where I have had success and those that require further nourishment.

Principle #2 Humility is one of my challenges. I've often expressed my confidence with arrogance and pride instead of appreciation and thankfulness. After listening to the discussion on Humility, I realized that God hears my voice when I call on and depend on Him. But I am separated from Him when I let pride and selfishness come between us.

Principle #10 Joy is my favourite and I live my life in a constant state of Joy. As mentioned, Philippians 4:4 "Rejoice in the Lord Always" is always on my lips. I freely share this verse with others to help them see God's love through His creations. Although it is challenging to rejoice always, it is important to keep this verse in mind and come back to it every day. You will soon realize how different your life will become.

There will be times in your life when you do not feel particularly joyful, but I've found a few songs which always lift my spirit. Kirk Franklin is one artist whose uplifting message and beats gets me going no matter what. "Smile" is one such song. When Kirk reminds me that Jesus is the sunshine after the rain, I know that I can do all things through Christ who strengthens me, and my trademark smile emerges.

We are in control of our happiness. Every day we make the choice to be either happy or miserable. May I suggest that you decide now to live a life of Joy. The fact that you have life is a reason to rejoice. God has created us in His image and has promised to provide everything we need to live a great life. Acknowledge this and express thanks and gratitude to Him. Express gratitude to someone today. Challenge yourself to call someone in your life and thank them for being there for you in times of need.

The feeling you receive when you randomly express gratitude to someone is perhaps more rewarding to you than them. Do it. Pick up the phone now and speak to your mom or dad and ask them for forgiveness, and then tell them how much you love and appreciate them. For someone who does not have a relationship with God, this exercise will reveal who God truly is. There will be a spirit, which will consume you and that person. That area of your being is where your joy lives.

Release your inhibitions, put away your pride. Give birth to your joy.

Your life will change forever. Mine did.

Charles Duncan Waterman | Bio

Born and raised in the Tropical Paradise of Barbados, Charles Duncan Waterman relocated to Toronto, Canada in 1982 to pursue his education.

With a background in Fashion and Image Consultation, Charles always found Joy in transforming the lives on Men through his keen eye for detail in their appearance.

An additional career in Hospitality and now Real Estate, Charles has been successful in all areas of his business life.

His Spiritual life began as a young boy, and with early personal tragedies, Charles made the commitment to trust God to provide the hope and Joy which Charles now shares with all who come in contact with him.

Charles currently serves as Warden at the Church of The Messiah in Toronto, and sits on the committee of the Black History Association in Ajax, Ontario.

Charles and his lovely bride, Audrey, have four children and feel truly blessed to share His Joy.

Charles lives by the verse of Philipians 4:4

"Rejoice in the Lord, Alway.. And again I say Rejoice…

Charles can be reached at Charles@cdwaterman.com or www.cdwaterman.com

CHAPTER 11

One Step Closer

By Dionne Malush

Growing up in a small town South of Pittsburgh, I thought from a young age that I would have to work hard to get where I wanted to be. I started working at age 16 and had 3 jobs while attending the Art Institute of Pittsburgh. At 15 years old, and again at 18, my doctors found tumors in my left breast. I went from being a child to an adult instantly due to the fear of the unknown. It was frightening and my family and I were all very scared. As I approached high school, I was a bit more rambunctious than most kids. I was very self-confident and I think that the surgeries gave me the feeling that I could win and beat this foreign object in my body.

Around the time I was 18, I went to a seminar in downtown Pittsburgh that featured Zig Ziglar and I was immediately hooked. At that point, I bought my first of many copies of Think and Grow Rich by Napoleon Hill but I didn't read it. I didn't know that book would become such an amazing part of my life. After graduating, I knew quickly that I could not work for anyone else. I was too strong willed and independent. I decided to start my own graphic design business after having a few jobs.

In 1999, I met Jason. He was so different from other guys I had known. He was amazed by my work ethic and he didn't try to hold me back. He truly believed in me. He didn't drink or do drugs like many people did in my area. He was kind and willing to step back and let me flourish. As Jason and my sister joined me, the design business grew to $1,000,000 in yearly sales, which was quite impressive because the average ticket sale price was only about $400. In the early 2000's, I decided to partner with a few men and buy another company. It seemed a great fit. After about 11 months, my partner lost his job at the local hospital. He basically came to us and said – we have to decrease salaries and eliminate employees because I have to make the same money that I was making at the hospital. At that time, we had 11 employees. It was a horrible day as I watched my 2 partners, one-by-one, tear apart my company. Again, I proved to be the tough guy … I quit, too. In fact, I gave them 90 days' notice and let them run the company into the ground. On the 89th day, we went in and took all of the equipment and I left my partners a letter … they called the police and the police said – it's her company, she can take whatever she wants. It was a civil case, not a criminal one. The partnership destroyed my company and almost destroyed me. I was devastated to the point that I thought that I was having a heart attack and had to be hospitalized for days to find out that it was anxiety from my business loss. In the next 2 years, I lost 14 friends and family members including my best friend. Once again, I was so saddened. I felt like a failure and had such incredible loss that I did not know what to do. Thank God I had Jason and my family by my side, as I entered some of my darkest moments. They all helped me through it and never gave up on me. To this day, they are my biggest supporters and I love them all dearly.

At that point of losing my business, I had many months without income. I knew I had to find something else. I hadn't saved a dime. I was just living on what I made never foreseeing that I would lose it all. I had always had an interest in real estate so I thought about adding that as a part time job to my graphic design career. It took months to close a deal but once I did, there was no holding me back. I could use my creative skills to enhance my real estate business. It's a great marriage of two industries.

In 2006, as Jason and I vacationed with my parents in Key West, I knew that I was in financial trouble. I had just enough money to pay half of the next month's bill. I didn't know what to do, so I went home and watched The Secret. From that day forward, we have always let mindset training guide us to the next level. Since I was a visual person, "The Secret" really hit home with me. I showed it to Jason and he, too, was mesmerized by the message. We realized that "Think and Grow Rich" was the next step. So we both started reading it and listening to the audio. I had affirmations all over the house and dream boards, too (I still do – in fact, I am watching many of my dreams come true). I spent every morning in the shower listening to Napoleon Hill. My life was changing and I just kept listening. I was getting my second chance. I was just a girl from a small town. I was called names and made fun of and when I was 14 years old someone spray-painted terrible words about me on the Church steps next to my house. This had affected me negatively for many years.

I didn't know that I could change my life with my mind. I didn't know that I could change my finances with my mindset. I had to believe in me …

In the years following that time, I have read and listened to many books, audios, videos, and more. From Wallace D. Wattles to John Kehoe to Napoleon Hill to Grant Cardone and much more. I try to keep my mind on track. I even masterminded with a few friends, Erica and Lisa which was so intriguing and fulfilling.

I then wrote my Definite Purpose before I met any of the following men that influenced my life: "My definite purpose for my life is to be able to help my family as well as many others through my studies, my finances, and my love. I believe you have to give to receive and I am giving my whole heart into becoming so successful that I can reach my goals with incredible faith in God. I earn over $1,000,000 per year and also maintain a happy and healthy lifestyle with the man of my dreams. I will share my secrets of success plus will continue to learn from the teachings of Napoleon Hill, Andrew Carnegie, Wallace D. Wattles, Bob Proctor as well as today's modern teachers of the law of attraction. I will study daily to become a better more-rounded person. I want my energy to enlighten everyone that I meet, and my positivity to radiate onto them. I surround myself with like-minded people to further ensure that I am learning from the best so that I can pay it forward. I will keep God close to my heart at all times in my journey. I plan to become A Real Live Santa Claus". - Dionne Malush, March 24, 2012, Revised 8/31/2016

In 2013, I met James Spooner who was a former instructor for The Napoleon Hill Foundation. I met him at a time that couldn't have been better. I was working for another real estate agent and he introduced me to a friend of James – when I heard that James knew so much about Napoleon Hill, I couldn't resist wanting to know more. Since meeting James, we have spent many days together discussing how to change my mindset and keep it on track. His knowledge and passion for "Think and Grow Rich" has been a true inspiration to me.

2014 – Tom Cunningham – I saw this unique man on Facebook and instantly, I had to follow him. His story is one of my favorites, he truly is a passionate, dynamic personality. I am so honored to be working on this project with him.

2016 – Jim Shorkey – 3 years ago, I heard of a very successful local businessman that was a huge follower of "Think and Grow Rich" so I Facebook messaged him to find out more … fast forward to January of 2016 when one of my colleagues told me about a man that read "Think and Grow Rich" 100 times. How could I be so close to someone that had absorbed all of this knowledge? And I had only reached out to him one time before this. Well, this time, I wasn't letting him pass by … we met at a local coffee shop and he introduced me to "Think and Grow Rich" again … I am working with him to grow in ways that I hadn't known I could.

Are these coincidences? I think not. All of these amazing men came into my life through the law of attraction. They are my guides to take me to the next level. Riding this "Think and Grow Rich" train at this point in my life and seeking expert counsel will be the turning point for me. I am on my way and would love to share and mastermind with any one of you.

Back to 2015, I had my best year ever and even sold a house to one of our hometown Pittsburgh Penguins. I was ecstatic; I was finally turning the bend to the next level. Then BAM! I had a personal issue that completely crushed me. My mindset was ruined and my self-esteem was destroyed. I was a basket case. I didn't want to listen anymore. I have never been so sad and hurt in my life. I was thinking negatively and those that know me knew something was terribly wrong. 2 months later I ruptured my Achilles tendon – 100%. **I didn't walk or drive for 12 weeks.** I fell into a horrible place … remember, **I know** that the mind can achieve whatever it believes and I still fell short.

I am always on the go as walking and driving are critical to a real estate agents job and this was a real shock for me and truly knocked me down a bit. I haven't been very good at asking anyone for help so this too was a struggle. I know that things like this happen to make us stronger and it's working. I must say that my appreciation for mankind is off the charts. I saw a side of humanity during this that I had never seen before. People of all ages treated me so kind and went out of their way for me. Many times it brought tears to my eyes.

Well, here I go again. I had to pull myself back up. Why do I have to keep falling down? Why can't it be easy for me? "Easy for Dionne" … that's not what I believed. After all the training and listening, I believed that I didn't deserve success. In fact, the day that I sold my largest property was literally one of the worst days of my life. A coincidence, no! It was me. I had it somewhere in my subconscious mind that I don't deserve all of this. I didn't deserve success. So the universe, let me know that I was right. My business suffered terribly in 2015 while having the best year of my career. I was so focused like a horse with blinders on but when it got TOO good, I fell apart. I didn't believe in me.

Early 2016, I am still deep in depression and not walking. While in physical therapy, the therapist finally says, "Take a step, it's time for you to walk", I said, "I am scared" but guess what? I did it anyways. I took that step and started back on track. It was a rough start to the year but finally; I was one step closer and was going to be OK … no matter what. My heart was mending and my leg is mending. There is a pain every day to remind me and it will be there for a while, but I am Dionne Malush and no one, not even myself, will keep me down.

I started training with Jim Shorkey (featured in this book) and his partner, Chuck Bolena (also featured in this book). I am very excited to learn their ideas. Jim almost lost everything and then successfully rebuilt his company 10x better. We even have a weekly mastermind group. Napoleon Hill would be proud. So this is my goal for 2017 - to surpass my goals and to show the World what so many have before me that you get knocked down but you always have to get up … with that, I will leave you with this, one of my favorite motivating quotes from Rocky Balboa:

"The world ain't all sunshine and rainbows. It's a very mean and nasty place... and I don't care how tough you are, it will beat you to your knees and keep you there permanently, if you let it. You, me or nobody, is gonna hit as hard as life. But ain't about how hard you hit... It's about how hard you can get hit, and keep moving forward... how much you can take, and keep moving forward. That's how winning is done. Now, if you know what you're worth, go out and get what you're worth. But you gotta be willing to take the hits. And not pointing fingers saying: You ain't what you want to be because of him or her or nobody. Cowards do that and that ain't you! You're better than that!!!"

— Rocky Balboa

I have had personal issues, medical issues, incredible grief, stress and even a major business failure. I have been flat on my butt but I always get back up. Then enters Napoleon Hill into my life and I realized that the only thing that I had complete control over was my mind and my thoughts. When I changed the way I looked at things, the things I looked at changed. I searched and studied endlessly with friends that believed like I did, for the information that would enable me to make my dreams come true and through all of this, I keep getting up and I persevere. I know I will get where I want.

But I have to stop here and clarify the book. "Think and Grow Rich" and Napoleon Hill's writing is not written in today's language. It's amazing to me how relevant it is now 90 years later. There are no references to computers, email, the internet, Facebook, social media, credit cards, or even TV — because none of those things existed when he wrote this classic self-improvement book. Yet somehow the book has managed to sell more than 100 million copies over the past seven decades. To receive all the wealth in the book, you have to get over the fact that "Think and Grow Rich" was written so many years ago. As a country, we were right out of the Depression and the stock market crash of 1929. World War II was in full swing, the mood of the country was nervous, and Napoleon Hill was screaming, "Make friends, be positive, believe in yourself, be influential, develop a goal and a plan, articulate yourself clearly, dedicate yourself to excellence, take directed action and encourage others to do the same." Pretty cool, isn't it?

These books aren't 70 years old; rather they were 70 years ahead of their time. Maybe that's why Napoleon Hill's "Think and Grow Rich" and Dale

Carnegie's "How to Win Friends and Influence People" have been on bestseller lists for 70 years.

I am now an owner of a real estate company with over 20 agents on my team. Jason joined me in pursuing his real estate license too. It takes work but it is so worth it. We did it together, and you need to believe that you can too. NO MATTER WHAT.

Dionna Malush| Bio

Dionne Malush is a listing and marketing specialist in the Pittsburgh area. In real estate since 2004, she calls herself The Almost Famous Realtor. With a creative background (over 27 years as a graphic designer), she has been able to climb to the top in her market utilizing her artistic ability. Dionne is a 1989 graduate of the Art Institute of Pittsburgh. Since starting her real estate career, she has been coached by many of the top real estate coaching companies in the country.

She was ranked in the Top 500 Real Estate Marketers in the US and Canada. Dionne is a Certified Home Selling Expert, which entails hours of training each week. Her graphic design background and many years of training help to set her apart in an industry where anyone can become a real estate agent but becoming a successful agent is a much bigger challenge. She is able to really showcase her listings because of the marriage of graphic design and real estate. Her properties stand out for many reasons including utilizing professional photographers and treating a home as a product that deserves the very best marketing.

She has achieved the prestigious Centurion Award from her 5 years at Century 21 Frontier Realty. Ranked in the top 1% in sales at Coldwell Banker Pittsburgh over 1,000 agents, the #9 REMAX Agent in Western PA and now is an owner of Northwood Realty 201 Associates which she ranked #8 Northwood agent in the entire Pittsburgh/Ohio region in 2015. She consistently sells between 55-65 homes each year when the average agent nationwide sells between 8-12. In 2015, her best year ever, she closed 74 transactions while being injured for the last 2 months of the year. She also closed her biggest transaction of her career by selling a home to one of her beloved Pittsburgh Penguins. She has also co-authored "The New Rise in Real Estate", a book that has reached #1 on Amazon.com's 2012 Best Seller List. Malush just recently published "25 Tips for Selling a Home in Pittsburgh" which is also sold on Amazon. She has trained and masterminded in various groups with Bravo's Million Dollar Listing Agents, Josh Flagg from Beverly Hills and Fredrik Eklund from New York City learning their techniques to compete in the luxury real estate market.

Working with her team, she is able to dedicate her to time to focusing on what she needs to do daily to get a house sold. She has a large Social Media reach. Dionne studies the law of attraction daily and maintains goals in writing to help her get to each level of her success. Part of her daily routine is studying many great books written by Napoleon Hill, Bob Proctor, Wallace D. Wattles, Grant Cardone and many other mindset authors. Dionne is a VIP member of Dan Kennedy's local marketing mastermind too. An avid sports fan (Steelers, Penguins & Pirates too), she also loves Corvettes, Mercedes, Bentleys and Drag Racing. Enjoys going to beaches especially Key West, Myrtle Beach, Outer Banks and Santa Monica. She loves spending time with Jason, her longtime love, just going jet skiing and snowmobiling, reading, and snuggling with her pets, Isabella and Hulk.

Her mission statement for her business is this:

It is my mission to create customer delight by outperforming the industry in ways that sell my client's home faster, more efficiently and for top dollar. My dedication to this industry and making it better as well as myself is an ongoing pursuit. My graphic design background makes my client's homes "stand-out" in the marketplace and I am committed to putting their property in front of millions of potential buyers through my extensive online strategies. I learn daily and share my knowledge to help others as well as my sellers and buyers make educated decisions. I am honest with my clients creating long term relationships that enhance the growth of my business as well as myself. I know my weaknesses and strive hard to overcome them through endless training from the industry's leaders. I demonstrate uncompromising integrity in all things at all times. No exceptions, ever. My positivity radiates to people in my life creating a positive experience for everyone.

Contact Dionne Malush:

www.DionneMalush.com

724-554-3514 cell

dmalush@gmail.com

CHAPTER 12

Keep Smiling-The Magic of a Positive Attitude

By Piseth Kham

"Nothing can stop the man with the right
mental attitude from achieving his goal;
nothing on earth can help the man with the
wrong mental attitude."

— Thomas Jefferson

A positive attitude leads to happiness and success. Our attitude controls our lives. It determines the way we look at things and how we respond to what happens to us every day. A person with low skills and a positive attitude has a higher chance of becoming successful in life than those who have higher skills but a negative attitude.

If you look at the bright side of life, your whole life becomes filled with light. This light affects you and the way you look at the world, and it also affects your environment and people around you.

I was in a room with some Asian authors, speakers, coaches and consultants. We were discussing the top qualities that contribute to a person's success. Many ideas came up such as skills, knowledge, attitudes, and strategies. To clarify what most important we did a simple exercise. Each one of us took a piece of paper and wrote down the top ten qualities of a person we would want to be our substitutes in our business for one year. It was a surprise for everyone because we all came up with:

- Positive Mindset

- Integrity

- Honesty

- Hardworking

- Confidence

- Influential

- Strategic Thinking

- Positive attitude

- Courageous

- Persistence

- Humble

The lead facilitator asked us "Are these qualities, skills, knowledge or attitude?"

Of course, everyone answered **ATTITUDE**.

Sometimes we need someone who has more experience than us to see the unique quality or gift that we possess in life. Once we realize those qualities inside of us we need to update them and empower them so that they support us at a higher level.

One of the visiting professors from Australia who was teaching at Maharishi Vedic University of Cambodia found a unique quality inside me. He told me that I have a natural gift that will bring me more success and happiness in life. He kept reminding me of this gift, "Smiling".

I always use this gift. I realized that people found it hard to recognize whether I faced difficulties or not because I always smile. I was often invited to give interviews on TV or newspapers. I am always wearing good clothes and a big smile on my face for the interviews. I talked about how to lead a successful life. I encourage people to talk about their goals and dreams no matter how hard their lives are. And I have seen those who follow this single advice turn their lives around for the better. They attract positive people and great opportunities into their lives.

People often thank me for the educational and inspirational messages.

Turning Passion into a Business

"You have to be burning with an idea, or a problem, or a wrong that you want to right. If you're not passionate enough from the start, you'll never stick it out."

— Steve Jobs

Prior to reading Think and Grow Rich, and the Law of Success I was working as management advisor to non-for-profit organizations (NGOs) in the areas of leadership, management and fundraising.

I started to see things differently after I read Napoleon Hill's books.

My wife and I started to have a dream of running a successful business. We want a business that inspires and transforms other people's lives for the better. We came up with an idea to run an educational business. We combined our names Piseth and Malay for our company's name "PM Leadership" Our mission is "To Lead Humanity into Success and Financial Growth".

Nowadays, people are inspired by how we started our company. We did not have enough capital. We did not have an office for the company. To get started we asked one of our friends to use his house for us to register the company. We had 400 Dollars as our capital. We ran our business in our living room from 2011-2013.

We faced many financial challenges during the first two years. We perceived our challenges as a God given exam for us to qualify ourselves to see if we were ready for more success in life. We passed the universal exam by not violating our core values of Integrity, Honesty, Love...

When people ask me how I got started I tell them it was because I have a mastermind group. Like Napoleon Hill wrote about and suggested, my wife is my best mastermind partner. She is the power beside me. I often advise single men and women to; "Choose your spouse wisely".

Another key to my growth is masterminding with other like-minded people. In 2012, I started running a monthly Mastermind for Success group. We had people from all walks of life join our sessions. We shared our life experiences and the knowledge we learned from training and seminars. Many of the mastermind members had become our team members in the company.

In 2013, I became one of the Founding members to kick-start the very first Business Network International (BNI) Chapter in Cambodia. I always give credit to my late mentor Mr. Bellum Tan for his guidance and encouragement to join BNI. It was a life changing decision. Since then I have served in leadership positions of the chapter many times including one as the President of the chapter.

In 2014, I became the first Director Consultant of BNI Cambodia to receive a "Hall of Fame" award from BNI Headquarters.

In 2016, we won a TOP business award "Business with Passion" from International Business Federation (IBF) Singapore.

Become A Leader and Inspire People

"Your Significance will remain forever obscure to you, but you may assume that you are fulfilling your purpose if you apply yourself to converting all your experiences to the highest advantage of others."

— Buckminster Fuller

I initiated a study group while I was in university. I had students from the first year and second year to join my class. It made me feel great to share with them what I had learned. In return, I gained respect from them as a senior student and as a brother. I did the same thing when I was working as a management advisor for NGOs. I organized a learning group during the weekend. I encouraged those who have higher experiences to develop the lesson plans. I reviewed their lesson plans and gave ideas for them to share with their coworkers. I feel proud seeing them grow. Many of them are highly successful in their careers and lives now.

Since day one of my business I have never had more than ten people working in my company. I have set a goal to turn what I am doing into a cause. My intention is to inspire people to come and support our mission to help more people. We attract awesome people from high net-worth families in the country, top executives, and business leaders to work with us as volunteers. They feel inspired by the work we do. They have opportunities to give back to other people for their journey to success and financial growth. They receive love and friendship in return. The quality of their network becomes stronger with the business community nationally, and internationally.

One of our team members, Mey Thir, shared why she started supporting our mission "The very first reason is because I feel the essence of Love, Integrity, Fun, Vision and Commitment to uplift humanity from the founder Kham Piseth. And then after the first few times, I continued because I felt an essence of Love and Fun in the team as we learned and worked together.

All of this combined with access to mentoring, coaching, opportunities, a great network, and higher and higher benchmarks and commitments to the original vision - to lead humanity to success and financial growth."

Having A Mentor

"Whatever it is that you lack in education, or knowledge, or influence, you can always obtain it through somebody who has it. Exchange of favors and exchange of knowledge is one of the greatest exchanges in the world."

— Napoleon Hill

When we study many successful people we see that they have mentors who guide them and support them.

It has been said that "Success Leaves Clues". I always tell people that if you want to be good at playing football like Ronaldo, I would recommend that they 1) learn how to play football with Ronaldo himself, and 2) find out who are Ronaldo's the teachers or coaches and learn from them.

I believe in having mentors and learning from them is a fast way to learn and climb the ladder to success.

I have been searching for some of the top minds in personal development and business growth strategists. As a result, I have met and learned from people like Tony Robbins, Les Brown, Robert Kiyosaki and many others. And when I study them they mentioned one book that has had a huge influence on their lives. That book is "Think & Grow Rich." I follow their paths. I read the book and I listen to audio. I started to study some of the names mentioned in the book. I personally consider Think & Grow Rich as a form of mentorship that Napoleon Hill had created for me and other people all over the world.

I know that reading books, attending seminar and trainings is not enough. I need to have coaches and mentors. I watched a TED Talk video where Bill Gates talked about the importance of having mentors. His famous quote is; "Everyone needs a coach".

One of the best mentors I have had is the late Rich Dad Asia Mr. Bellum Tan who passed way in September 2016. He had a huge impact on my life. I first met him in 2012 and he gave me a clue about my life path. He said; **"Piseth! You are on the right path"** It was very touching to hearing this from him. I knew what my true north was.

Later in 2013, he introduced me to advanced personal development and business development programs. He told me; "Don't be cheap". If you want to be successful you need to pay the price. Invest in yourself.

My life has changed dramatically since I met him and had him as my business partner and mentor. He always reminded that "Rich People Work as a Team".

He connected me to other great masters and mentors who still guide me in business and investment. Within one year working with him I grew my income to six figures.

He reminded me to "**Always have coaches and mentors**"

Work To Learn Not Just To Earn

"Surround yourself with people who love life and learn."

— Lorii Myers

One of my all-time favorite books is "Rich Dad Poor Dad" by Robert Kiyosaki. In Chapter 7 "Work to Learn - Don't Work for Money" he wrote about his decision to join the Marine Corps because he wanted to learn leadership skills and how to fly. He later resigned from his position in the Marine Corps and started working at Xerox because he heard they had a world-class sales-training program. He vowed to learn everything about sales and, once he was successful, he would move on. In 1977, he formed his own company, beginning the next phase of his career, and the rest is history. He is now a global successful businessman, investor, self-help author, educator, motivational speaker, activist, financial commentator, and radio personality.

Since my second year in university, my friends and I have worked as volunteers for three to four months for companies or non-for-profit organizations during our holidays. We work without getting paid. We wanted to have work experiences for us to find jobs. Interestingly, many of my friends were offered high paid jobs even before we left university.

I got offered a paid job when I was in my fourth year of university. I worked at the same time I went to university.

I remember during the interview for the position of Assistant to Management Advisor that the interviewers asked me "Why did you apply for this position?" I replied; "I want to be a management advisor. So I need to start as an assistant to the management advisor. Working hand in hand with the management advisor I will have the opportunity to learn from her and the senior management team of the organization." I worked very hard during that time. I used my pocket money to pay for my Master Degree and other work related programs. I volunteered to help different departments if they needed my support. Within one year I was promoted to the Management Advisor.

In one of my seminar "Be Rich Seminar" featuring my late mentor Mr. Bellum Tan he shared how important it is to learn everything you can while you are working for someone.

After college, Bellum Tan gave himself five years to work for others as an employee to learn the trade. While working for others, he was very helpful and volunteered his service to other departments because he wanted to learn as much as he could about the business. Soon, he started his first company, a part-time business. Then success begat success and he became a successful contractor. He was living a successful life as an entrepreneur and investor. He travelled all over the world to teach people financial education. He always reminded us that "Work to Learn Not Work to Earn"

I asked him why he was so passionate about travelling to many countries and teaching people even when he did not get paid. He said that "The highest form of MONEY is Spiritual Money where you give back what you get. The more you teach the Richer you will become"

I found out that my mentor read Think & Grow Rich when he was young.

Everything Speaks – The Magic of Self Confidence

"With realization of one's own potential and self-confidence in one's ability, one can build a better world."

— Dalai Lama

Most of the time people believe that skillsets and strategies are the most important for one to become successful. Therefore, they focus on developing their skills and expecting things to become better in the long run.

However, when we study the lives of great men and women we see that they are very good at managing their mind. They have unshakable psychological strengths. This can be apply to businesses and corporations as well.

One of my coaching clients is a top executive from Cambodia's branch of a multinational and multi-billion-dollar corporation. In Cambodia for the past two years they had never exceeded 60% of their target. Interestingly, they hit 93% of their target in September 2016. When I worked with one of their top executives for four months I focused on building his inner strengths, confidence, personal responsibility, positive and can attitude, and good habits toward saving and spending money. I also coached him how to share what he learned from me to his fellow senior executives in the company.

I have another client from a top insurance company in the country. He came to me with two goals he wanted to achieve after he had tried and failed. First, he wanted to become a trainer for his company. He told me that he had proposed to management that he organize training and retreats for sales staff in the company because he saw that it would help the company to grow more. For over two years the company did not give him the opportunity to train their staff. I found out that he has great potential and a unique gift as a trainer and coach inside him. Yet, his level of self-confidence blocks him from doing great things. So we worked on discovering his gift and building his inner strengths and self-confidence. The mantra for him was "Everything Speaks". After working with me for two months he was granted the opportunity to lead the capacity development retreat for the whole company's sales team. After seeing his great level of performance as a retreat leader the company gave him the opportunity to train all sales staff in the company. He told me that he felt so happy and grateful that he has the chance to do what he loves in the company. He is often invited to share his experiences to the public and students of famous universities in Cambodia. Moreover, his leader called him for a meeting and offered him a higher position in the company with a bigger reward. The fact is he did not request a promotion. "Everything Speaks". His self-confidence communicated to his leader that he deserved a higher position and a higher reward.

His second goal was to start a part-time business. He felt hesitant to start a part-time business because he had failed in a restaurant business that put him into debt. With the new level of high self-confidence he did a joint venture and started a business that brings him a secondary income. The great thing about his new business is that other people run it for him so he has the time to work on things that he loves and matter most to him and his family.

Piseth Kham| Bio

An Award Winning Entrepreneur, Piseth Kham, is the founder of PM Leadership, Cambodia's leading seminar organizer on success, business and wealth creation. He is the Master Facilitator of CashFlow Club Cambodia supported by Rich Dad Asia.

He is famously known for starting his company with $400 and turning it into a national brand within one year. Piseth served as a Director Consultant of BNI Cambodia from 2013-2015. He is the first Director Consultant of BNI Cambodia who received the "Hall of Fame Award" from BNI headquarters. He successfully launched a BNI Chapter "BNI Cambodia-Millionaire Chapter". He served as the President of the BNI CEO Chapter in 2015 and several times as a member of the leadership team. He acted as a Management Advisor with German Development Service (DED) in 2007-2008. He served as Program Manager for CDPO for almost five years. Piseth develops his personal success and business skills through his interactions with some of the top minds such as Jay Abraham, Robert Kiyosaki, Tony Robbins, Blair Singer, Rich Schefren, Bellum Tan, and more... He has appeared on CNC, SEA TV, TVK, Hang Meas TV, Bayon TV, Radio Australia, National Radio, Phnom Penh Post and others.

Piseth can be reached at pisethkham@gmail.com

CHAPTER 13

From Desperation To Inspiration

By Inez Blackburn

Beyond beliefs

*"The only competition you have in life is who
you were yesterday"*

— Maria Wahlberg (Inez's Grandmother)

I have struggled with self-esteem for most of my life never feeling truly comfortable or confident. My obsession with feelings of inadequacy compromised so many opportunities because I placed more importance on how I was perceived rather than what I believed. No matter what I accomplished in life, I never fully celebrated my success. When someone complimented me, I always found a way to dismiss it, looking for what was wrong with me rather than what was right.

When I look back at my life, I realize that deep down I felt guilty about my success, that somehow I did not deserve it and in many cases sabotaged many of my accomplishments. I lived my life on auto-pilot, always striving to live up to the expectations of the people around me while losing myself in the process. Somehow, I believed that for people to accept and like me, I had to look a certain way, behave in a certain way, and constantly do things for people even when I felt that they were taking advantage of me. I spent a lifetime searching for answers and drifted in and out of depression in a constant struggle to hide my feelings from the world. I often wondered if my depression was hereditary since my father suffered from manic depression and suicidal tendencies for over 50 years.

It took a lot of energy living in two worlds; one where everyone perceived me as a success, being happy and prosperous, and in another world where my insecurities defined my purpose. Looking back, trying to survive on coffee and an apple a day to achieve the perfect weight was a disaster because the benefits were short-lived and had a devastating impact on my health. The compliments I received for my unrealistic weight were insignificant compared to the price I paid for it. My thinning hair from lack of nutrients and weak immune system were often the casualties of my obsession with my weight. I am in disbelief when I think about the number of times I starved myself to lose weight for an upcoming event. One of those events was a beauty pageant where there was a cash reward, and all I had to do was look thin and answer questions intelligently. The fact that I could sing well was a bonus for the talent portion. Winning the talent competition and the cash made me feel happy for a fleeting moment until I started eating regularly and regained all the weight I lost. A mirror became my judge and jury in the self-imposed purgatory I created for myself.

It is hard to admit that my life was defined by how other people perceived me rather than how I perceived myself. Embarking on knowledge adventures and my love affair with books gave me solace and hope. Believing that books would help me to re-enter the world from a position of confidence resulted in an incredible library of self-help books. My journey of discovery and relentless pursuit of answers made me realize that I had created a tsunami of limiting beliefs that had become my reality. My dictionary of flawed ideas was extensive and mortgaged my purpose in life.

When my good friend, Tom asked me to write a chapter in his upcoming book, I embraced the opportunity to tell my story in the hope that if it helped just one person, it would have been worth it. Tom reminded me of Napoleon Hill and his success principles and how Napoleon's book changed his life. He told me that many of us place greater importance on our limiting beliefs and allow other people to define us rather than discovering our purpose. We face so many challenges in life and often lose our way in our pursuit of happiness. Suddenly, a book I read so many years ago took on a new meaning. I hope that my story will help you to face adversity boldly and emerge triumphant by refuting the limiting beliefs that hold you back.

"No one is inferior without their consent"

— Maria Wahlberg

Flawed Belief #1 – I have to be smart because I will never be pretty.

When I was ten years old, my older sister and I were getting ready for church, and I was looking for a beautiful dress to wear. I looked in the closet and noticed that my sister, Lucia had a lovely green dress, which I desperately wanted to wear. I pulled the dress out of the closet to try it on, totally oblivious to the fact that Lucia was very petite and I was a little chubby. I struggled with the zipper for what seemed like an eternity, but it would not move. Utterly defeated, I sat on the floor crying until my father came into the room and tried to comfort me by saying, "Don't worry, Inez. You are the smart one and your sister is the pretty one." I sat on the floor feeling completely shattered. Moments later, I began charting a course that would allow me to define myself by my intelligence rather than my appearance. After all, this was my father giving me advice so it must be true. From that day forward, I would gain acceptance from my dad by being the most gifted child in the family with the best grades and a love for math. I believed my father, so I reinvented myself as the smart one and propelled my sister forward as the pretty one. All through middle school and high school, I lived in my sister's shadow by always playing down my looks and favoring intelligence.

I remember being in grade 7 and asking a boy to a Sadie Hawkins dance (where girls ask the boys to a dance) only to be ignored by him because he said he thought I was asking him on behalf of my sister and that I was too chubby to be his date. I left the dance in tears feeling devastated and swore that I would never put myself in that position again so no other boy would ever laugh at me for how I looked or what I was wearing. This experience still haunts me to this day as I will often try on multiple outfits for any event and will usually change my clothes just before leaving. My confidence was shattered again because I felt I had, even more, evidence to support for my father's prophesy. I spent the next four decades struggling to fit in and continued to allow myself to be defined by how I looked and what I wore even though I was so much more.

Flawed Belief #2 – You have to become something that you are not to gain acceptance

Moving to Canada from Lagos, Nigeria was very hard for my dad as he had to leave an excellent job and wonderful life. He held a senior position with British Railways, and we lived in a beautiful home. My mother ran a nursery school on the property, and I learned to read when I was three years old. We had no choice but to leave Lagos because my father's life was in danger. One of his employees put rat poison in his sandwich, and he was hospitalized for weeks before he was well enough to leave. Despite the challenges, I loved living in Lagos, and it was very hard to move and adjust to our new life in Canada.

When I emigrated to Canada with my family in the late 1960s, we did not have a lot of money and struggled to pay the bills and put food on the table. My father had a tough time finding work and suffered from multiple bouts of depression. Every time he had any setback, he spiraled back down into a state of hopelessness. It is important for you to understand that my father was born in Bombay, India and was a very proud man. As a child, he dreamed of becoming a doctor and was forced to give up that dream when his father passed away, and he had to support his family. He often spoke to me about how my life would be different if he were a doctor. My father was an accomplished engineer forced to work as a janitor to support his family when we left Nigeria.

When we arrived in Quebec, my entire family experienced the challenges of a new country, climate, and culture first-hand. Most people in Quebec spoke French, and my father struggled to learn the language. We also faced a lot of racism because we were a mixed-race family. I remember my older sister dyeing her hair blond to hide the fact that she was half Indian. Many of my siblings struggle to this day with their ethnicity and sometimes suppress who they are. I, however, decided to take a different route as I was proud of my Indian heritage. I remember many incidences when something we owned was vandalized and my father always encouraging me to turn the other cheek. I remember one particular snowy day when someone slashed our tires and his words echoed in my mind. "Turn the other cheek, Inez." Seeing his sadness and frustration infuriated me so much that I ran as fast as I could toward the perpetrator. It happened so fast. I did not think about what I would do when I got there. Seconds later, that bully was airborne into the snowbank as I yelled as loud as I could, "Kiss my ass!" I was 11 years old, and this was my interpretation of turning the other cheek.

I felt empowered because, even though I was not and am not an advocate of violence, that single act turned the tables for me. My grandmother believed that evil prevails when good people do nothing. I took a stand and made my point. I'm happy to report that this was the last time that someone slashed our tires in that neighborhood.

While the harassment in my area subsided, the bullying at school continued. I remember so many times when I was teased at school because I would take delicious Indian curries to school for lunch rather than peanut butter and jam or a ham sandwich. They teased me because they did not like how my food smelled. Some of my classmates would throw my food in the garbage and laugh because I had nothing to eat. These experiences left a lasting impression and fueled my insecurities.

Ironically, the bullying at school about my lunch triggered my love for cooking and celebrating my ethnicity. Reminding myself that I was Indian and British with some Swedish and Portuguese thrown in became a cause for celebration and triggered my obsession with cooking. I started cooking when I was 11 years old and baked my first loaf of bread and made delicious Indian dishes. Being a creative cook was a necessity because my parents only bought what was on sale so we could never follow a recipe since we never could predict what they would buy. I gave dishes cool names like Batman Hash so my siblings would eat it. Batman Hash has become a favorite for my children and of all of their friends. I also learned to make blueberry jam to sell to tourists and kept costs low by picking the blueberries and charging prices based on the car they drove. It is no coincidence that I pursued a career in marketing and retail!

Cooking gave me confidence and acceptance with my family and friends. My love of food helped me to develop a strong understanding of how to use and combine spices from around the world to create delicious meals. Spending countless hours in bookstores reading and memorizing recipes from expensive cookbooks that I could not afford to buy became my favorite pastime. Cooking became my personal sanctuary that would offer comfort and salvation on my darkest days. Opportunity often emerges from adversity, and as such, I am a fantastic cook today because I would not compromise on who I am. My cooking reflects all of me, my ethnicity, my knowledge about nutrition, my travels, my family and my friends.

My culinary skills also played a pivotal role in my education as I ran a catering company in University, which helped me to pay for my education. Cooking a delicious meal for my family and friends is one of my most favorite things in life because of how it brings people together in an environment of love and appreciation. Cooking with love for the people you love can bring so much joy to you and the lives you touch.

About five years ago, I called my friend; Sara to wish her a Happy Thanksgiving, as I knew her husband was coming home from the hospital after a successful battle with cancer. I called her around 11 in the morning and said "Happy Thanksgiving! How are you?" I listened for an answer and thought that there was something wrong with my phone until I heard what sounded like tears. I asked Sara what was wrong and she mentioned that she had totally forgotten about Thanksgiving with everything going on. I told her not to worry because I had a 20-pound turkey in the oven as part of a huge feast I had prepared. I told her that all she had to do was come over with a big pot. A few hours later, she arrived with the largest pot I had seen in a long time. We filled it to the rim! She and her family enjoyed a wonderful turkey dinner at home, and her family was so grateful for this simple act of kindness that we became the best of friends. I was honored to help and inspired to this day by the experience. After all, we lift ourselves by lifting others.

*"The man who enters a storm is a very different
person than the one who emerges"*

— Maria Wahlberg

Lost my job and discovered my purpose

There were some very stormy times in my life. I found myself always having to evolve and adapt as I trudged through them. No matter what job I had, how much money I made, how many lives that I touched in a positive way, I still felt insecure atop a complete inability to celebrate my success to the point of self-sabotage. Writing best-selling books, teaching at four universities, running a successful company and holding numerous vice president positions did not negate the failure I felt when I looked in the mirror. I struggled to see a successful, confident person. I saw someone who was never enough, that is, until the day I lost my job and had to come face-to-face with my reality.

At 5 PM on March 22, 2016, the president of the company I was working for called me into his office to tell me that he did not feel that I was a good fit and decided to eliminate my position. I stood motionless and in total shock and seconds seemed like hours. What would I tell my family? What would I say to my husband and my son who just got a baseball scholarship at a Division 1 University? What would I say to my daughter who is just embarking on a new career in New York? So many thoughts raced through my mind. Is this a sign from the universe telling me that I do not deserve success? I somehow managed to keep it together and gathered my thoughts as I was directed to meet with personnel in another office to discuss my severance. My head was spinning from the shock. So many questions and challenges raced through my head as I tried to concentrate on what was said. How will I tell my husband? What will he say and what will he think of me? I managed to compose myself as I searched for the right words and questions. Then suddenly and without warning, I heard the voice of my grandmother in my head.

*"Never to be defined by a situation but rather
by your beliefs and actions."*

"No one is inferior without their consent."

*"Sometimes things just happen, and you don't
know why they happen and how they
happen."Think about who you want to be in
these situations, not what you want to do."*

"Have faith and not fear."

*"The only thing you need when you're in a dark
room is a match to find your way."*

*"No matter what happens to you, always look
for a positive aspect of the situation."*

My grandmother passed away when I was 19, but at 54 years old, it was as if she was standing right beside me and guiding me with her wisdom. I was able to keep my composure and went back to my desk to get a few things all the while I feeling ashamed and sad. I could barely make eye contact with my incredible team. It took everything I had not to burst into tears at the thought of leaving them behind, never to return and unable to let them know. I was given a few minutes to gather my things before leaving, and it felt like walking the plank at the Spanish inquisition with nothing to look forward to but the abyss of the ocean.

When I look back at that time, I do not know how I managed to exit the building without falling apart. I now know that I drew strength from all the people in my life who love me and those who still watch over me. I thought of my father, who left Nigeria in the sixties with his family and limited belongings, leaving behind the life he had built to start over in a new country. He was 56 years old, almost the same age as me. I thought of what he went through, being poisoned and almost dying and being forced out of a country and life that he loved. I remember the sadness on my mother's face when she realized we had to leave and start over. I remembered her courage and commitment to creating a new life for her family.

Finding sunshine in the shadows

I was walking out of the building desperately looking for a shelter from my emotional storm. I walked to the end of the street to find a quiet spot to call my husband. I dialed his number twice and hung up before getting through to him as I searched my brain for what to say. How do I tell him that I just lost my job? What will he think of me? Am I a failure? Every insecurity ran through my mind. When he answered the phone, I paused at first, searching for the words and struggling to hold back the tears. He immediately sensed that there was something wrong and asked me if I was ok. It all came out at once; "I lost my job, and feel scared. What will we do?"

He offered to come downtown to meet me and asked if I was okay to drive home. He told me not to worry; it would be ok and that I was very talented with tremendous potential. He said I should have faith in myself. It was like my grandmother was speaking to me except it was my husband who was saying the words. I will never forget how kind and understanding he was as he reassured me that we would be okay and that this was an opportunity to go on a journey of self-discovery to find out what I wanted to do and accomplish in life.

I stood motionless while hoards of people around me rushed to their next destination. I was still wondering which way to turn. Then, I looked up and saw beautiful clouds and the sun beaming through them. The sun gave me hope and a sense of peace and optimism. I decided that I would go to the nearby coffee shop before going home. As I headed towards it, I noticed a man sitting on the sidewalk holding a sign that said," I'm hungry. Please help." Seeing that poor man made me realize that my life was truly blessed. I had a family that loved me, a beautiful home, and my faith. I stopped to talk to him and said I was going to the coffee shop and asked what he would like. His eyes filled up with tears as he told me that he had been sitting on this corner for months and no one had ever stopped to ask him what he wanted. I told him that I had just lost my job, so I was not having a good day but, I always believed that a single act of kindness could change the world. I went into the shop to buy him a sandwich and coffee and rushed back to the corner to give it to him. He was very gracious and thankful and wished me good luck in finding a new job. I realized then and there that no matter what life throws at you, you must always stay aligned with who you are.

Always remember that who you are is so much more important than what you do for a living or what you have. My grandmother said, "Compassion and being grateful will always bring you the greatest joy." I do not think that the homeless man realized how much he helped me that day. He reinforced my grandmother's belief that a simple act of kindness can change the world. I also remembered the words of Napoleon Hill who said that a positive mental attitude and pleasing personality would pave the fastest route to success, especially when combined with passion and purpose.

As I turned to walk down the street to my car, I saw my reflection in a store window. I was wearing one of my favorite pink floral dresses which I wore in honor of my sister, Jackie, a breast cancer survivor. I had received so many compliments that day about how beautiful I looked and never really appreciated it until that moment. I stared at myself for what seemed like forever and realized that my priority should be finding and discovering myself before looking for a job. Ironically, losing my job could be the best thing that ever happened to me.

Losing my job propelled me on a path of discovery to determine why I saw failure when other people saw success. Conducting a personal audit would be my exercise in salvation. A personal examination would allow me to calculate my real value by separating my assets from my liabilities. Relentless best describes this experience as all flawed beliefs or liabilities would be scrutinized. Understanding the source of my insecurities required a complete personal inventory and audit.

I was shocked to discover that bullies, braggarts and well-meaning family and friends were the catalysts for my flawed beliefs. This exercise was one of my most difficult, challenging and rewarding tasks because it allowed me to break free from self-imposed constraints and helped me to pursue the life of my dreams. I was determined to find that spark, the light that would offer hope in the darkest room.

My grandmother was the light that guided me. I only knew my grandmother for a few years, but no one has had a greater impact on my life. I was 17 and in University when my grandmother came to visit me in Canada. I remember picking her up at the airport and being overwhelmed by her poise and beauty. She was a woman of few words, but when she spoke her words, they changed lives. She reminded me that the only real competition you have in life is who you were yesterday.

We talked endlessly about life and the challenges she faced in Europe during the Second World War and how she fell in love with a British soldier, my grandfather. She spoke about what it was like being pregnant out of wedlock in the 1940's, and the shame she caused her family, and the guilt foisted on my mother. She also spoke of how she let my mom down by leaving her with her grandparents to raise her, only to take her from the only home she ever knew when she gave up on the love of her life (my grandfather) and married someone else. She was the best listener that I have ever met and still find comfort in her words. Her wisdom was vast and all encompassing. She told me that, "The only thing that needed to be separated by color was the laundry." and not to worry about having an Indian father and British mother. She said, "The combination just made me more perfect. Love is color blind, and we are all God's children."

Napoleon Hill believed that you should have a definite purpose and passion for what you want out of life. My grandmother also told me that you will have either discipline or regret and that happiness is wanting what you have not had what you want. It was like my grandmother and Napoleon Hill had joined forces to mentor me, protect me and keep me safe.

Losing my job was one of the most challenging and empowering events of my life as it forced me to change the way I viewed myself and my life. I believe that when you change the way you look at things what you are looking at changes. When I discovered that I could not back up my flawed beliefs with actual evidence, I was forced to let them go. No longer would I succumb to a mirror as my judge and jury. I learned to celebrate even the smallest of my accomplishments.

Being loved and appreciated is the one thing that all humans crave and loving yourself is the first step. A healthy lifestyle would be my focus with exercise, eating a balanced diet and taking time for myself. Restricting myself to coffee and an apple would never happen again, no number would ever define me again. My passion and purpose would guide me combined with the love of my family and friends. My journey to real success is just beginning. I am so excited about what the future holds and am overjoyed by what I have learned.

- Overcoming adversity and pursuing your dreams is why we are alive
- Complacency will never be the catalyst for a change in your life
- Understanding that a thought that you think long enough will manifest into a belief, and a belief that becomes your truth will eventually influence your behavior.
- Choosing faith over fear and living every day like it was a gift has helped me to overcome any adversity
- Wake up every day feeling grateful, thankful and inspired by the quantum of potential that exists when you overcome limiting beliefs.

Just imagine what you could do and be if you knew that you could not fail!

I hope my story inspires you to identify and eliminate flawed beliefs and help you to overcome adversity with passion and purpose.

Happiness is a choice

I believe when we are born
We join the human race
With a number on our back
And a name to match our face

We become what we think
We sometimes lose our way
When we fail to see our true selves
And just exist each and every day

We all have a choice
Break free from what life seems
Live life in the sunlight
Rather than the shadows of our dreams

— Inez Blackburn

Inez Blackburn| Bio

Inez Blackburn is a best-selling author of Pride Passion Profit – 7 Steps to Category Development and is a serial researcher. Inez has spent the bulk of her career studying retail and consumer behavior even though many of her research projects conclude that consumers don't behave. Inez has worked with many Fortune 500 companies and held many executive positions to help businesses launch products that consumers need and want and develop marketing messages that say something meaningful and significant because she is fed up with advertising that answers questions that no one is asking.

After spending over 25 years helping companies to succeed, she decided to embark on a journey of self-discovery and address all the self-imposed constraints that forced her to live her life in the shadow of her dreams. She loves to read and is always on the lookout for new recipes as cooking has often been her salvation. She is proud of being a nerd and often studies medical books as a hobby as well as books about natural cures and ancient civilizations.

Her wonderful husband and children don't seem to complain as her love of cooking have resulted in hundreds of dinner guests, and her daughter has benefitted from her vast shoe collection. When she isn't reading writing or cooking, she is most likely singing or watching a documentary on Ancient Aliens or the brilliant Game of Thrones.

You can connect with by visiting her website: inezblackburn.com, to sign up for emails about new recipes, stories of inspiration or sign up for her blog or email her at inezblackburn@rogers.com

CHAPTER 14

The Faith Factor

By Michael Hecktus

When Tom Cunningham, a Certified Instructor from the Napoleon Hill Foundation, reached out to me to be a contributing author to the "Journey to Success" series, I was blown away. I was excited at the idea of writing a chapter about my journey but I was also scared as hell. I knew parts of my journey were probably something many could relate to, but how many people would have handled the situation the same way I did? Or better yet, how many would step out and put it on paper for all to read? Some of you may find this journey to be more of a failure than a success, but I've found my life to be filled with lessons that made me a much better person. To me, this has been a very successful and lesson-filled journey. So here I am sharing my rollercoaster-of-a-story in hopes that I can make an impact on both the generations of today and tomorrow.

I sat down and looked at where I had come from, the lessons I had learned and how I would put it all on paper. The only writing I had ever done had been through text messages, e-mails and most recently personal blogging. I was not a writer, but here I am. I hope you enjoy my Journey to Success!

The Sure Thing

My name is Michael Hecktus and I am an entrepreneur. In all honesty, that wasn't always the plan. In fact, my guidance counselor and parents had something much different in mind back in 1977 when I left high school. You see, I grew up in the industrial manufacturing age. We made stuff and we built stuff! Both of my parents left school at a very early age because they had to go to work to support the family. It was the many years of hard labor and dedication that my dad put in that opened the door for me to obtain my summer job. At the age of 16 I started working at the local meat packaging factory, making

$9.00/hour, which in 1975 was damn good money! (But I knew it wasn't where I belonged…. I always envisioned myself in a suit.)

That being said, my future seemed like it was already planned. I was never really pushed to achieve great grades. A 50 was a pass, so that was my goal. If I obtained a 50 by the end of the year, everyone was happy.

As you can imagine, that didn't get me very far. In my final year, I failed to get my passing grade of 50 in English. I hated English! I hated reading books. I could read the words and I was a great reader of words, but because it wasn't something I was truly interested in, nothing stuck. There were too many other conversations going on in my head to absorb what I was reading. Shakespeare? Are you kidding me? Who talks like that?! Unfortunately, Shakespeare won that round. I finished one credit short! But all was good because my career path was already in line for me. I was going to work in a factory for the rest of my life…diploma or not.

Was This What My Future Looked Like?

One morning I woke up and a small thought popped up inside my head: "Do I want to work in a factory for the rest of my life? Do I want to wear a lab coat, work boots, a freezer jacket and hard hat?" It wasn't until a school buddy who was destined to follow the same career path called me about jobs opening at the local distillery that the possibility began to seem more attainable. An uncle had put in a good word for him and they were looking to hire two mail clerks. It was an office job, with great potential for me to move up the ladder and wear that suit I had always envisioned.

In 1989, after being with the company for 10 years, I had moved up the company ladder as promised. I started as a mail clerk, moved up to the accounts payable department, promoted into purchasing, and reached the level of purchasing manager. I worked hard and it paid off. At this point I was married, had a beautiful daughter, a brand new custom-built home, and a dog and a cat to boot. I guess you could say all that was missing was the white picket fence.

Life was good and I was having a blast, but that's where things took a bit of a turn. The distillery I was working for was about to be shut down, so it was time to look for something different. Was I devastated? Was I upset? Actually, I wasn't. What I found strange was that I was excited about what the next chapter in my life might look like. I had no idea how we were going to survive or what my new career path looked like, but I knew that I was being given the chance to seek new challenges and opportunities. Most people would have been scared or stressed, having a new home, a mortgage, a daughter and another baby on the way, but I knew the Universe had something in store for me-- something even better.

It was now when I began to study the power of an optimistic mindset. I started following positive motivational speakers and applying their material to my own life. This really hit a chord with me. I was always a positive thinker, always the guy with the glass half full. Well-maybe it wasn't half full, but I knew I was the one pouring the water.

Bringing Opportunity To Life

I thought long and hard about my next career move once I left the distillery. I know that one sector had always intrigued me—sales! It seemed like the sales team was always having fun and I wanted to be a part of it. But there was one thing in my way...one thing that would have stopped many right then and there. I had zero sales experience and no grade 12 diploma.

However, just as I envisioned a better career outside of the factory job, I envisioned being great in sales. People were always saying I had great salesman qualities- I was positive, I always wore a smile and I knew how to build great relationships. "You're not qualified" was not going to stop me. Unbeknownst to me, a friend recommended me for an open sales position and a week later the job was mine. I was now a sales representative for a promotional products company that was on the rise to success.

I had no experience and no education to fall back on, only a burning desire and a vision. I was led to the exact position I had created in my own mind! It's true-- what you think about, you bring about! I wanted it so bad...I created it.

Time for Growth

Things in sales were going very well, and I was now able to support our family financially. And while our situation was comfortable, I knew there was always more opportunity for growth. With 4 years in sales under my belt, I realized we were never going to become abundantly wealthy with me being a salesman. I had to step out and create my own company and my own income...the income I believed I could create. Building my own agency would allow me to create that income I envisioned. This was my first step to becoming an entrepreneur. This was my first step to being self-employed and creating the life I truly believed we were meant to have.

Creating Lessons From Roadblocks

After four years of making an impressive income, a business of my own sounded pretty good-- it was the cash flow highs and the cash flow lows that I failed to manage. The high months, we lived high. The low months-- oh yes-- we continued to live high, always assuming that it would turn around. One day we were so far in debt, that after speaking to financial advisors we realized we were in trouble. We were embarrassed and we felt like we had failed. And yet, inside I knew this was a turning point for us and something great was ahead.

It was at this point that I did some real soul searching. I knew I needed to work on me. I needed to leave my ego outside and I needed to stop trying to "Keep up with the Jones'" as they say, and change the way I was looking at things. I had to change my attitude and create a positive mindset by surrounding myself with positive, successful people. I needed to find a mentor, someone to guide me and make me accountable. I began reading a lot of positive motivation and positive mindset literature. (Yes, you read that correctly. The guy who left high school, one credit short of graduating because he hated reading, was now reading books. Go figure.)

I heard the phrase; "Leaders are readers." I began to listen to motivational speakers and started studying how the subconscious mind worked. I attended seminars on positive mindset and personal growth and this was when I bought my first edition of *"Think and Grow Rich"* by Napoleon Hill. I read books by Louise Hay who is a spiritual motivator and I read the biography of Lee Iacocca and Donald Trump, among others. I began to read about tapping and self-hypnosis to clear old thoughts and create new thoughts. I immersed myself in an online personal development course. The founder of this company is, to this day, still one of my mentors. I follow him and learn from his teachings daily. I knew my mindset was changing. I was feeding my subconscious mind positive thoughts.

I began seeing things with clarity and I found I had much better focus. My sales agency was once again on a high and I was being head hunted by some of the best in the business to work for some pretty big players in the promotional marketing industry. I knew what I was good at and now others were seeing the same thing.

"If you've never fallen you've never challenged your potential!"

— Visca

This was around the same time that The Secret hit the scene, so you can bet I started drawing up my vision board. I started following people like

John Assaraf and Bob Proctor and began studying my strengths and how I could make a difference in this crazy world.

It didn't take long before I had a call from the national sales manager from one of the biggest writing instrument companies in the world looking for a Regional Sales Manager. We sat down and instantly hit it off. I was told there was a good chance that if and when the time was right I could possibly be considered for the national sales manager position. The company loved to promote successful individuals and create a positive atmosphere and positive growth. That excited me. If I worked hard and built strong relationships and showed my leadership abilities, I could be up for an opportunity to become the next national sales manager, an executive position with a global company. It was an amazing position-- my mentor and boss was now a very close, personal friend. I was traveling for trade shows, entertaining clients with an expense account and enjoying award-winning years with sales growth. It was just a matter of time before they would see my potential and the corporate ladder would become that much easier to climb.

Much of my time was spent in the car, so I had lot of time to listen to tapes on topics that interested me. Once again, I created a vision board with the dream house we always wanted. My vision was clear. Our home had a big bedroom for each of the girls, a spare bedroom for guests and an amazing master bedroom and on-suite for my wife and I. It also had a huge kitchen (My wife loves cooking!), a great room for entertaining friends and family and a separate office that would be my space to be able to work and have some quiet time to work on me.

This dream home had to be put on hold for a while, because to be able to afford this dream home I needed to hold the national sales managers position that was in my future—or so I thought. Unfortunately, the company did some restructuring and my opportunity to take on that role was no longer part of the corporate plan. I was destined to be a regional sales manager forever. Forever is a long time with no opportunity to move up the ladder, so once again I put it out to the universe that I was looking for a national sales manager position -- the position I knew would someday be mine.

Never Say Never

Shortly after this disappointment, another company approached me at a national trade show. They were up front with me, explaining that they had been watching me; they had done their homework contacting clients, and they had an opportunity I might want to look at.

I told them I was always interested in new challenges and opportunities, and suggested we talk. What do you know? They were looking for a national sales manager. It was a position where I would lead a sales team across the country, a team they would encourage me to inspire and motivate to reach their goals. I was now in a position where I could have an impact not only on the company's growth, but the growth of a sales team.

To no surprise, this position was something I had on my vision board. It was a picture of me addressing the sales team, inspiring them to find that inner spark—moving them to greatness, encouraging them to take ownership in the company and to make decisions they felt were in the best interest of the company and our clients. I wanted to teach them the importance of building strong relationships, which were the backbone of our success. Well, successful we were. The company experienced double-digit profits for 2 years running and became a leader in the industry.

"Whenever the spirit of teamwork is the dominating influence in business or industry, success is inevitable!"

— Napoleon Hill

With this newfound success, my personal life was once again very positive. We broke ground on the new dream home I spoke of earlier. My vision, along with faith and desire had helped us to achieve yet another goal. I was starting to see a pattern; if you set goals and believe you can achieve them, you can be, do, or have anything you desire. The quality of our lives begins with the quality of our minds. I was starting to see that I needed to focus on my thoughts. Positive thoughts created positive results!

"Positive mental attitude is the right mental attitude in all circumstances. Success attracts more success while failure attracts more failure!"

— Napoleon Hill

I was never going back to where we once were. I was now controlling my own destiny. Negativity was no longer a part of my makeup. I would work on my conscious thoughts, but also work on reprogramming my subconscious mindset.

I absolutely loved my new position. The owner of the company and I became very close friends. We shared a very strong passion for making our clients feel special. We spent a lot of time entertaining and treating clients to special outings and we rewarded them for being our partners. Our growth was the result of this shared passion.

And what happened? People started to see a change in me, a very positive change. They started to notice that I was not only working on being a very positive person, but I also started to take on a new physical well-being. I started hitting the gym 4 days a week. I began eating better, making better food choices and seeing a change in my physical appearance. In 2010, I competed in my first bodybuilding competition and placed in the top three. People started to ask what I was doing. They felt this positive energy and they wanted some of it! I was receiving calls from clients asking me for fitness tips and diet advice. It was as though I was a health and wellness consultant, which got me thinking...perhaps I could help others find success not only in their careers, but in their personal lives as well!

Business was going well, but a relocation moved headquarters to the east end of Toronto. My hour-long ride into the office became 2-3 hours, depending on the weather. Aside from the extra travelling, my personal and family life was suffering. Yes, you're correct, I needed a change. But what was I going to do? I loved my job, the industry and the money was great. However, it was my 50th birthday party when my wife Vicki expressed her daily worry about my drive to and from the office. Well, happy wife, happy life folks! It was that conversation that led me to once again resurrect my own agency.

My agency allowed me to work from home, creating my own income and spending more time with my family. I started my own marketing and consulting company and I helped clients that I had known for the last 15 years create marketing campaigns as a consultant. I was happy to help new sales people create strong relationships because it's not about the sales...it's about relationships!

My agency is now in its12th year as one of the top in the country. With multiple seven digit sales every year, it has been a breath of fresh air to look back and see how far I've come from someone who left high school and almost lost everything 20+ years ago.

The Final Piece to My Journey to Success

As I said in the beginning, I've been an entrepreneur for over 25 years now. What stuck with me all this time? One of my mentors taught me that financial abundance comes to those who know how to align themselves to create extra streams of income. He also made it clear that it is necessary to find a business that fits your personality, your passion, and your vision or, invest in a product or company that you are passionate about. So in a nutshell, I began searching for that extra stream of income. I wanted to create an income in my spare time, an income in an industry that I was passionate about. It had to be an electrifying company, (my personality); in the health and wellness industry (my passion); with a legacy mindset (my vision). My search commenced.

I started by practicing meditation and visualizing the life I wanted to live. I started to study a number of experts in this field, looking at what others had, that I wanted.

Another one of the mentors I aligned myself with gave me a simple message: "Don't just read books on personal development. Take the time to study them, study them and apply the lessons they offer". From our conversation, my newfound favorite book became "Think and Grow Rich." I think the biggest thing this book has taught me, is that everything starts with DESIRE and the BELIEF that you can, in fact, achieve your dreams. The message was very clear: I am a product of my own thoughts.

I found that extra stream of income with a leader in the health and wellness industry. This company was leading the way in the health revolution. They promote positive, mental attitudes, natural products and amazing compensation packages that reward leaders for building others up and guiding them to success. A company that was built on the principles I always stood by.

"If you're not making a difference in other people's lives you shouldn't be in business, it's that simple!"

— Richard Branson

So here I am today with a very successful marketing agency that I love, which has been built from incredible relationships with some amazing people who are more like family now than clients. I have also added that extra stream of income that I was looking for, which enables me to live a fit, healthy and abundant life with the opportunity to help others achieve the same. My goal is to walk side by side with them and build this legacy together. I now surround myself with some of the most amazing people on both career paths, on a journey with like- minded individuals and like-minded goals.

Does my journey stop here? Well, they say home is where your heart is-When you wake up and can't think about anything else, you're home!

"Developing and establishing positive habits leads to peace of mind, health, and financial security. You are where you are because of your established habits and thoughts and deeds." Napoleon Hill

Michael Hecktus | Bio

Michael Hecktus is a very successful entrepreneur. After trying the 9-5 lifestyle, Michael knew he wanted to work for himself and create his own destiny. In 1990, he started his own marketing and consulting company to assist corporate buyers in promoting their brand and the message they wanted to share. Michael has found great success in this field and it's because of his strong relationships that his businesses continues to prosper. The creative opportunities in this field make every single day exciting and fresh, but where Michael truly flourishes is in appreciation for building strong, personable relationships.

From a very early age, Michael has always been driven by mental and physical health. At the age of 50 when encouraged by friends, he decided to inspire others his age to be proud of their bodies and embrace their health. Michael has stood on both the provincial and national stage as a bodybuilding and physique competitor, finishing in the top 3.

Now 57, Michael continues to be a strong advocate of abundant health and wellness, as well as financial freedom. He has started his own company, Extraordinary Life Starts Now, as well as being a distributor for ZIJA International. Most recently, Michael won the Rising Star Award for having the fastest-growing business in Canada. He believes that you are only as successful as the people you surround yourself with. With that, Michael finds himself surrounded by the most successful, influential people in the Natural Health Revolution.

Michael lives by one simple rule: If you're not helping others find success, you shouldn't be in business. It's that simple!

Michael can be reached at www.mikehecktus.com and https://ca.linkedin.com/in/mikehecktus

CHAPTER 15

Outwitting the Devil

By Roger Weitzel

Pivotal Moment

Everyone can look back on their lives and pinpoint a pivotal moment when things changed. Radically changed.

These life-changing moments are different for every person; but the similarity is that it became a life-changing event. For some, it may have been a long-dreamed-about accomplishment – you completed that marathon, for example. For others it might have been a special encounter with a special person – you just knew it was going to be a life-long friendship (or a life-long romance).

Your pivotal moment may have been when you were alone in nature – at the beach, in the forest, or on a mountaintop – and for a brief moment of time, you felt at one with the universe, and your heart was forever changed.

Perhaps it involved a disaster that changed your entire perspective about life. It may have been the death of a loved one that gave you reason to pause and consider your own immortality.

For every person these moments are different. For me, it was a book.

It was a Book

Hm. A book? Sounds too simple, right? Almost blasé. But it's true. And here's the fascinating part of this pivotal moment – my introduction to this particular book has led to a number of subsequent pivotal moments.

And from where I'm at in this moment of my life, there's no end in sight.

That's a pretty exciting prospect – would you agree?

Outwitting the Devil

You're probably wondering what book could there be that could have such a powerful impact on one person's life?

The book is titled, Outwitting the Devil, by Napoleon Hill. Many of you may recognize Hill's name from his classic book, Think and Grow Rich, published in 1937.

Outwitting the Devil was authored by Hill a short time after *Think and Grow Rich* but, due to its controversial nature, his family kept it out of circulation for over 70 years. It was finally published by The Napoleon Hill Foundation in 2011.

More details are wrapped up in this fascinating account of how this all evolved, but with a little research you can easily learn all that on your own.

Let me share with you how this book did indeed bring me to a pivotal moment – a defining moment – in my life.

The Account of Hill's Lowest Ebb

In the opening segments of the book, Hill describes how he had to literally escape for his life. He had been friends with a newspaper publisher who courageously spoke out about organized crime. That publisher was murdered by the mob and Hill – by association – was at the top of their hit list. He would be next.

Hill received a warning to leave town within 24 hours and he ran for his life, going into hiding with relatives in West Virginia. For more than a year he lived in constant fear, barely daring to come out of the house.

You have to realize, that at this time in his life, Hill had already spent years conducting an intensive study of successful businessmen and had compiled what he called the 17 Principles of Personal Achievement, and yet here he was, overwhelmed with discouragement, disillusionment, and doubt.

Listen to this quote from the book:

> *"For nearly two months I suffered with the worst of all ailments; indecision. – I knew the seventeen principles of personal achievement but what I did not know was how to apply them."*

Discovery of "Other Self"

At this lowest ebb of his life, Napoleon Hill discovered how to tap into what he came to call his "other self." He also calls it "source of power," and "strange force".

While he was in prayer, or meditation, whichever way you might view it, Hill heard this admonition:

"This is your testing time. You have been reduced to poverty and humiliated in order that you might be forced to discover your 'other self.'"

It was through his "other self" that he did learn exactly how to apply those 17 principles of personal achievement.

Hill went on to create a fortune during the Great Depression by listening to, and heeding, the guidance and direction of this Infinite Intelligence that came by way of his "other self."

Interview with the Devil

Now you may be wondering about the title of the book. Why would he refer to outwitting the devil? It's because the greater part of the book is given over to Hill's one-on-one interview with the devil.

(You heard that right – the devil.)

Page after page is filled with Hill's intense interrogation of the devil covering any and all subjects you can think of.

Before I can continue, we must put an issue to rest. And it is this: It is totally immaterial whether or not you believe that there actually is an entity known as the devil. What we can agree on is that each of us battle with personal demons almost every day of our lives.

This is where the book affected me in a powerful way. Because I knew that I had demons that needed slaying. I had become weary of allowing them to conquer me.

My Intro to the Book

I first came across *Outwitting the Devil* a year and a half ago. I listened to it on CD and, to say the least, I was enthralled – and captivated. I didn't listen just once. I listened several times. Every time I listened, another truth seemed to grab hold of me. It was, to me, as if I had just awakened from a deep sleep.

As a side note: the entire unabridged version of the book in audio takes 5 hours and 51 minutes to listen to. This gives you a better idea of the amount of time I devoted to soaking myself in the philosophies of this book. I'm not saying this so I can brag or boast, but rather to convey how absolutely captivated I was.

From there, I took on the task of reading the nearly 300-page book.

I could sense my attitudes and perceptions changing even as I listened and read. It truly became a pivotal event in my life.

Concept of Fear Versus Faith

One of the primary concepts that affected me in this book was that of fear versus faith.

As I listened to the audiobook, my mind turned to areas of my own life where I had allowed my personal demons (the devil, if you will), to cause me to shut down and succumb to fear. Here was the biggie.

I was in my fifties and because of fear, I had never married. I was dating a lady I cared for very much, but at the thought of marriage, I froze.

As I read what Napoleon Hill had to say about how the devil comes in and causes us to be stuck in a "hypnotic rhythm" (one of Hill's terms used in the book), it became clear to me that that was exactly where I was at.

I had allowed my fears to suck me into that hypnotic rhythm where I dared not step out into the unknown. It was as though I had been lulled into a behavior pattern that could not be shaken.

When at last the wedding date was set, I shut myself away and read the book yet again. The principles, the concepts, the underlying philosophy became even more clear.

This has now become my "happily-ever-after" story, because we were married in May YEAR. And we are very happy. I am enjoying a level of happiness and contentment that I never thought possible. And I would never have experienced this had I not come to embrace the concepts that Hill outlined in his book.

Notice I said I "came to embrace" the concepts. Had I simply read the book and took no action, nothing would have changed in my life. I would still be in the state of "hypnotic rhythm."

Here's another great quote from Hill's book:
As I sat there in front of the Lincoln Memorial,
reviewing
in retrospect the circumstances which had so
many times
previously lifted me to great heights of
achievement, only to
let me drop to equal depths of despair, a happy
thought was
handed over to me in the form of a definite plan
of action by
which I believed I could throw off that hypnotic
feeling of
indifference with which I had been bound.

"A definite plan of action." One never comes upon a plan without the need to step out and take action. It's not enough to acknowledge truths, they must be acted upon.

Change of Direction

When I was in my 20s, young and inexperienced in the game of life, I was certain that success and financial independence was what I was searching for. And, to a degree, I went after it.

However, just like Hill talks about in his book, I discovered that material gain didn't cut it for me. Those types of achievements were empty and did not enrich my soul.

By the time I reached my 30s, I realized that I must find a purpose in life. Hill refers to it as **definiteness of purpose**.

But just because I changed my desire in life, doesn't mean I was taking action to move toward my purpose. I did not.

Why?

Because I was still stuck in the hypnotic rhythm. I was still drifting through life with no purpose at all.

When I say drifting with no purpose I mean those words in the most serious sense possible. Many times I entertained thoughts that since I had no purpose and no direction, I was of no use on this planet.

The next connected thought – as you can imagine – was the wish to make my exit. I wasn't strong enough to just kill myself – oh no, not me. I thought it might be simpler to go by way of something legitimate. What would that be?

Well, I reasoned, cancer might be legitimate.

Ever hear the phrase, "Be careful what you ask for"?

Cancer

In February, 2014, a growth appeared under my arm which was then diagnosed as cancer. I was even told that it may have already metastasized. If that was true – if the cancer was indeed spreading – the medical world was using language like: "Possibly six months…"

Six month to live? I can tell you that rocked my world. Suddenly a spark of life was awakened within me. I realized how much I **wanted to live.**

What a surprise.

My Diagnosis and the Book

This diagnosis that I faced, and my discovery of *Outwitting the Devil* are intricately intertwined. Here's how that came about.

I have always been a lover of self-help books and am constantly shopping for new ones. As I was browsing through self-help books on Amazon, I saw a book by Napoleon Hill that was new to me. I didn't think that was possible – I was familiar with all his writings. Then I learned that it had been under wraps for decades. I saw what Brian Tracy said about the book:

> *"While Napoleon Hill's Think and Grow Rich*
> *provided a roadmap to success, Outwitting the*
> *Devil will help you break through the barriers*
> *that may be holding you back."*

That was good enough for me. I ordered it immediately

As I already mentioned, I devoured the book. But here's the kicker. I truly believe my recent diagnosis of cancer prepared my heart and mind to be receptive to Hill's message.

Would I have discounted a book about an interview with the devil before cancer came into my life? I can't answer that. All I know is that I was ready for all this book had to offer me. I refused the route of becoming the typical why-me-victim. I now knew that my life mattered.

The principle of fear versus faith broke down many barriers for me. But then this concept was another life-changer:

> *"There is a seed of equivalent advantage in*
> *every adversity."*

That concept caused me to believe that good could come from my being diagnosed with cancer.

I can stand here today and tell you that the medical world finds no sign of cancer in my body!

How's that for a pivotal moment?

Here's yet another example of how the book changed my thinking and changed my behavior – and subsequently my actions.

In the Workplace

In Hill's book, he defines a drifter as one who "has a total lack of major purpose in his life." His description clearly defined me in my workplace.

My expertise is in the field of mechanical engineering, and I served as a Machining Instructor at the Pueblo Community College for a number of years. Throughout my tenure, my most prevalent goal was to try not to get fired.

That's it. That's as far as my vision would take me. (Sounds like the drifter, right?)

After reading Hill's book, something inside me (that "other self"?) began to rise up. I wanted to become a contributor and not just a taker in society. I was no longer content to sit back and serve as a "worker bee," but rather to become a positive influence. To make a difference. To have a purpose.

I came up with the idea to create an initiative offering machine shop apprenticeships to our students. In my enthusiasm, I circumvented those in authority, and went to the city planners to lay out my plan.

Eventually, this led to my dismissal. I found it interesting that my dismissal came on the very anniversary of my 30 years with the school, which effected my early retirement.

Because of all I had learned from this book, I did not see it as a negative. On the contrary, I saw it as the working of the Infinite Intelligence. No fear came into the picture at all.

Seeds of Opportunity

While some might have looked upon this dismissal as adversity, I did not. I had learned from Hill's book that I was no longer a victim of my circumstances. I had moved out of my old victim mentality. I knew I was in control of my life. As with my run-in with cancer, I chose to see this event as a seed of opportunity, rather than something bad that was "happening to me."

Take-Aways from the Book

As I began to move through the days of my life with more awareness of the philosophies set forth in *Outwitting the Devil*, several of the principles just kept surfacing in my mind and heart. It was mainly these three:

1. **In every circumstance we're faced with the choice of faith or fear. It's the essence of free choice. Once you are aware, you can stop and weigh it out in your mind which one you will choose.**
2. **There are certain levels of "hypnotic rhythms" in our lives. More for some than for others. We are put to sleep, so to speak. Those hypnotic rhythms cause negative vibrations. It's time to break out once and for all.**

3. The drifter is the person who can't, or won't, make decisions. They just go with the flow. This described me to a "T."

Schools and different religions, often promote drifting. People give up their power of reason and thought, following what they are told.

For the most part, all our schools demand of students is the right answer. We have a generation of students who have ceased to love the process of learning. They have ceased to be independent thinkers.

Outwitting the Devil showed me how much I needed to unlearn. I'm on a quest to do exactly that.

1. I make the decision to choose faith over fear
2. I make the decision to take action and break out of hypnotic rhythms
3. I make the decision to take back my power of thought and reason – and cease to be a drifter.

Vivid Example

I recently experienced a vivid example of allowing my "other self" to step in and take over in a frightening situation. I was on a tubing trip on the river where I, and several others, had three tubes lashed together. The tubes became lodged amidst a large fallen tree, causing the situation to quickly become perilous.

At first – and quite naturally – fear wanted to take over. But I knew that I had a choice, and I refused to allow the fear to rule. I intentionally moved over into my "other self," and let that faith person enter into the situation.

In his book, Hill notes that discovery of the "other self" often comes as a result of an emergency when a person is forced to think their way out of a difficulty. He notes the many times that his "other self" guided him and then transcended him into the realm of faith.

And so it was with me. In spite of it being a terrifying situation, I remained calm and as I did, a plan formed in my mind.

I was able to get out of the tube that I was in, and make it to the shore. I walked upriver a short way and then swam down through the turbulent river toward the tubes. My plan was to come from behind and dislodge the tubes.

This was by no means a simple or easy maneuver. I was forced to grab onto a branch of the fallen tree, then to yet another branch, to get to the tubes. As I continued to function in the realm of faith over fear, I was able to force the tubes free of the fallen tree. Within a few minutes, we were on our way again with no one harmed.

And – quite naturally – the ego in me was expecting thanks and adulations from the others in the group. But all were silent. As I look back on it now, having had time to reflect, I know that they were in a state of shock, realizing just how close they had come to a possible fatality. At the moment, those thoughts had not occurred to me. I was dealing with my own ego struggle.

I was quite amazed, however, at how quickly that struggle was resolved. It dawned on me that it had been the Infinite Intelligence that stepped in and took over. It was not to my credit at all.

I also realized that I had just experienced an answered prayer. That, too, was a triumph in my life. I could rest in that – no ego stroking necessary.

Is This Journey for You?

If what you're reading appeals to you, if you, too, would like to move out of your drifter position and embark on a similar journey, here are a few tips.

1. Become Aware

When fear tries to rear its ugly head, step back and take the position of an observer. Fear is the red flag that you should always be on the lookout for. Cultivate this observer position and let it serve you.

2. Desire to Break Out

Develop a strong desire to break out of the hypnotic rhythm syndrome. You have to want to make a change. (I can attest that a diagnosis of cancer caused me to want to change.)

Take inventory of your life. In what areas are you not making the progress, or the breakthroughs, that you long for in your life? Begin here and apply the principles that Hill teaches in his book.

3. Become Friends with Your "Other Self"

When you reach out and become friends with your "other self," it will expand your life. It means you will become emotionally open and honest with who you are and where you are. And where you want to be.

Not for Everyone

I'm fully aware that this kind of journey is not for everyone. No matter how clear the path may be laid out, not everyone will choose to take that path.

Because my life has been so affected and so changed, it has caused me to want to share this philosophy with as many people as possible.

It's my desire to be helpful without being critical. For those who choose not to take this path, they are free to make that choice without being judged.

For me personally, when I discovered my "other self," it made all the difference in the world. It was at that moment, I connected to what Hill refers to as the Infinite Intelligence.

My life today stands in stark contrast to where I was only a couple of years ago. My life is fuller, richer, and more fulfilling that I could have ever dreamed.

I feel as though I truly have "outwitted the devil."

I have slayed my demons!

Roger Weitzel | Bio

Colorado resident, Roger Weitzel, by his own admission, spent a good part of his life with no purpose and no direction.

So directionless was his life that at one time he despaired of life itself and contemplated suicide.

At least that was the case before Napoleon Hill's book, *Outwitting the Devil*, came along.

Roger comes from a background of engineering and manufacturing, his education being in the fields of mechanical engineering and business administration.

As one who is highly analytical, Roger confesses that his life was filled with fear and indecision. These patterns of fear and indecision kept him in the hypnotic rhythm that Hill describes in the book.

Outwitting the Devil came into his life at a desperate time in his life – when the diagnosis of cancer had the medical world announcing he might have only six months to live.

It was a now or never point in his life.

Already a proponent of motivational books, Roger happened to see *Outwitting the Devil* featured on Amazon.

He was surprised because he thought he knew all of Hill's writings.

Beginning with the audio version, he immersed himself in the book until the concepts and principles were enmeshed into his being.

From there, he moved over to reading the full text several times.

Today, not only is Roger healthy, he is also now happily married – a step that for years he feared to take.

His life is brimming over with purpose and direction – and new adventures, all due to taking action on the principles and concepts outlined in *Outwitting the Devil.*

Roger can be reached at....

Roger Weitzel

4407 Turnberry Crescent

Pueblo, CO 81001

goodenrule2020@hotmail.com

CHAPTER 16

Fell Down 8 Times Got Up 9. Stronger And More Committed Than Ever.

By Paul Morris

Reading Napoleon Hill's Think and Grow Rich first as a young man and consistently through to middle age benefited me and others as I shared some of his lessons and gave away many, many copies of his wonderful book. He has a great quote that stayed with me until at one point it felt like there was only that quote to look at to hang on to faith itself!

> *"Every defeat, every disappointment and every adversity carries with it the seed of an equivalent or greater benefit."*
>
> — Napoleon Hill

I was born in Boston, MA. to parents that provided me with all the love and material things that one would need to be comfortable and stable in this life. From the earliest of ages though I seemed to have a pattern of clearly seeing every loss as the certain building block for my next win. I don't recall meeting another person much less a child who from the age of 3, when asked what they wanted to be when they grew up, never varied one time ever in their response. I wanted to be a erMajor League Baseball pitcher.

Blessed with health and good athletic ability, this faith that any loss could motivate me to a win, manifested itself and those endless days of competition in every major sport created in me the desire to NOT LOSE! Notice I did not say a burning desire to win because, for a long time in my life, I did not know that what truly drove me was a tremendous fear of losing. In fact, losing had so great an effect on me that as an 8 and 9-year-old baseball pitcher I would get very quiet and turn almost completely inward following any loss. During those times I would sit in that uniform and not feed myself and remain quiet until I was able to work through why I lost and what I needed to do better next time in order to win. This pattern was pretty true in all competitive things and I gained an intense self-loathing for anything less than not just winning but performing very well. As time passed, I firmly believed that I would play major league baseball, without a doubt, and I mean without ANY doubt. How could a little boy from age 3 forward not have that doubt? Because I could not afford to have any doubt. I was a bit undersized as an athlete and the FACT that no major league pitcher since before World War II was inducted into the baseball Hall of Fame under 6 feet tall only meant to someone 5' 8" that he would be the first. The fact that the average major league pitcher probably threw at a velocity in excess of 88 miles per hour and on a great day I could reach maybe 81 miles per hour did not figure into any real sense of what my skills were because I knew that through my positive mental attitude my growth spurt to greater than 6 feet was assured! A positive mental attitude was probably my greatest strength but learning that any defeat I suffered carried the seed of an equivalent or greater benefit was my truest self. Because if I ever took the time to really logically look at what I was up against to succeed in a field that relies so heavily on physical tools I simply did not have enough to go to the highest level I would never have attempted that, let alone many of the other challenges I have attempted or been faced with in my life. I seemed determined to never take the easy way, or aim low or, for that fact realistically in many ways. I believed that if I wanted anything badly enough I could do it. I never woke once in my life and thought, "Hey today wouldn't it be great to be average."

Sounds like the perfect Think and Grow Rich laboratory of a person doesn't it?

But, rather than accept one of many scholarship packages offered by colleges, I thought it would be better to play in a league that pays its players so I could be considered a "professional" and thus lose my eligibility to play in any U.S. University. The only reason I could think of to attend college was to play baseball so I could get on with my life and play Major League Baseball as a pitcher. Why was pitching so important? Because I did not understand that I had developed a true need to either win or LOSE. And those words are upper case intended. Because just winning wasn't enough, and losing was all encompassing, and as a pitcher most of your they put a W for a win next to your name or an L for a loss, that appealed to me. Every defeat could be a greater benefit until the time that at 22 years old someone lets you know you are not good enough and they don't believe you can go any further. Then you have to figure out how on earth this adversity will help you find that greater benefit that I know is there.

The obvious answer was to get married young while baseball still seemed like an option then go full force into a career working more than just full time in corporate life, go to night school and decide that you want to be an attorney. Why settle for a 4-year program when you can aim for 7 years? The challenges just seemed to get bigger but this will surely work out because, unlike baseball, I don't have to be the right size, or throw harder than most people on the planet. I would work very hard with a great attitude, set my definite goals and work towards those goals with a laser like focus, and I did just that. Until I came home from work one night 14 hours after I left our apartment and was told through tears that I was not wanted in her life anymore because she felt she married too young and frankly I was just too intense and she could not figure out how I knew what I wanted all the time. She didn't know that I was feeling like a complete failure and now this made the two things in my life I had completely committed to and my second major failure by the age of 22. I was only sure that at that point in life I had never met anyone who had two LIFE failures.

This was the time that I started to identify with the Rocky character created by Sylvester Stallone. Everyone loves Rocky and admires him but not because he wins but rather because, no matter how bad the circumstances, he always gets back up! With moderate success in corporate life I decided not to pursue being an attorney and figured I could find that special place in the business world and that winning and losing would replace being a failed athlete. A failed athlete and failed husband and this was just when everyone seemed to be getting started and I seemed to be getting finished.

It was at this time that I was getting my car serviced and I asked what the manager of the dealership how much salespeople earned and he said about $30,000 - 35,000 on average. Again, there was no average goal in life so I asked if he thought I could do that job? When he responded, "Well you just made a complete sentence in English didn't you?" I probably should have guessed that the requirements of the industry were not especially high, so I promptly quit my corporate job with excellent benefits and a salary and took a 100% commission job even though I had never sold anything before because I figured they would train me and if not I could learn it myself. One month selling cars and doing just fine without virtually any training other than getting yelled at for what I did wrong, I already had achieved my first goal towards being a car dealer. I was going to learn the Finance Manager's job and do that. And with 4 months in the car business I was appointed the Finance Manager mainly because I was the only one that could operate a computer at all in 1986! Finally I was moving forward again and with all this motivation I decided to get married again because well in every defeat....

I do not make fun of the principle, in fact I knew somewhere down deep that every failure was just my next chance to win so I was now back in competition and this time I could not lose. I doubled my income in the first full year in the auto industry and the next year I doubled that again so we bought a house and started a family. With all these things going so well I couldn't wait until my third full year in the car business. At the end of 1987 a little event happened on October 19, 1987, which was called Black Monday in the stock market, but I was in the car business and cars wear out and disposable items can't possibly be affected by stock prices, or could they? Things started in 1988 the way they had left off which was really good and seemingly I finally had found something that talent and effort would directly in proportion reward me. Then we noticed a little fluctuation, meaning sales fell 40% seemingly overnight and my performance had to dramatically increase in order to try to break even from my previous year. After a lot of hard work I was down 25% in earnings and that was achieved by improving my overall performance greatly!

By 1989 I knew that I could not financially survive in my job and changed jobs to another dealership to fix their considerable problems. They knew they were hiring an expert and sure enough those major banking problems got corrected and they offered me a pay cut!

I decided that with no money at all and facing bankruptcy, a 3-year-old and a wife at home, the only logical thing to do was start my own company. I would simply write a software program that would automate the very best process for automotive finance departments and sell that program with the training to dramatically improve dealer's profits! The only obstacles were no money and no computer coding experience at all. But after a week of working on it I had a draft on paper of what it would look like and I went into computer stores to find someone who was smarter than me in computers and coding (which was roughly anyone) and I made them a deal to pay them $10,000 to write my program, payable in installments based on sales and in 90 days it worked. Somewhat without crashing at least, and when it did crash I asked the customers if they had been having problems on THEIR system? This system was reprogrammed two additional times and parts of it were "adopted" by manufacturers.

I did freelance training with no training experience and I decided that summer of 1988 that I would put on the refrigerator a sign that said simply $100,000. Without realizing it, as I had not yet read Think and Grow Rich, for the first time in my life I had a definiteness of purpose. Now I had never earned $100,000 before and wasn't entirely sure how that would work but I was sure I would. And amazingly enough, after driving almost 75,000 miles and flying another 30,000 miles AND working incredibly long hours in 7 different states I earned 100,000 in one year! If anyone had told me that 95% of small business startups failed I probably would have told them I feel bad for those 95% but after some failure in my life I was ready for success and I had a very positive mental attitude.

Remembering that I wanted to be a dealer, I sold my company and took over a small auto group in Western New York, far from my Massachusetts roots and moved my now two young children and wife away from everything they knew so that I could climb the next mountain. And within 4 years that small group grew into 16 dealerships and I was President of the auto group at age 35. Finally, Rocky could stay standing but then he wouldn't be Rocky without hitting the mat yet again. As soon at things were reaching what felt like a peak I was really feeling like it was time for a new challenge. What could I do next?

A crushing divorce, and in search of a new business challenge and a debt load that would bankrupt a small country was a good start. By now Think and Grow Rich was a part of my vocabulary but not yet part of my heart, and having read it several times I was wondering beyond the definiteness of purpose what I needed to do to invite the success that I was seemingly in search of perpetually.

I ran some companies over the next few years, always on contract because I did not like the feeling of working for someone else because my experience had been a belief that if I did very well for them they would "take care" of me. Making good deals for them and not for me was not going to work anymore so limiting my time with a company was a really good fit for several years. The more in distress the situation was the better I liked it and the more I believed that this was at last my greatest benefits of years of on and off struggle and challenge.

After ending yet two more long term relationships and being with a company for 4 years and seeing it grow only to be told that after they hired someone to really grow that company much more than I was capable of, the company almost went completely under so the two most expensive people the fix it man brought in and me had to go.

The new plan had another life twist. After 20 plus years of not drinking alcohol I started to drink in a way that brought me to the longest 8 count possible from life's referee. I was feeling hopeless and defeated and the only certainty I had was that I was not happy to have woken up that day or any other. I was homeless, feeling helpless, unemployment insurance was running out and I was sleeping in a car that was about to be repossessed and that broke down completely. The words I remembered from a dealership service manager rang true to my soul when he told me, "Paul it is not worth it to even try to fix it." I had something in common with my car at that point. Both broken down and hopeless to even try to fix.

A friend took me in and after 2 months I decided to get help, face my problems and try to build a plan in my life that made sense. It took several months to get myself back to training people and feeling good about the chances of using my adversity to achieve an equivalent benefit at that point sounded great to me much less a greater benefit.

Well, I found a woman I love more than I can describe and have a relationship that is beyond what I even could have dreamed of. I have 3 beautiful children and a precious granddaughter that have provided me with a many blessings and purpose in life. I have a job I love and after 3 and half years this better me has benefited from so many of the 17 Success Principles that I am working on raising my career level and training to a level higher than it has ever been. I am finding ways to be of the greatest service to my fellow man and to provide the best service from the heart in all I do. The "magic" was always right there in front of me, I just was not looking in that direction. If we are not walking in faith, then we are walking in fear. When we truly learn to believe deeply within we can bring it out to the world and manifest these great principles into our lives. At last I am ready to receive such a thing and have found that "success" is not one or two of these principles but in part all of them together. Rocky is finally back up in the ring but now with life experience and 17 Principles that proved the more training we put in and less fighting for survival, we are so much the wiser for it. The fear and feeling of not being worthy is gone, and the commitment to reaching the greatest of my heights is my daily passion.

Thank you to my Amazing friend Tom Cunningham for the inspiration, the guidance and the example you have set for so many of us.

Paul Morris | Bio

Paul Morris was born in Boston, MA and through high level competitive sports he was able to develop the truest sense of self-discipline and teamwork. He was able to transfer that undying love of competition and self-development into business in founding a consulting and training company.

Having had the privilege of serving as President of 4 companies, Executive Vice President of 3 companies, C.O.O. of 2 companies, General Manager, Director and V.P. of Training of another he has enjoyed the greatest of experiences in training and developing people in 3 countries. He firmly believes that, "you rarely hire greatness, you develop it."

As a father of 3 wonderful children and a grandfather of 1 the lesson that there are no ordinary moments has only enhanced his dedication to living in the moment and reaching for his greatest potential. As such he is a certified practitioner of N.L.P., and a 25 year fan of Napoleon Hill and Think and Grow Rich.

The culture of a company is the soul of its leaders.

Paul can be reached for personal or corporate development, in company leadership management, or motivational speaking at:

Paulemorris2016@gmail.com

(814)-449-1899

CHAPTER 17

Achieving The Impossible Dream Through 17 Proven Principles of Success

By Jeffrey E. Feldberg

"Congratulations Jeffrey!" said the excited lead investment banker, Charles, who continued, "It's official. The deal is closed, and the bank wire is on its way."

I hung up the phone, took a deep breath and relaxed for the first time in eighteen months. I leaned back in my office chair and admired the hot summer day. It all felt surreal.

To outsiders, I was a 37-year-old "kid" who was an "overnight success" because I was at the right place at the right time. My talented business partners and team would tell you otherwise. In fact, if I had a quarter for every mistake I made it would just about equal the bank wire!

But I'm getting ahead of myself. Let's start at the beginning of this epic journey.

Find Problems And Solve Them

I was the youngest in my MBA program, which I had just started, and eager to get into business after witnessing my Dad and Uncle blaze a trail of business success.

My wise Uncle often said, "Jeffrey, create YOUR success by finding and solving problems. The more people you help, the better!"

It didn't take long for my group to find a "problem." Our MBA program was full of Type A personalities all striving for top marks. After meeting before and after classes, weeknights and weekends we stumbled on a recipe ensuring we were the worst group and miserable! I started my MBA program with a full head of hair only to lose most of it from stress! I was barely into my program when the thought of quitting or ending up in the hospital spurred me into action.

Being a super geek, I created a system that allowed my group to work from anywhere, save time, enjoy the program and learn! Today this sounds simple. But remember that the Internet was a few years away, and the only web was a spider's web!

My group rapidly went from the worst to the best and earned straight A's. I introduced my system to the school in the second semester, and it spread like wildfire. It turns out we weren't the only one with this "problem."

Opportunity Knocking

As my 25th birthday and graduation approached my friends and family rallied hard for me to find a lucrative job to get business experience. I felt like a bird in a cage in the only job I ever held, as a summer intern. I would have fired me on the first day!

I'm all for hard work. In high school, I sold water purifiers and in University I started a video production company that filmed bar-mitzvahs, weddings, and the occasional corporate production.

And then it hit me like a ton of bricks -- start a company to solve the same "problem" at other business schools. A week before graduation, e.mbanet, short for "Electronic MBA Network" was born. My next challenge was finding customers.

"Hey Jeffrey," said my operations professor Roger with his usual smile, "rumor has it you're commercializing your system!"

Smiling, I said, "Prof, news travels fast. If only finding customers was as quick!"

Intrigued, Roger said, "I was recently President of the association for business school deans. I'll call in a favor and secure a presentation for you at their upcoming conference!"

Before I could thank Roger, he was already down the hall.

Later that day I picked up the phone, "Jeffrey," Roger excitedly shared, "You're on the program! That said you're the last presentation on the final day of the conference which is only six days away. Still game?"

"Prof," I said half excited and scared, "I can't thank you enough."

Chucking, Roger said, "Just remember us little people when you make it big!".

Enrolling In THE School of Hard Knocks

I worked around the clock and finished just before I set out on the two-hour drive to the conference. I was accompanied by my biggest raving fan and cheering section of one, my girlfriend Waleuska.

With visions of grandeur fueled by my lack of work experience and from the letters after my name, I envisioned signing up the entire room. As for my presentation being the last one, I figured the organizers saved the best for last!

I gave the presentation of a lifetime, at least in my mind, and braced myself for everyone to bolt over the tables and signup. The only shuffling of tables was from people making a beeline for the exit.

Seeing me in my speechless stupor, the conference organizer put his hand on my shoulder and said, "Jeffrey, don't let them get to you. They can be a tough crowd."

Little did I know that this failure needed to happen if I was going to be successful and that I had just enrolled in the most prestigious school of all, The School of Hard Knocks.

The Forbidden Three Letter Word – J.O.B.

Walking back to the car, the naysayers were whispering in my ear, "Who do you think you are starting a company right out of school! Be like your friends and get that corporate job". Waleuska interrupted my thoughts and said, "That was a tough one, Jeffrey. I've been in sales most of my life. Your idea is great, but your presentation needs work. I was planning to start law school, but I'll postpone for a semester to help you".

I stopped walking and said, "Waleuska, that's really generous. I'm touched. Let me think about it".

"Of course," said Waleuska, who continued, "just don't let those grumpy business school Deans get you down. I see the future, and it's e.mbanet".

The car ride home was quiet as I replayed that disaster of a presentation in my head. That night, as I cried myself to sleep, I had a moment of weakness and considered giving up and getting a job. Maybe the naysayers are right.

The Book That Changed Everything

My father was a dream customer for infomercial marketers. Most nights Dad worked late into the evening from his home office with the TV in the background. Perhaps my dad was tired, loved a great story or wanted to support the local economy. Whatever it was, those late nights were a perfect storm for Dad to buy just about everything he saw on those infomercials!

I was a teenager when Dad came to my room one Saturday morning and said, "Jeffrey, here's something I bought you from an infomercial."

Dad and I talked about business and life for a while before he left. I eagerly opened the package and laid my eyes on Napoleon Hill's book THINK AND GROW RICH. From the title alone I was hooked. As I read the last page that same day little did I realize that reading Think and Grow Rich would become a lifelong ritual.

Ideas Are Great But Action Is Better

Before you could say 'good morning' I found my copy of Think and Grow Rich and tore into it. I internalized the first principle, 'Definiteness of Purpose.' Mine is to enable business school faculty and students to save time with an easy-to-use system allowing them to collaborate anywhere at any time.

With Waleuska now on board, I implemented the second principle, the 'Mastermind Alliance,' in which we worked in complete harmony to achieve every business school using e.mbanet.

Hill's third principle, 'Going the Extra Mile,' reminded me of my Dad and Uncle who often said, "Jeffrey, always do more than what people expect, and do it with a smile." On the spot, I resolved to go the extra mile for everyone AND expect nothing in return.

The fourth principle of success, 'Applied Faith,' was a game changer. Ignoring that I lived in my parents' attic, lacked formal business experience and capital, and was violently rejected by my target market, I saw opportunity where others saw failure.

Through 'Applied Faith,' I felt the feeling of having more customers than I could count, owning a building for my operations, and employing a team of amazing people.

If It Were Easy, Everyone Would Do It

I was interrupted by a phone call from my MBA buddy Don who was hired right out of our program by a Fortune 500 company. I was excited for Don who shared that he just received his third promotion and with it the lavish corporate perks, salary raises, and extended vacations. That said, I felt anxious. I was six months out of my MBA program with nothing to show for it, and yes, I still lived in my parent's attic. As I headed downstairs for a late dinner, Dad just arrived home.

"Jeffrey," said Dad, "I see you're working another late night. Not sure if you've had dinner, but why don't you join me either way."

We grabbed some of the leftovers from the family dinner we missed and headed to the table.

"How goes the battle?", said Dad.

"Battle? You mean slaughter!", I sighed.

"Slaughter"? Dad said. "Sounds like you're in a rough spot."

Frustrated I said, "I'm giving e.mbanet my all and going the extra mile on everything. Between myself and Waleuska, we're speaking to anyone who will listen, but it's still not enough."

Dad broke into a huge smile and laughed before saying, "Jeffrey, I'm laughing with you. One day you'll look back and see what I see."

"See what you see?" I asked puzzled.

"Son, you've just begun. I don't understand what you do, but from what I've seen you're on the leading edge."

"Yeah," I said, "So what."

"The apple doesn't fall far from the tree, son," Dad said still grinning. "When I started my pharmacy I wanted everything yesterday and became angry if it didn't happen as I imagined it," said Dad lovingly.

Continuing, Dad said "Jeffrey, if it were easy everyone would do it. Son, the path you've chosen isn't easy. Yes, the rewards for helping people and succeeding in business is like nothing else. But to get there, you need time, persistence and patience."

In my heart, I knew Dad was right.

Lost in my thoughts Dad interrupted and said, "Jeffrey, the other day I saw you carrying around that Think and Grow Rich book I bought you a while back."

"I love that book! It's the best present ever", I said with a grin.

Dad said, "That was one heck of an infomercial. If I had that book when I started, it would have saved me a lot of heartache and time as the principles of success transcend culture and time."

"Go on," I said riveted to my seat and anxiously waiting to hear pearls of wisdom.

"For me, there are five Principle of Success that stand out. Let's start with a pleasing personality," Dad said in an excited tone.

"OK," I replied.

"Jeffrey, know that most people don't care about what you're going through as they're more concerned with themselves. This may sound harsh, but it is what it is", Dad said in a stern voice.

Dad continued, "always remember Hill's principle of a 'Pleasing Personality' and be friendly, happy and agreeable. While you're at it, Hill's principle of 'Enthusiasm' helps you focus on what you love most in life so it can energize you."

On a roll, Dad continued, "always look for the positive in every situation no matter what. My biggest so-called failures eventually prepared me for success. Hill calls this a 'Positive Mental Attitude,' and he's right on the money. And the last two principles, 'Personal Initiative' and 'Self-Discipline' have you complete essential tasks while building up the habit of making the right choices."

With affection, Dad said, "Jeffrey, always remember you have what you need within you, right now. That said, why don't we pause our business talk and enjoy dinner. Not sure about you, but I'm famished."

We had a dinner to remember as we talked about life, told stories and enjoyed quality father-son time.

Thinking My Way To Success

I forever remember that night when Dad gave me the motivation I needed. Four years later, I'm out of my parent's attic in a six thousand square foot office, with an incredible team helping to change the world, one student at a time.

But even this space is overcrowded from e.mbanet's growth. Now don't get me wrong, getting here was a slog and one of the hardest things I've ever done. I trained myself to become excited when a prospect said "no" because it brought me closer to a yes. Through trial and error, I found the sweet spot – Executive MBA Programs. And let me tell you, once I cracked this nut I never looked back. e.mbanet became a trusted advisor to business schools. e.mbanet's name changed to Embanet as good news travels, and before I knew it, we welcomed in all kinds of distance learning programs.

And the 'secret' to my success, you ask? It's a symphony of things. My definiteness of purpose is my guiding light. My mastermind alliance, which now includes people outside of my industry provides me insights I would otherwise never have. I go the extra mile, no matter what, while expecting nothing in return through providing more services than I'm paid for.

Great times or not, I keep my faith, put my best foot forward with a pleasing personality, and sprinkle enthusiasm and a positive mental attitude everywhere. My self-discipline and personal initiative helped find a way when the naysayers said it's impossible. Best of all, Embanet is profitable, and a nice nest egg is accumulating.

Embanet's service helps schools keep students in their seats through our hosting and 24/7 live technical support. The bottom line is the bottom line. Students, mainly working professionals, complete their online programs and forever change their lives for the better while schools benefit from higher completion rates.

Everything was going great, until a phone call that changed everything.

Putting Yourself Out Of Business

"How's my favorite tech whisperer?" said a familiar voice over the phone.

"Hey Jon," I said with enthusiasm. Jon took a chance on me when I had no track record and became my first client.

"We wrapped up our weekly marketing meeting, Jeffrey, and I need your help," said Jon in a grim voice.

Concerned, I said, "Of course, Jon, tell me more."

"With Embanet, our student retention levels are the highest ever. In fact, I was promoted, and our MBA program is the university's golden child", said Jon with pride.

"Jon, congratulations! But with all this great news, what's bothering you?" I said confused.

"Our enrollments are down as my competition has set up shop in town and through the Internet.", said Jon in a dark voice.

Knowing I needed time to think, I confidently said, "Leave your worries with me Jon and rest assured, I'll figure it out."

"I knew you would rise to the challenge!", said Jon in an upbeat voice.

While hunting down a solution for Jon, I realized that keeping the students in their seats was about to take a back seat as technology became easier and cheaper for schools to do themselves. I was at an inflection point and realized that I needed to put Embanet out of business so I could embrace the next big thing of filling the seats. Better this is done by me instead of a competitor!

Stop Growing And Die

In what seemed like the blink of an eye six years have passed from that inflection point. Embanet expanded with the Embanet Knowledge Group and leads the industry in filling the seats, keeping those seats filled, and having the highest graduation levels. Our Definite Purpose is to change the social fabric of society by enabling working professionals to better their lives through graduate education.

Sitting back in my office chair I smiled. What started in my parents' attic morphed into a 6,000 square foot office that led to a 52,000 square foot building. But I'm getting ahead of myself.

Jon's plea to help fill the seats became my obsession.

Hill's tenth principle, 'Accurate Thinking' came to the rescue. I flew across the continent attending conferences, had phone calls at all hours and took more research notes than I could count. I separated the information, as Hill prescribes, into "important" and "unimportant" facts in as clear and accurate a manner as I could.

I wholeheartedly listened to the opinions of everyone I spoke to but reserved the final decision for myself. The easy thing was to do nothing, but this would cause Embanet to stop growing and die. As one Dean told me, "Jeffrey my IT department provides the same services, but for free. They may not hold a candle to your team, but you can't beat their price"!

I reminded myself that Betamax was superior to VHS but lost the war. Same for the Mac OS losing to Windows.

As painful as my discovery period was, I followed Hill's eleventh principle – 'Controlled Attention.' I kept focused on my desired outcome –

helping my clients fill their seats – and ignored everything else. It wasn't easy leaving my family and business as I traversed the country looking for answers. When the thought of traveling to yet another conference seemed too much, I asked myself one simple question, "Jeffrey, have you found your answer yet?"

Against All Odds Fate Intervenes

Had it not been for the mastery of 'Controlled Attention' I wouldn't have taken a cross-country flight to San Jose, California for another industry conference. Amidst the jet lag and confusion on the tradeshow floor in San Jose, something magical happened. I came to the conference looking for a marketing solution. Little did I know that another man, Steve, showed up looking for a hosting, technical support and course delivery solution for his marketing service. Steve shouldn't have been at the conference if not for a last-minute set of events that ultimately changed the course of history for both of us, and the industry.

And this is where Hill's twelfth principle, 'Teamwork,' enters. Steve and I shared our thoughts in an open and willing manner to help each other. I remember as clear as day when leaving I said to Steve, "Call me crazy as I just met you, but I have the strangest feeling that we're going to do great things together." With a twinkle in his eye, Steve nodded in agreement.

The next step represented a huge risk. Applied Faith saved the day as it enabled Steve to give up ownership and a financial future in a company that was going places, and for me, to put that sizable nest egg at risk for "Embanet II."

Transform Adversity Into Success

Embanet's mastermind expanded to Steve, Waleuska and me as we poured our hearts and souls into turning our dream into a reality. Waleuska held down the fort and pioneered a course development system that was second to none while Steve and I took to the road to spread the word.

Although "Embanet I" was humming along, "Embanet II" was having challenges. Steve and I racked up countless air miles as we flew across the country pitching our solution to Universities.

"Gentlemen," said Edward who was the President of a University in the Northeast, "I appreciate you flying out, but I can't afford your marketing, the copyright of materials isn't owned by my faculty, and besides, I have people who do what you do. I'm sorry, but I don't see a fit."

Our seventh rejection in as many weeks. Napoleon Hill said in his thirteenth principle that, "Every adversity, every failure, every heartache carries with it the seed of an equal or greater benefit."

I didn't yet realize that our ultimate "formula" was the phoenix rising out of the ashes of our "failures." We were down but not out thanks to 'Creative Vision.' I remember that dinner talk I had with Dad who nonchalantly said that if something were easy everyone would do it. Something had to change if we were going to succeed.

And then it happened.

And I knew.

During one of our long philosophical talks that we usually had after getting our butt kicked, Steve said in a defiant voice, "Let's go through every one of our rejections, get creative and eliminate those objections, so we get to YES!"

Give People What They Want

Although it didn't happen that night, it didn't take long before we had our "formula." Looking back now we would have failed if not for the fourteenth principle, 'Creative Vision.' We let our imagination run and took a chance on us.

It was a bet the farm decision. We decided to provide the marketing, course development, hosting, technical support, and copyright for FREE!

It cost the school nothing, and we even paid for the faculty's time. The university is profitable from the first student onwards. Through revenue sharing, we recouped our investment over time if and only if students enrolled and stayed in the program.

When The Unbelievable Becomes Believable

I pinched myself to make sure I wasn't dreaming. "I'm sorry George," I said hoping to not give away my excitement. "Could you repeat what you just said," I asked.

George was the President of a prestigious and influential University in the Northeast.

"Sure Jeffrey. I was saying that I loved your presentation. I came in with an encyclopedia of objections. But after hearing you and Steve present my only question is how soon we can start?"

The Embanet Knowledge Group had its first customer! With the wizardry of Steve and his marketing, the elegance of my technical solution, and Waleuska's brilliant course creation system, we had a great story to share. And people wanted to be part of that story.

We put the original Embanet out of business, just like we planned years back. Once again Embanet led the industry with the highest completion, graduation and enrollment rates.

By no account was it smooth sailing as success breeds its own challenges. That said, Hill's Principles of Success came together like a well-tuned symphony to help us make music that had people smile.

Three Overlooked Principles That Have Everything To Do With Your Ultimate Success

Oh, I almost forgot. At first blush, Principles like 'Budgeting of Time and Money,' 'Maintenance of Sound Health' and 'Cosmic Habitforce' sound boring if not 'woo-woo.'

If not for Budgeting of Time and Money, which had me scrutinize every purchase to build that nest egg, the Embanet Knowledge Group (Embanet II) would not have happened. And remember that Embanet II made Embaent I look like a rounding error.

And I'm far from perfect. Too many plane rides, not enough home cooked meals and lack of exercise is the perfect storm for being unhealthy. Just the thought of lacking energy, having a body that aches and brain fog makes me shudder.

Never again.

And when it comes to Cosmic Habitforce let's turn that famous saying on its head and say that 'seeing is NOT believing.' Lots of things exist that aren't visible!

Hill said it best when he penned, "you are where you are and what you are because of your established habits and thoughts and deeds."

Amen.

Full Circle

As I sat back in my office chair on that hot summer day, I felt like the song from the 'Man of La Mancha.'

I dreamed the impossible dream ... to follow that star ... no matter how hopeless ... no matter how far ... to reach that unreachable star.

And on this day I feel I've reached that unreachable star. Countless lives changed for the better because of a dream and a lot of help from many talented and caring people.

I grin ear-to-ear knowing that I played a small part in helping a single mother to a President of a Fortune 100 company to a high ranking government official achieve their educational goals and dreams, and in the process, enabling them to change the social fabric of society ... one graduate at a time.

Jeffrey E. Feldberg | Bio

Jeffrey Feldberg is a passionate entrepreneur whose personal mission is to be a deliverer of happiness. In addition to running his companies, Jeffrey provides insights, strategies, education and tools to help you flourish and succeed in both your personal and professional life.

This is accomplished through private mentoring, through business advisory and Jeffrey's Curation of Success post.

Jeffrey can be reached through hello@jeffreyfeldberg.com and promises to personally reply.

About the About

So glad you made it this far. Bio and About page etiquette suggest you prop yourself up and strut your stuff for the world to see. Let's change it up and make it real. If you see me in public, be sure to introduce yourself. If you have a question, send me an email through hello@jeffreyfeldberg.com and I will personally answer. Either way, I don't bite. I promise.

Jerry can be reached at: hello@jeffreyfeldberg.com

CHAPTER 18

A Journey of Discovery in the World of Business

By Santosh Krinsky

I did not set out to be successful in business, or even to be in business at all. When I attended Michigan State University, my thoughts were focused on philosophy, psychology and sociology. I was interested in how to understand the principles of living and how those principles could be applied to creating a more balanced, harmonious and peaceful world. Business, per se, did not factor into my thoughts at the time.

Many people define success in the world as "making money". It is quite certain that this is a deficient definition of success. In my early search for meaning, I recognized that everything has its place, including money, and that goals set for one's life had to be larger than a paycheck. After undergoing a near-death experience toward the end of my second year at MSU, I officially became a college dropout. With two years of study under my belt, in fields that had no "career path" for college dropouts, I left for Europe armed with several books on the practice of Yoga and no specific destination in mind. Having sold everything I had, the funds I assembled were clearly not going to last long. Hitchhiking across Europe, sleeping in communes or in some cases, abandoned buildings; I nevertheless had time to pursue my studies and practice. I took jobs when I could get them, including bussing tables and washing dishes in the US Army Hospital Cafeteria in Frankfurt, Germany for a while. Eventually I joined up with several other individuals who were interested in pursuing their spiritual practices and we moved to a farmhouse in a small village and I spent my time immersed in Yoga and walking in the woods. During this time I encountered the writings of Sri Aurobindo and recognized that life was more than being a cog in the business machine and a consumer. I devoted my time whole-heartedly to the study and this led me eventually to reside for about 10 months at Sri Aurobindo Ashram, in Pondicherry, India.

During my time in Pondicherry I was able to meet people who had led very successful careers in fields of business, engineering, science, education and government, yet kept their attention on the evolution of consciousness and the integration of a new consciousness into the relations of society and planetary harmony. My goal was defined for me clearly during this period. I also had a chance to visit the community of Auroville which aspired to be a model of a new form of social order based on higher principles, and doing away with artificial separations due to race, skin color, creed, gender or other superficial characteristics. I met people from many countries around the world, working together, struggling to overcome differences and misunderstandings through an embracing goodwill.

I returned from India in early 1974 with no money, no job, no career, no college degree and no clear idea how I was going to carry out the aims I now had for my life. I got a very short-lived job as a delivery driver, and soon found out that I was not cut out for that career! A friend had worked as a file clerk at a collection agency and when she quit that job I immediately applied for it. I was told that "there is no job opening here". They expected a woman to do the job.... I responded that I KNEW there was a job opening and they could give me any test they wanted. If I passed, I expected the job. Sometime after getting the position I learned that they thought I must have been from the Equal Opportunity Division testing them for discrimination! After cleaning up their file room, I was asked if I could type. So I entered into my career as a professional typist by day.

At this time I recognized that many people could benefit from the kind of books I had found so useful in defining my life and goals, so I started my first company by borrowing $108.00 and buying some books for resale. I went to a local bookstore and sold the books. When the owner agreed to buy them, I asked him to tell me how to go about doing it as he was my first customer in my first business endeavor. He walked me through the process of invoicing for the books. When we came to payment he told me that normally they would pay in 30 days. I mentioned to him that he now had my ENTIRE stock in trade and that I really needed to get paid right away. He agreed, and I thus had funds to buy a few more books and repeat the process. Over time I added more books, incense and other products imported from India, including some Ayurvedic products, and the company was launched, but it could not stand on its own feet, so I worked my day job typing and handled the budding enterprise evenings, weekends and holidays.

I went to work at an advertising agency business owned by my parents and took on the "legal" division to protect businesses who were being treated unfairly in the yellow pages industry. This led to numerous hearings in front of the Public Utilities Commission and serious study in regulatory requirements, and legal briefing techniques. The yellow page companies did not like losing cases, so they did what they could to put the agency out of business, which they eventually did. Litigation followed and I wound up drawing an expense check from the law firm handling the case while it slowly proceeded. I had to read, understand and categorize hundreds of thousands of documents and organize for the attorneys the basis of the case. My original business continued on the side. After deciding to get married and move across the country, it was handed off to a non-profit organization so that we could make the move unencumbered, and thus, start over again. Shortly thereafter a settlement of the litigation gave us a small fund to start a new business, which focused on publishing books, importing and natural personal care products.

As the first business had grown and added products, I became involved in the natural products industry and recognized that we were killing ourselves, and wreaking havoc on the planetary balance through all the toxic chemicals in the products we put on or in our bodies. After moving to Wisconsin, then the idea was to provide viable and useful alternatives for people to meet their personal care needs with safe, natural and humane alternatives. Lotus Light wholesale distribution was the result and we soon found that this type of business, in the Midwest, was not yet recognized and it was difficult getting customers. I wound up working day and night, developing customers, writing orders, doing the bookkeeping, picking and packing orders, ordering replenishment, and paying the bills. Eventually the business took hold and grew and I was able to add employees, managers and products as we developed customers for our selection of products nationwide. Today Lotus Light is 35 years old and employs approximately 75 people.

We found that other similar companies around the country were having difficulties sustaining themselves as well, for various reasons, much of which was due to undercapitalization and consequent lack of all the staff and skill sets needed to operate a quite complex business. We set out to try to help them survive and in some cases shipped products for them to their customers to help them tide over rough patches in their cash flow. Many of these companies nevertheless went out of business, and we acquired assets of some of them, while others turned over to us voluntarily their customer accounts. We thus gained a nationwide footprint and expanded product selection.

We experienced a major challenge early on when one of the biggest product brands we distributed successfully, and on which we relied for a good portion of our revenue stream, was sold to an animal testing lab! We were both shocked and appalled and decided, together with several other similar distributors around the country to drop the brand and boycott it on the basis of the animal testing connection. We had to quickly figure out how to replace the revenue in order to meet the overhead and payroll while taking this stand.

In 1992 we began to recognize the issues of complexity within one business structure. We were trying to be a wholesaler as well as a brand manufacturer and marketing company on the other; while simultaneously publishing books under our Lotus Press imprint. This led to an important realization and we spun off Lotus Brands to handle the brand manufacturing and marketing along with the publishing division and set it up with its own management, facilities and staff. This simplified the operations of Lotus Light so that we could focus on operating that business profitably and finding a way to survive when other similar companies were failing regularly. At the same time, Lotus Brands and Lotus Press now had a clear and dedicated mission with a team of people who could carry it out, allowing our brands and publishing efforts to grow much more effectively than previously.

Around that time our companies had a "near death" experience as well. We had acquired assets of another distributor out of bankruptcy and along with those assets we hired some of their key management personnel. We soon found out that despite having schedules of assets submitted to the Court "under penalty of perjury" there was a lot of confusion and bad reporting involved and we acquired far fewer assets than we had anticipated. We were also operating three warehouses (East Coast, Midwest and West Coast) at that time and the manager involved was shuffling funds back and forth so we could not get clear oversight. Once we got oversight we were shocked! We were losing $90,000 per month and would soon be bankrupt ourselves. We took immediate action and after firing the manager, closing the two satellite warehouses and paring back expenses radically, we were able to "right the ship" and continue our journey of discovery in the world of business. I remember calling the managers in and laying the facts on the table.

Nothing is quite as easy as it sounds. As the businesses grew, we now had personnel issues to understand and resolve, ever-larger financial resources to borrow and deploy, new challenges on the regulatory front to understand, and competitive forces in the marketplace to address while at the same time, remaining true to the guiding principles and working to keep a collaborative rather than competitive approach to others engaged in similar activities. We acquired some brands that just did not fit our profile and thus were eventually written off. Our lack of formal training and education in the field was showing! We acquired other brands who claimed to be compliant with regulatory issues. We soon found out otherwise and had to clean up regulatory messes that were not of our own making. Time, focus and money were invested in these various areas and along the way, we have educated ourselves and developed protocols and procedures to educate our staff, on how to meet the regulatory requirements while operating the companies effectively.

In late 2002 we received a phone call from one of our larger customers in the publishing division, New Leaf Distributing Company. Their long-time CEO and leader had recently succumbed to a drawn-out terminal illness. The company had been without strong leadership for some time as a result, and they were on the brink of bankruptcy. The caller told us that if we were not prepared to buy New Leaf immediately they would have to file bankruptcy. We had no contingency plans to deal with this situation, but after discussing it my wife and I decided to give it a try. The additional challenge was that the company was operating on obsolete software and systems, was serving a fast-changing marketplace with the rise of online bookselling and was located in Atlanta, Georgia so that it would not be a "hands on" management for us. We jumped in, borrowed a sizable sum of money and took the risk on the basis that New Leaf, in our view, was an important cog in the wheel of providing spiritual literature and access for hundreds of publishers to the metaphysical market, which also relied heavily on New Leaf. So not just New Leaf and its employees were at stake, but many thousands of others, and the dissemination of conscious living literature as well.

The New Leaf adventure started in 2003 for us. It was a decidedly difficult project. We had to develop new software and systems to handle the complexity of the company as it existed and as it would exist in the future. We had to clean up the bookkeeping that was filled with inaccuracies, and we had to write off huge amounts of inventory that was gathering dust. We had to re-instill focus and purpose in the company and the staff, and bring expenses under control to keep it operational, all while dealing with a declining market as long-time customers went out of business and moved on in their lives. This process of reinventing New Leaf continues even today, 13 years later. No one expected the process to be easy, but we did not imagine that 13 years of efforts would be needed to reach a stable platform that could once again start growing in new directions.

In 2004 we purchased the Eco-Dent brand of oral care products. The brand had originally been developed in Europe about 70 years prior but was struggling as a small brand in an industry that was becoming "big business". We felt that by bringing it under the Lotus Brands umbrella, it would have a good chance of both survival and growth and we invested heavily in that project. Today it is one of our leading brands with a strong and loyal consumer base which we have cultivated by providing effective products that avoid the "sulfates" and "parabens" that are in most commercial oral care products, and by developing products and packaging that were substantially more friendly to the environment than commercial products. The brand met our criteria for adhering to the core principles of balance, harmony and environmental concern.

Having survived "near death" experiences several times in our business lives, it is interesting to note that we also had some positive opportunities to help us along. One of those was related to our Ancient Secrets Nasal Cleansing Pot. We designed and patented a "neti pot" that we believed would work best for a regular routine of nasal cleansing. We put it into distribution and achieved a fair amount of success with the product. Then we heard that one of the other products in the market had arranged for Oprah to do a feature on using a neti pot. (She actually did a follow up show several weeks later as well.) We immediately contacted our supplier and asked them to put us in the production queue and start airfreighting goods to us without delay. While the airfreight would eat up the profit, it would keep the market alive. Even though it was not our design being featured, we knew there would be a solid impact. Within days we were sold out, but our airfreight shipments started coming in and for several months we were bringing in airfreight consignments weekly. We had obtained this service by promising to buy 1.2 million pots by the end of the year (around 7 months), which was far beyond anything we had ever sold before. In the interim, we found out that the other vendor had run out after the first day, but had no air freight shipments and no consignments coming in by sea for months, so in effect, our product was now on all the shelves in the industry while the others were "out of stock". We made the commitment after researching the methods behind the "Oprah effect" and we determined that Oprah always did "re runs" of popular shows later, so we expected to see a second effect to take advantage of our now virtually universal availability in the health food market and our strong in stock supply. By the end of the year, Oprah did her reruns and we were able to sell through our stock of pots in the months that followed. Surprisingly the other vendor had not planned on a 'second showing' and was quickly out of stock again so once again, we had coverage at the store level and product to fill the pipeline.

A local newspaper sent a reporter down to write up the story and she laughed when she indicated that a "one time" fluke of this sort was not real success, and that we would essentially be crying when the boom was over. We had, however, no illusions on this score, and used the funds from this opportunity to acquire several additional brands, including Beauty Without Cruelty. This was a brand dedicated to "no animal testing" and it fit our philosophy perfectly. We could use the brand to expand the message of living life in harmony with nature, and to provide products that both promoted consciousness and gave people viable alternatives to commercial personal care products, with natural ingredients, high quality products and a cruelty-free message. Beauty Without Cruelty, started originally in the U.K. in 1963, was the first brand to make an issue of animal testing of cosmetics and provide options. The brand is also entirely Vegan and at the same time provides great value and outstanding products that really work for people.

People believe that when there is an economic "boom" it is easy to succeed. A "boom" tends to attract a lot of competition and attention, new money and innovative approaches based on the new investment capital coming into the market. We have watched the natural products industry grow from the time of the mid 1970's to today. It has "boomed" and today major companies, publicly traded, multi-billion-dollar entities tend to control the manufacturing, distribution and retail ends of the business. Small, family-run businesses have a hard time surviving in this environment.

It is, however, even harder for small companies during economic "bust" cycles. Lenders cut back on available funds. Businesses fail and competition intensifies. Larger retailers tend to work with larger wholesalers who tend to work with larger manufacturers. Meanwhile, employees have to be compensated fairly, benefits such as health insurance have to be provided, and somehow, the small companies need to find ways to keep their heads above water.

We have been through several "boom and bust" cycles and recognized that the best strategy is to stick to our core competencies, assemble a team of highly skilled and dedicated people to carry out the company mission, and provide fair value and service to our vendors, our customers and our employees. We are grateful to the many individuals who have stuck out the good times and the hard times with us for 15, 20 or even 25 years! During this time, we have also recognized that things never remain the same, and thus, we have reinvented and renovated our operations, our brands, our platforms and our marketing directions to embrace changes in the marketplace.

One of the recognitions we gained during the economic downturn in 2007-2008 was that Lotus Light as a wholesale distributor needed to diversify away from selling just national brands in the natural products industry, which were being sold by the publicly-traded distributor who served the vast majority of the industry. We recognized that there was a solid niche to bring to the USA leading natural personal care brands from Europe primarily that had no US-footprint for their brands. These companies had very high quality standards, clean ingredients, met our "no animal testing" requirements and had diverse product offerings that would be valuable and interesting to consumers in the USA. This direction is now the core focus of Lotus Light, while the company continues to distribute a vast array of national brands, and it is quickly becoming the key to the future success of Lotus Light.

Without intending to be in business, and without a background in business, it became clear to me that my contribution to the evolutionary effort and development of a more harmonious world would be through the implementation of business. The goal has not been to become rich, and we have turned down a number of "buyout" offers over the years. We continue to focus on "products that promote consciousness" and "products inspired by Mother Nature" which are our key guidelines. We also continue to expand our publishing effort, such that Lotus Press is now the leading publisher in the USA of books on Ayurveda and Reiki, as well as contributing valuable books in the field of alternative health and wellness, herbology and spirituality.

I recognize that no journey goes on forever, and that eventually a future needs to be determined for this work that does not involve me. To that end, I have worked for the last 20 or more years to develop a dedicated and effective team of people who can run the companies without my direct involvement, when necessary, and to develop protocols, procedures and guidelines that will help maintain the focus, energy and dynamism, and core principles for which the companies were founded. My daughters, one of whom is actively involved in the business, have committed to the continuance of our corporate mission and focus. I have confidence in the management team and our dedicated staff to be able to effectively continue into the future whether I am involved or not. And in the end, when we recognize that we cannot take it with us, it is important for us to practice non-attachment to the fruits of work, whether in the form of wealth or business and to use whatever opportunities are given to us to promote the core principles, by which these businesses were founded, of harmony, growth of consciousness, and environmental balance, because in the end, this is the real legacy we leave behind us.

Santosh Krinsky | Bio

Santosh Krinsky has been working in the natural products industry since 1974. During the ensuing 30+ years, he has acted as a book publisher, importer, manufacturer, wholesaler and online retailer through a number of business entities. His work involves the integration of spirituality into daily life and the incorporation of new paradigms for addressing the problems of health, wellness and fulfillment on the planet.

Santosh has a unique educational background, having majored in psychology, sociology and philosophy at Michigan State University. He then studied spirituality and yoga at the Sri Aurobindo Ashram in Pondicherry India. After returning to the USA, Santosh became involved in the natural products industry and book publishing and has subsequently studied Ayurveda through the Institute for Wholistic Education. He is an active writer on spiritual approaches to solving social issues of the day.

CHAPTER 19

Success Illustrated-The Beginning

By Spencer Iverson

I have been an entrepreneur for all of my adult life. Some know me as a sports attorney. Others have come to know me as a business development consultant., while others follow me as a motivational speaker, trainer and global leader in the industry of network marketing. I guess I got the "bug" from my father, John Iverson, Sr., who is a minister in Valdosta, Georgia. As a child and teenager watching him, I loved how he could manage his time so as to always be there for important family functions and trips. I loved how he could further use his time to visit the elderly and sick and participate in charitable causes. I loved how he controlled how much, or how little, he earned all because entrepreneurship gives you one of life's most valuable commodities...time. Time affords you the ability to have options. One of the options that I exercise with my time is indulging in reading. While all readers are not leaders, it is true that all leaders are readers. In 2012 I was introduced to a magnificent piece of literature, one that would ultimately go on to change my life.

Napoleon Hill's book, Think and Grow Rich, and the Success Principles contained in it, have done more for my personal and financial development than any other book I have read during my lifetime besides the Bible. I read these principles. I study these principles. I train thousands of people worldwide on these principles. I live by these principles. Why? Because you should never view success as a "mystery." Creating wealth for you and your family is not some hidden formula buried away in the dark recesses of carefully guarded manuscripts, access to which is only given to a privileged few. No! Success is readily attainable by the masses. You just have to know where to look for it. That's what Napoleon Hill did. He probed the minds of millionaires and billionaires and found that they all had several things in common. He memorialized his findings in a book. Now, these practices serve as a roadmap for anyone desiring to achieve more in life. The average millionaire has read Hill's book 3 times. Oprah Winfrey, a billionaire, has read Think and Grow

Rich 13 times and attributes much of her success to Hill's teachings! As an attorney, this is what I call "a clue!"

My "journey to success" has not been a straight road, but rather a long, circuitous, winding path. More than 10 years ago, I was doing a motivational seminar in Columbia, SC. The gentleman who was hosting the event was preparing to introduce me to the audience of about 500 people and he said, "Spencer Iverson is one of the best speakers and trainers in America. When you look at his initials, S.I., that doesn't stand for Sports Illustrated, he's Success Illustrated!" Well, from that moment on, the description sort of stuck. The ideaology is that you should live your life in such a way so that when others see you, they see the very embodiment of success. You become the illustration of success and achievement that they have always dreamed about and aspire towards. In the pages that follow, I will share with you some stories of how Hill's principles have become manifest in my life.

Irrational Faith

By most accounts, Napoleon Hill was not known to be a particularly religious man. However, he saw the value of faith and placed a high value on it in achieving success. What Hill calls faith is in fact a type of self-confidence that borders on religion. It was a principle that he once learned from his mentor, the steel magnate and Andrew Carnegie, the 2nd wealthiest person in history.

Carnegie once said, "I believe that every failure carries within it—in the circumstances of the failure itself—the seed of an equivalent advantage. If you examine the lives of truly great leaders, you will discover that their success is in exact proportion to their mastery of failures. Life has a way of developing strength and wisdom in individuals through temporary defeat."

I know all about defeat. The old saying goes, "Be careful what you pray for, you just might get it!" Well, I know and recognize that I am deficient in so many areas of my life, one of which is patience. I am very impatient. I walk fast. I talk fast. I think fast. I eat fast. I make fast decisions. I drive fast cars. I ride fast bikes. To me, life's too short to be slow. I want to do more, see more, experience more and I want to do it all right NOW! That's fine, but I know that is not always advantageous and could become counter-productive as I work with other individuals and organizations in an effort to help them reach their maximum potential. So I began to ask God for patience. James 1: 2-3 states, "My brethren, count it all joy when ye fall into diverse temptations; knowing this, that the trying of your faith worketh patience." In essence, James is telling us that to have a full appreciation for and understanding of the practice of patience, you must necessarily experience some problems.

In 2008, at the beginning of what we now recognize as America's greatest economic downturn, my business was hit with a series of unfortunate events. I watched my income go from more than $120,000 a month to $0 in a matter of 5 months. It seemed as if everything I touched or tried failed.

I owned several cars, one of which was a black, fully loaded, show car ready, Mercedes Benz CLS 550 sedan, but times got real tough real quick. I ultimately agreed to what they call a "voluntary repossession" where I just told the lienholder, "come and get it." Trying to balance between buying groceries to feed my family and making a payment on a luxury vehicle had become too much.

Then, a nutritional company that I had built a very large organization with and made a lot of money for, turned around a filed a wrongful $1.2 million dollar "breach of contract" lawsuit against me and a partner. Even though the allegations within the complaint were totally false, we still had to provide an answer and a defense. I contacted an attorney from the state of Utah who had dealt with this company suing other distributors in a similar fashion before. He said he needed a $20,000 retainer! I think I only had $20 so that wasn't going to work for me! I made the decision to defend the case(s), pro se, on my own. I defended both my case and my partner's case simultaneously, so I had to do every brief, every answer twice! It seemed like I received correspondence and court filings daily, each of which had to be answered, submitted and filed. I pulled my best "Johnny Cochran" and was successful in arguing and winning the first round of proceedings when I moved the venue to Georgia, but that didn't stop them. They just kept pounding us with paperwork. I got tired. I was tired because for almost 2 years my life had become consumed with fighting this case, and I couldn't focus on building a profitable business for my family. I was under constant stress, I was not eating right and I was not looking well. I finally made the decision to file for bankruptcy to extinguish the lawsuit. For some reason I was so embarrassed, because I was that person who was supposed to have it "all together." Why was I feeling like such a failure?

Things just continued to get worse and worse. Our 2 kids, Brandon and Hayley, were attending a private school that cost more than $17,000 per child, per year. This was the only school they knew. This is where all of their friends attended. This was the center of their social world, but I could no longer afford to send them there. So we had to make the decision to put them in a public school near our home. That hurt.

It hurt because what was happening to me financially was not the kid's fault. Brandon and Hayley were making "A's" in school and dad was making an "F" in life. However tough things got for me, I didn't want the kids to sense or feel any loss in the quality of life that they had come to enjoy. For example, my wife, Tonya, and I typically like to go out to eat for dinner on Sundays after worship. Well, during that time, I was having to make a decision if I could even go to worship because I couldn't afford a round trip tank of gas. I'm a pretty good golfer, and would often times go to the course with about $20 in my pocket and hustle up a game where I would win $200 - $300 just to have some money to survive on during the week.

So, with a little money in my pocket, we would go out to dinner as per our custom on Sundays. Tonya would order, Hayley would order and then I would just cringe as Brandon, who was growing like a weed and eating everything in sight, would order the "full rack of rib dinner combo" for $18.99! Come on man! Anyway, I would never order. I would always come up with some excuse as to why dad was "still full from breakfast" or "couldn't find anything I really liked on the menu." I would quell my hunger pains by simply eating whatever the family had left over (or sneaking some extra communion wafers into my pockets from that morning's worship service - forgive me Lord.)

I prayed for patience and the Lord sent me problems. But as I pressed forward, I slowly began to realize that these were not problems. No, these were passageways. Passageways that would lead to a recognition that God wasn't just building my faith, he was giving me an "irrational" faith. That's the kind of faith where losing is no longer an option. That's the kind of faith where the word "failure" ceases to exist in your vocabulary. That's the kind of faith that allows you to become "more than a conqueror." Despite the storms I was living in, my faith was being renewed and grew in strength every day. I learned how to compartmentalize my problems. I stopped having pity parties for myself and realized that although I was going through a tough time, somebody, somewhere was going through worse.

I watched God allow my Mercedes to be taken, but He still provided me with transportation. I witnessed God permit my kids to change schools, but blessed them to go on to meet new friends, develop new relationships and for Brandon, earn a full, all expenses paid scholarship for his undergraduate and graduate studies and even make an appearance with his partner, Jordan Williams, on The Steve Harvey Show! I waited on God to make me experience hunger, only to be filled with an insatiable spirit, passion and desire to dig deeper, reach farther and go higher. Today, I am a survivor. God has navigated me successfully through so many storms of life that I am now a qualified tour guide for somebody else.

Make A Decision

The inability to make a decision is ultimately what kills the squirrel that is trying to cross the road. You see, had the squirrel simply made the decision to continue quickly all the way across, or rather commit to going quickly back in the direction that it started, the squirrel would have lived. But no, the squirrel is indecisive, hesitates, and ponders and then BAM! The squirrel is killed by a

Honda Accord.

This phenomenon exemplifies Hill's principle of decision. It is closely related to his high value of leadership. I discussed this same point in my book, The 3 CEO's Formula, and entitled the chapter "Pull The Trigger." Here is a sample of what I wrote.

"Often people sit in their offices or cubicles at work and stare longingly outside or simply "daydream" about being somewhere else, living their fantasy, fulfilling their life's dreams. Why are some people living their dreams in life while others are not? The answer a lot of times is that the successful person, at some point in his or her life, stopped talking about doing something different and did something different. We call this, "pulling the trigger."

Stop sitting around the house talking about losing weight and "pull the trigger." Develop a plan and commit yourself to a regimen of healthy eating and exercise. Stop complaining about how stupid your boss is and "pull the trigger." Have the confidence it takes to look for a position that will allow you to display your abilities and talents. Stop looking at the screensaver on your computer of the Tropical Island and aqua-blue water and "pull the trigger." Check your finances, go online and start saving for and planning your dream vacation. The point is that you must do everything in your life with a sense of purpose and a sense of urgency. Otherwise you will look at yourself in the mirror one day and won't be able to recognize the aged face that is staring back at you!"

Leaders make decisions quickly and stand behind their decisions. Such people, Hill writes, "know what they want, and generally get it." That is because "the world has the habit of making room for the man whose words and actions show that he knows where he is going."

The more important lesson may lie in what Hill has to say about indecision.

"Indecision is a habit which usually begins in youth. The habit takes on permanency as the youth goes through graded school, high school, and even through college, without definiteness of purpose."

I am very confident in both my skills and abilities. As such, I very rarely take a long time to make decisions. I process information quickly. I gather as many of the relevant facts as necessary to aid in making a quick decision. I also contemplate and consider how or if this decision is going to affect my spiritual and family life. For me, all of these things are happening in my mind simultaneously.

In life, I see people missing out on great opportunities all the time because they cannot make a quick decision. They are just like the squirrel - they start, they stop, they think, they think some more, and then BAM - life happens. Something happens in your life that now precludes you from taking advantage of an opportunity. Understand this, opportunities don't go away, they just go to other people.

Further, the people that you spend the majority of your time with, i.e. your inner circle, can also be a negative influencer as well and subconsciously play a role in your inability to make a quick decision. How? Well, it has been proven scientifically that people tend to associate with others with similar likes, tendencies and habits. You've heard them all before, "Birds of a feather flock together, "evil communications corrupts good morals," and my personal favorite, "If you hang around four broke people, there's a strong possibility you're about to become number five!" If you follow this logic, this means that if you are an indecisive person, your inner circle is more than likely also indecisive.

It is really a study in-group dynamics. Do you notice that your group always has a difficult time making a decision where they will go for dinner? Do you find it frustrating that no one in the group can determine quickly which movie should be watched that night? Does it drive you crazy watching your friends stare aimlessly at the McDonald's menu screen and cannot choose from one of the twelve numbers from a menu that has not changed in fifty years? Begin today by making a decision to evaluate your inner circle. There are some people, right now, that are in your life that you think are assets, but in reality, they are liabilities and they are preventing you from reaching your fullest potential.

Program Your Mind Through Affirmations

The human mind is a fascinating organ. Here are some interesting facts. The average brain is believed to generate around 50,000 thoughts per day. Disturbingly, it is estimated that in most people 70% of these thoughts are negative. (How Negative is Your "Mental Chatter"?, Dr. Raj Raghunathan Ph.D.). Your brain's storage capacity is considered virtually unlimited. (What Is the Memory Capacity of the Human Brain? Dr. Paul Reber, professor of psychology at Northwestern University.) Think you are in control of your life? Think again. 95% of your decisions take place in your subconscious mind. (The Subconscious Mind of the Consumer (And How To Reach It), Harvard Business School professor Dr. Gerald Zaltman.)

Napoleon Hill was equally fascinated with the human mind, specifically the subconscious, and the role it plays in determining one's capacity for success. He discusses the idea of autosuggestion. It is familiar to most audiences today, whether in the form of affirmations or visualization. It is a technique that can serve as the very foundation for your belief. As Hill once put it, "If you do not see great riches in your imagination, you will never see them in your bank balance."

Hill's techniques of autosuggestion are quite traditional. He suggests repeating the mission statement aloud every morning and evening, while visualizing the goal in mind. If you desire to have money, see yourself in possession of that money. If you desire to have that big corner office with an executive assistant nearby, place yourself physically in that environment. If you are in sales and want to have a record-breaking quarter, visualize the dollar amount and tell yourself every morning, "I am so happy and grateful that I reached $1,000,000 in sales this month!" Here's the catch. The autosuggestion, or affirmation, process begins with belief! You can't fool your subconscious mind. Proverbs 23:7 says, "As a man thinketh in his heart, so is he." Even King Solomon, who wrote the book of Proverbs, understood the importance of belief. You can wake up every morning, look into the mirror, and exclaim, "I am so happy and grateful that I made $1,000,000 today!" While that is a nice declaration, deep down, you know you don't believe that. When that happens, your subconscious mind completely ignores you and simply detects that right now, you're just yelling in the mirror.

I did not know this, but I had been practicing Hill's technique long before I actually read his book. I remember as a first year law associate, I was working at my firm in Atlanta when a new associate was making her rounds introducing herself to everyone in the office. We developed a friendship and would often have lunch together and discuss cases and matters of the day. During one lunch meeting, I guess she felt comfortable enough to compliment me on the suits I wore and how my outfits were put together, but then she turned her attention to my watch. At the time, I was wearing a Swatch watch with a rubber band. I thought my watch was nice, even though it only cost me about $80. She commented, "You wear nice, custom suits to work, but you have that cheap watch. Why? You're a successful attorney and should have a much nicer time piece." Ouch. I never saw it that way.

So, from that day on, I took that "cheap" watch off and never wore it again. Instead, I began to study the history of fine men's timepieces like Breitling, Rolex, Patek Philippe, Ulysse Nardin, Audemars Piguet and others. I finally settled on Rolex. I located a picture of one that I liked, cut it out of a magazine, and stapled it conspicuously in my day planner. I used my day planner every day, so every day, multiple times a day, I would see and envision the object of my desire. At that time, I could not afford the price tag for such a nice watch, so I went two whole years with no watch. The repetitive visualization of the watch every day stimulated my subconscious mind. My subconscious mind then began to drive my actions. I became consciously aware to set aside a little money here and a little money there. I imagined how the watch would feel against my skin. I saw the watch on my wrist daily. I went into the jewelry store multiple times a week just to stare at the watch. Until finally, after closing a big deal, I went and paid cash for my Rolex.

By the time I actually owned my Rolex, it now seemed like everybody had a Rolex! What happened? Now, your subconscious mind is actively engaged and you have become consciously aware of other people who own Rolexes. Have you ever bought a car thinking that you are going to be one of only a few that has that particular make, model, and color, only to drive off the lot and now see that same car everywhere? It's the same phenomenon.

Now that I know how powerful affirmations and visualization are, I practice this on purpose! I have "vision boards" on my phone's screen saver that has 4 images. I created a "poster" that shows the number $1,000,000, there is an image of a Ferrari F458 Italia, there's an image that says "Debt Free" and a picture of a sunrise. The $1,000,000 represents my goal for the amount of liquid assets I want to accumulate within a certain time frame. The Ferrari represents, well, my next car! The poster that says "Debt Free," represents my desire to have no debt, aside from a mortgage. The sunrise is symbolic of this "happy place" I aspire towards in my life. I see these images every day. They are reminders of some of my goals and dreams. I have Post-It notes in my office that have these words written on them so I can see them constantly.

What goals do you have for your life? Are you speaking them into existence? Do you really believe that these goals can come true for you and your family? You must have the firm belief that you are successful long before the success begins to physically manifest itself in your life. Your "journey to success" will likely be much like mine, filled with ups and downs, twists and turns, thorns and bushes, but don't quit. Apply Hill's principles to your life, believe they will work for you and in time, you too will become "success illustrated!"

Spencer Iverson| Bio

Spencer Iverson is one of the most gifted and multi-talented business leaders in America. Spencer started his first business at the age of 12, attended Georgia Tech, where he earned a patent, attended law school at Mercer University and by the age of 28 had become the CEO of a publicly traded company. After law school, Iverson represented professional athletes in the NFL, MLB, golf and basketball as an agent for more than 10 years.

Iverson has appeared in Essence, The Atlanta Business Chronicle, Success from Home (twice) and other magazines and has also appeared in and written articles for numerous national publications, radio shows and television programs. In 2009, Iverson was named as one of "Atlanta's Top 100 Most Powerful and Influential Men." He is the co-author of the top-selling The 3 CEOs Formula and Breakfast with the CEOs.

Today, Iverson is the National Director of Sales and Global Business Development and leads the largest organization in Paycation Travel, one of America's most successful and fastest growing home-based companies. Iverson's new training modules, Success. Illustrated. Volumes I and II and The First 48, are quickly becoming top sellers amongst home business professionals and corporate executives in a variety of companies around the world. Iverson is also the Chief Executive Officer of a sports and entertainment agency that facilitates the representation of professional athletes, artists and actors, as well as participates in the development of music and film projects worldwide.

Spencer can be reached at worthyofmillions@gmail.com

CHAPTER 20

Truth In Clarity

By Tony Fevola

I'm sitting in a comfy chair feeling the warmth of the sun on my face as it streams through the window. As I begin to write, I am reminded of how I have always thought that things would just work out and that people would be honorable, honest and genuine in their agreements. Well, often learning the hard way, I have found out that this is not the case. Reflecting on my business experiences I see now that the business paradigm is more like that of a sinking ship: every man for himself. At this point I believe that I know a little more about how people, the world and business work. I have observed that what we think, both consciously and subconsciously, is what we become. We have now come to know this as the Law of Attraction, which has guided humanity through the ages. I find myself in the 21st Century looking at our world and seeing that this Law continues to be true in even larger ways. I have long seen myself as an intelligent person who has struggled with maintaining my integrity and growing businesses while simultaneously trying to discover my burning desire, white hot in my heart. I started a business when I was so young and naïve, and as much as I have learned about dealing with others while making sales and deals, I have learned the most about myself. While I am privileged to have the opportunity to write this chapter, I realize that I may not have the time to explain fully my intentions, as I know that I still have so much further to grow in both my business and my personal life.

Learning by Doing

I've had a series of small epiphanies recently, just tiny ones. Little blips that I feel within my chest but I can't quite find the words for, or if I do find them then they seem wanting in their ability to convey this new and nascent knowledge. What I hope to show you in this chapter are many of what I thought were struggles were actually the use of the Law of Attraction, along with the process of breaking down the paradigms that have programmed my mind and needed to be undone. What I had believed were struggles were quite possibly the greatest lessons of my life. I will also show how you can use some effective techniques that will aid in recognizing and achieving major shifts in your life.

One of the key components of success is having Purpose and using Imagination to guide you through your ventures. In my years of living and working, both in creating businesses and in consulting work, I have gained a tremendous amount of practical experience. This experience is the best teacher. The knowledge that I have gained has grown exponentially. I have read and discovered specific things I needed to know in order to grow and develop my businesses, but more importantly, who I am. I have been able to wed the ideas that I read with the creativity in my heart and mind. In this chapter I am attempting to transform and transfer my information and knowledge into pragmatic, practical ideas that will hopefully inspire some of you to think, create, take action, and grow as well. I will discuss why Purpose is the essential component of success and why it can easily elude us if we approach it without clarity. This clarity needs to be mental and spiritual as well or it will not serve you.

I know that whenever I have read many books, in order to understand and develop both my business and myself, I have always felt more productive and focused when they provide specific suggestions of how I can start to enact what I could see for myself. I will provide some practices that can enhance your own growth. As I relate some of my ideas, think of how they resonate in your own life.

Each of us has an idea, a goal for how to achieve and live one's life. Some of us have been proactive and written these goals down regularly with varying degrees of specificity. We might have written some goals in vague terms and they seem to still be unachieved, while others may have been specific, for example in an amount of money, but without the necessary exact, descriptive qualifications about the goal to have it truly manifested. When going through my nightstand recently, I found an old goal card where I had written the amount of money I wanted to earn at a business in one year. Needless to say the Universe granted this goal, the business had pulled in the exact amount that I had written down on the card. I was disappointed however, since what I had neglected to do was write down that the amount I wrote down was what I wanted in my pocket after costs and any other payouts. The Universe munificently provided the exact amount I had written. I now see that the generous abundance of the Universe is very much present! It was my lack of clear specifics in writing my goals and my personal understanding of the Law of Attraction at the time that I wrote them which prevented me from seeing them fully realized in the way that I now know is possible. I did not imagine the larger picture which I have a glimpse of now. I know to think and imagine.

To achieve these goals, we must recognize that each of us has desires, both conscious and subconscious. We need to understand that there will always be an obstacle or impediment to achieving our goals and these goals should ultimately be to acknowledge and understand our true purpose, to imagine and to create. There are and will be countless excuses for why and how we cannot meet or focus on our goal. There will always be something keeping us from having a laser like focus on it. Those excuses will always present themselves; we need to recognize them for what they are and look past them. Focusing on the excuse for not achieving will give the excuse weight and merit so that it becomes the impediment itself, keeping us further away from meeting that goal. Wallace Wattles wrote, "A thought is a substance, producing the thing that is imagined by the thought." So, when we allow ourselves to become distracted by and focus on the obstacle, we cement that obstacle in its place. What are we to do? I know for myself, I must acknowledge that it exists and consciously dismiss it. If I allow the obstacle to exist in the mind, it will certainly dig in its heels, guaranteeing that the goal and its pursuit will be thwarted. When you see the obstacle, take note of it but do not give it any undue energy.

Three Success Principles

I have narrowed Success down to three top priorities of the 17 Success Principles needed to make major shifts. The first is Purpose, to really define and crystalize what you desire out of life. Stop whatever you are doing this moment and think for a moment about what it all means. Are you thinking? Your situation may be one of happiness but with a bit of discouragement. It may be one of frustration and desire. To begin to understand I suggest you take a sheet of paper and write on it, day and night, making a list of all your desires. Do this day after day, in the morning and at night and you will see your ideas come before you as they crystallize and get into focus. Regularly review your list as if it were the most important document on this planet. Carry your most recent copy of it in your pocket.

This brings me to the second principle that will make you value your goals even more. Have the burning desire to acquire your wishes and goals and plant them deep into your subconscious along with all the other things that are already currently in your life. While planted there, your mind will actively work towards achieving them. The third principle is for you to create the desire to take action. Select a task everyday and move in this task daily to obtain your goal. Take specific steps everyday and create the habit to acquire your dreams. If you miss a day, start again; never give up! These three principles alone will accelerate your becoming and transform you almost without effort once you make these habits a part of who you are. And lastly, carry a copy of Think and Grow Rich with you at all possible times and read it everyday. Follow this practice and you will marvel at how incredibly your life will change. In order for the world to change, you must change. Work harder on yourself and your mind will expand. I know that this is one of my mantras and is part of what keeps me growing and learning every day.

When I was younger, I was not yet conscious of these principles. I was full of hope and optimism and I believed that I knew everything there was to know. I believed that my purpose was to create a successful business, not to attract the money and energy of like-minded people. I worked hard to achieve something I had not yet truly understood. I hope to explain how even though I was manifesting great success in my early twenties, I simply did not understand the great insights that Hill's Think and Grow Rich had to offer. I recall early in my real estate career (one of many careers) that success was coming so fast to me that I allowed my ego and the pre-programming of earlier paradigms to run my life. I was introduced to the recorded teachings of Earl Nightingale during my first mastermind meeting, and honestly, I had no idea who this man was. Once I started listening to this work about "attitude," I could feel a shift and the great knowledge coming upon me. I was opening my eyes indeed to the fact that there were great thinkers not only talking about meaning in life, but also how to control life through the practical understanding of our real power. It was s small shift into what others were projecting on to me, as well as the idea of what is truly possible through becoming and pursuing what we are created for. At that time, I felt that I learned that it is my world.

You've Got Nothing to Lose

I am not here to convince you to try something to improve yourself because I do not know what, if anything, you desire to improve. Perhaps you believe that there is nothing that needs improving since you find yourself perfect in that regard. Perhaps we don't even think about changing because we have been told to accept things for what they are. We follow the paradigms and patterns that our families and society have taught us. For example, in love we create the desire to be adored and loved by another. We can aptly describe the empty feeling we so perfectly feel when love eludes us. This common experience we tend to share with one another throughout life. This basic need of a human that we so desperately seek. Before we can create and be a purposeful success, we must answer the question: Who am I? Lacking an understanding of this and how to be creates another obstacle in the creative process of success. How to avoid or manage the distraction can be through the mindfulness of body and mind.

Breathing and Meditation

Among the things I have learned is that each of us has challenges, either perceived in our minds or as real as a train running off its tracks taking us out on our way to work. Challenges arise and need to be addressed; how it is that we choose to address them, that's the rub. That's the challenge. I have in the past found myself speechless but often able to come up with the words to meet the situation. The words have not always been the best, but they have gotten me through. A way that I know to assuage the challenge and refocus on creation is through breathing and meditation.

Meditation

Every challenge that we face brings with it tension causing resistance in whatever we are working towards. Learning to recognize tension or resistance is the first step toward releasing it and freeing yourself to pursue your best. Resistance shows up in the body in a variety of ways ~ tight muscles, a preoccupied mind, a rib cage that feels congested, a general feeling of holding on. All of these are indicators that your breathing is not flowing freely. When our breath doesn't flow, we get stuck in mental patterns that do not serve our highest good. This is part of the reason that meditation is so freeing to the mind ~ it moves energy around: we scan the body, increasing our awareness while enjoying deep expansive inhales and exhales.

How to Focus on Breathing

To bring myself into focus, I like to close my eyes and face directly inward, everything in my inner vision turning its focus on an orange glow. Inhale. Exhale. Scan the body. Inhale; relax the face. Exhale; let tension flow out on the breath. After a few rounds of this, it is remarkable how at ease the entire body becomes. Then the mind is cleared and connects through meditation and the Universe.

Cosmically, much is happening in our Universe. As is above, so below. Whether we acknowledge it or not, there is drama playing out in the energies that surround us. Daily, people are waking up with revelations and questions about how they have been living their lives. No doubt this is a process that takes time and practice to learn to navigate. The more we can learn to purposefully release tensions, the gentler this ride will be to our becoming who we are. We, in creating and realizing our purpose, are participating in the sacred.

Aren't most sacred things a little scary, at least in the beginning? Especially when they involve us living out our truth or searching for what we think is truth. Perhaps this is the alchemy of the heart, to take the scary things, our monsters under the bed, the opportunities life brings our way, the people who are converging and diverging along our path, the change that life's growing and dying and unfolding, and allow all of these things to be sacred. Imagination is the tool to creation and, whether you believe it can be accomplished or not, both will become true; it is in both your inner and outer world reflections. If you're paying attention, anyone can recognize the difference between doing something because you feel obligated to (for whatever reason ~ financial, personal obligations, etcetera) and doing something you deeply desire to do and doing it with an open mind. The focus engenders clarity that then creates an alignment between one's purpose and the Universe's abundance.

Visualization

Imagination is important when consciously trying to work with the Law of Attraction. I remember one time, before I knew of the abundance of money and all that the Universe has to offer, before I realized that the power to manifest those things I desire were present within me. I had unwittingly made use of the tenets of Think and Grow Rich. Someone I knew and viewed as being successful within my field at the time had offered me a ride. I agreed and we got into his Volvo 850, which I had seen many times before, unimpressed by its exterior. As I sat in the car, I cannot remember any of the conversation that we had as I was transfixed. I was enamored by the spacious interior, the sumptuous leather seats and the smooth ride. I couldn't believe this car. After I got out of it, I knew in my heart and mind that this was my next car. There was no doubt about it; I knew the color, the year, the mileage… and it was within weeks that I came across one in the newspaper that I purchased at the offering price. I enjoyed this car for a long time with my family and know that it was worth every penny. It seemed natural that I should have acquired and enjoyed this car. I knew nothing different from that. I knew what felt right and I trusted in it. It was natural because the Law of Attraction is a natural law.

Now, the acquisition of my dream car was a natural event. I had manifested it by being able to envision it and why and how I could see myself driving it. I call it natural because the Universe is what guided me, though I did not realize it at the time. I allowed myself to believe it was all me, not the subconscious in touch with the Universe me, but the Ego me that I was developing by watching many of the businessmen I came into contact with. There was the braggadocio of these men and it was infectious. This, I believe, was my first challenge that I came to face. It was my self. I am writing about this because I believe that this is the challenge that many of us fail to overcome. I recognize this trickster of an ego in me and now look to keep it at bay, not feed it.

The challenges we believe we face are the ones that come across as dangers, tragedies or traumas. More often than not they are brought on to us, rather than by us. Some may argue that we actually predispose ourselves to these situations. The outside challenges are ones that we unavoidably face because we are forced to face. They exist in every paradigm as a challenge. And we must acknowledge them, but we must certainly not be overtaken by the drama that they can demand and exact from us. When these strike, that's when the affirmations of gratitude and abundance come flowing like water out of our mouths. And it is not that we should not be aware of them; we should be cognizant of what is in our lives and the ever-present potential of creation in daily existence! It may be that when I am able to face the ego and conquer what it brings up in me, that I can become aware when a seemingly negative or bad thing occurs within life opening another door. The ego tricks us into complicating that which should be simple. I just want to shout out blame to the world when, in fact, the words of Viktor Frankl, on his time in the concentration camps in WWII can remind me that "Everything can be taken from a man but one thing: the last of the human freedoms—to choose one's attitude in any given set of circumstances, to choose one's own way." We choose to be and create our own purpose.

Seek Mastermind Groups and Hire Experts

I have also learned that while reading and writing by myself is beneficial, it is not the sole or best way to grow. It is important but I have realized that one cannot coach oneself effectively all the time and must see the value in masterminds and coaching from their mentors. Start with a coach- you will see a shift almost immediately. It's a challenge to look in the cosmic mirror and see our true selves. We are afraid to examine by ourselves what an honest other can show us.

First Pivot

Have you noticed that thinking about a thing we perceive as challenging or difficult usually seems a whole lot scarier than the actual performance of it? Remarkably, our anxiety seems to come before or after we have done what we thought we were so afraid of, not during the action itself. Every time we have the courage to do whatever that thing may be, we expand ourselves toward a new comfort zone, we are on our way to a new normal. But to fully arrive there, we must let go of the fear. Be open to the possibilities that change is offering us. It can be good, but only if we allow it. Being able to think clearly comes when the mind and body are in synch in pursuing and creating our purpose.

Health

While I find that Yoga is highly beneficial for the body, all physical practice is meant to aid in the focusing, cleaning and clearing of our thought processes and quieting the endless chatter and changing thoughts that can swirl incessantly in our heads. When the body is using and creating energy, the focus of the mind is able to enrich imagination by being in contact with the Universe. Yoga is quite simply about transcending the mind.

Part of my purpose has shown me that I want the challenge and the joy of my life to be in a space of sacred respect for all its glorious aspects. My heart knows what it feels like to be open. When I get too much into a negative vibration, then the opening comes with fear, reminding me to come to a standstill while I let the door swing completely open. Even tiny blips can echo across a valley, being heard and felt through its transformative power. Create your purpose, your true desire. The path will open and you will find energy throughout that will glow with the power of many lifetimes. Using imagination, you can sit and formulate goals and you will see pictures appear before your very eyes.

Think in the Now. I know that whatever I have been, wherever I am going, it is only being in this moment that gets me there. And worrying about whether or not the past has measured up or the right course is set for the future doesn't matter either. It is just my ego that thinks I should worry about having been or becoming anything at all. And when I let go of this seemingly third dimensional reality: illusion, I remind myself that it is a game. We are players, pawns, creators, gods, beings of light and dark. I am giving this all over to the Universe. I trust it conspires to bring me the true desires of my heart. May all of our lives be filled with a peaceful energy that leads us gently along the way. There is so much magic when one lets go. This is where freedom to live exists. Everything has a progression. Life doesn't manifest itself as a finished product. The starting place is the seed, the thought, the potential, and the idea that then needs to be nurtured in order to grow. So be grateful for the seeds and be patient with yourself. You need to give both room to grow and expand. I have discovered that life is full of whatever I "let in." Sometimes I'm conscious of it and sometimes I'm not. The goal is to keep expanding awareness of your state of being. You must see yourself through the eyes of the watcher. Whatever the 'thing' or obstacle is, you must make peace with it. You will discover what your purpose is when you are at most peace with your inner guiding system.

Peace is not a truce. Peace has no room for anger or resentment. This is why peace isn't easy, why sometimes we have to come to the end of ourselves, our ego, wear ourselves out with resistance to the 'thing' until there is nothing left, not even resistance. When every effort fails us, every turn thwarts our progression; anger has increased and can no longer be sustained, fatigue takes its place. Change seems absolutely beyond the realm of possibility. We break down. We give up. We stop caring and say to God, FINE, DO IT HOWEVER YOU WANT. There is always room to grow. So, recognize the fertile ground. Perseverance is not a quality of the faint of heart.

It is good to remind myself that I am not solely human. I am human and the truth is that under this facade of blood and bone wrapped up in a coating of skin, is a soul. This soul is well versed in lifetimes, not just here but here, there and everywhere. I don't know where it began or if it will ever end. But for the time being, here I am on planet earth, a 50 something male with a lot of questions about the Universe who tries his best to remember that this is temporary and we have a responsibility to reach our limit and our purpose. This is a journey, a play on a very convincing stage, but a play, none-the-less. Imagination is what allows us to understand and create the world we live in. Open your mind and your heart and you will see what you can be.

Tony Fevola| Bio

Tony Fevola, Entrepreneur and Branding Innovator

Tony Fevola stands at the forefront of the personal development trend, coaching and marketing services. He's spent the past 30 years evangelizing a shift to the positive thinking sector and has helped position many companies into big spaces.

A calculated risk-taker with deep experience and knowledge, Fevola has championed investments and services to his enterprise and consumer customers. His channel incentive models have motivated partners to embrace a positive attitude and is recognized for designing and branding businesses and leading the strategic strategies of partner Incentives programs for Enterprise Services.

Throughout his 30-year as an entrepreneur, Fevola has built a reputation for developing business strategies, incubating new business models, and building out channel programs.

Embracing the core values of integrity, innovation, and growth, Fevola consistently ranks among the top in creative Startups and branding. Tony Fevola is a successful businessman who has 30 years experience and worked in all areas of businesses, from starting several successful brick and mortar pizza delivery stores, also developing marketing and growing sales for each of them to consulting others in their fields. He has had the opportunity to work in sales achieving awards for his productivity and success. He has been an investor and developer in several companies. He has coached and consulted others on how to develop and grow their own businesses. He has created merchant websites and brand developing. He now utilizes his vast experiences and knowledge to consult and creatively market for his clients. You can reach him by email at tony@essenceOfProsperity.com

CHAPTER 21

You Can Do It If You Believe

By Nathan McCray

27 years ago, as a young man of 20, I married a beautiful, loving woman and started a family. People rarely plan out every aspect of their lives, but they will say they did in an attempt to seem as if they have it all together. We had nothing together, so we were pretty much flying by the seat of our pants. My Military Career started right out of High School. My Definiteness of Purpose was wrapped up in serving my country and retiring, everything that I had done mentally and physically up to that point had prepared me for military service. My JROTC class in high school prepared me well for a fast start, which would in my mind lead to an illustrious end to my military career with a chest full of medals! I met the love of my life Pam at Walt Disney World just before leaving for basic training. Love is a powerful thing because it has always been the foundation of our relationship. Fast forward three months later, I found myself trying to figure out how we could be together, where there's a will there's a way right? Pam transferred from a University in New Jersey down to an all-female college in Texas, closer to me of course. We started dating, I proposed, and two months later we were married. A year later we had our first daughter, Briana. She was all that we had imagined she would be; she was beautiful, smart and funny, but very, very talkative! We had fun trying to imagine what she would be in life. You could imagine that this was quite the shock to our little Love duo because now there were 3. I was in the Military with a meager military salary. Pam worked small jobs for a lot less than she was accustomed to.

It started to become apparent that if we wanted more we were going to have to earn more, but how? As many couples do in life, we confined our aspirations to what the system told us we could have. Since I was in the Military and clearly not doing anything different for at least three more years, I could only hope to increase my pay grade. Pam could be a bit more creative on the other hand; she could finish school, or learn a trade. There were so many things running through my head that needed to be in place so that my girls had all that they needed and most of what they wanted.

Over the next seven years, we took on the world together, trying to defy the odds and make an amazing life for our family. In that seven-year time span, a lot happened and the 3rd year of my military career proved to be the most challenging. Rumors of war became the reality of war. I found myself leaving my family behind to fight a war in a foreign land. At this point, like many others, I found myself questioning my decision to serve. Operation Desert Storm was a pivotal time in my life. That War taught me that life is short, it taught me that things aren't always as they seem on the outside, and most importantly it taught me that Life was valuable! It was there in the deserts of the Middle East that I made my decision to end my military career. The timing could not have been better because I was quickly approaching my re-enlistment date. The stress point at that time was getting back on US soil before I was forced to re-enlist during a wartime situation, which would give me six more years of service. I began to pray for the war to end quickly and my prayers were answered! The war was over, and I was back on US soil exactly 32 days before my ETS date, 30 of which was needed to process out of the military. The next 30 days were exciting and somewhat scary for me because I was starting a new chapter in my life.

The next couple of years were absorbing. With a Major in Search and Destroy and a minor in Communications, I had to find work related to my military training, which I knew would not be easy. I tried several things to make ends meet, none of which were reflections on my military training. One moment I was an exterminator conquering the insect and rodent population, the next I was a factory worker pulling bread and frozen items. I even tried my hand at dock work, loading and unloading trucks saddled atop of a diesel forklift! Search and destroy didn't seem so bad all of a sudden. Shortly after that came my introduction to Wireless Network Engineering by my brother in law. He put me in front of his OPS manager and said the rest is up to you. At this point, I knew that I needed to show and assemble an attractive personality that showed my positive mental attitude if I was to land this job. I didn't have much experience in this field, so I needed to give the person sitting in front of me a great experience during this interview, so that's what I did. He realized that he was talking to someone that wasn't as qualified as his typical applicants, but he was talking to someone with enough drive, personality and aptitude to by far exceed his expectations of his best employee. He gave me the job based on what I offered to learn and do as opposed to what I already knew and had done. It was at that moment that I started my career in Engineering. I did all that I pledged to do. I was exceeding all expectations, and I kept my humility and integrity intact. I always remembered and thanked those that have helped me and gave me the opportunities to excel. My Engineering career took off from there. I was able to command my wage because I was in demand. Not my skill set, but my Positive Mental Attitude, my Enthusiasm, and my Pleasing Personality. Things were finally looking up, and I felt like I was finally in control. Success to me has never been measured by the amount of money I can make, but by the number of people I can influence! Shortly after my start in Engineering we were introduced to the industry of Network Marketing and all of its glory. I heard the statistic that this industry had created more millionaires than any other industry in the world. It was at that time, at the beginning of my 20-year timespan as an Engineer that started my Mastermind Alliance with my wife, Pam. Our mindset was crystal clear and unshakable. If millionaires were abundant, then we would be a part of that statistic. We started dreaming about having more and becoming more, thinking outside the box. We began to realize that there was much more space outside of the box than inside of the box! It was at this moment at 25 years of age that we started to become psychologically unemployable. A tricky place to be in when you are working a job that's needed, and you know that there's something else out there that can get you out of the box, you have to be strategic in your actions. I quite frequently reference the movie The Matrix, contrasting how NEO felt while he plugged into the Matrix. He knew there was something out there calling for him to step outside of the box. He couldn't let everyone around him know because then he would be kicked out of the comfy box. General perception says that life outside of the box is hard, but if you can take the hits and keep getting back up the rewards are plentiful! So the trick for me was to work the job from 9 to 5 and work on our dreams from 5 to 9. The most important part of the mastermind plan was to allow my wife to explore all that the industry of Network Marketing had to offer full time. The idea was simple but would require some sacrifice; the sacrifice of living as a one-income family. The sacrifice was short term for a long-term gain. The very first opportunity that we were introduced to was in the Telecom industry. As you can imagine, with my background in communications, this was right in my wheelhouse! Like everyone else, we just knew that this was it, but we quickly realized that it wasn't. There were at least 14 other companies that we were a part of and they all contributed to our growth. I don't believe in bad mouthing other companies, specifically because I don't like playing the blame game. I have learned to take full responsibility for everything that I do or allow in my life. We have always believed that Failure and Success creates growth. Is failing hard, yes, until you adopt the Positive Mental Attitude that nothing happens to you, it all happens for you! Over that 20-year timespan, we encountered a lot of failures, not always easy to swallow, but growth happens. So we had a lot of opportunities to grow over the years. The reality is that we were and still are in our process, and we hadn't created the right equation for financial success. Even now, we are still in our process because there is so much more in store for us. We needed the right connections, the right company, the right products, the right compensation plan; all tied together with the right Mindset of Belief, Passion, and Consistency. This equation is what would allow us to be a part of the Network Marketing Millionaire Club! We knew that Creativity creates momentum, which creates excitement, which yields income! How would we pull all of that together and when?

There came that moment in my life where a sense of uneasiness set in because I knew we were living paycheck to paycheck, and more importantly I started to face the fact that we were slowly drowning in debt. I could no longer command my wage because the industry had become so saturated that my employers had their choice of individuals with the same skill set that did not demand their worth. I was no longer the hot Engineer with all of the answers because I could no longer thrive or recreate myself inside of that box because of my mental state. We decided to create our box, a box that would allow us to step out in faith and do something different, something drastic. We decided to pack everything that we could carry in the SUV and start fresh and new in Miami Florida. We only knew one person there, and that was our friend Stormy Wellington. We were working with her on another opportunity at that time, and it seemed very promising, and we were excited about our future with this company! We liquidated all that we could, 401K, checking & savings and struck out for Miami. We visited my parents for a few days, telling them we were moving to Miami and we had it all figured out. The kids were excited because it was the McCray family adventure to them, so it was all smiles for fast food and games on the trip. We planted our flag on a vacation rental there and went to work on this new opportunity. I was doing project management at that time so that I could work from anywhere. The money wasn't what it used to be, but it was money. Six months into that opportunity is when I received the news that my contract was ending and there was nothing else available! I got that nauseating feeling in my stomach, and I realized that this could get bad really quickly. There was no severance, no check in the hole, no 2-week notice, the money just stopped!

I have always heard the old saying, when life gives you lemons make lemonade or, when you get knocked down if you can look up you can get up, or keep smiling through it all! These sayings are easy to say and good to hear but are often challenging to live! We all talk about humility and how we want to stay humble through different situations in our lives. Seldom do we look forward to being called on it the way that I was. I didn't realize the level of humility I would need to bridge this enormous gap. My choices were sink or swim! Something happens to you every time you move out of your comfort zone; you find a new and more focused kind of Strength, Belief, and Passion! I no longer had the luxury of working on my dreams part time. I was forced to shift into a full-time mode. I asked myself, how, what, when, where and why! Well, the why was apparent, we needed the necessities, food, shelter and clothing. The remainder of the questions answered themselves in a very nontraditional fashion. The old saying is, "If you want something different you have to do something different." Everything in me said to reach out and get another contract somewhere else, which would mean me going back on the road again, away from my family! If we were going to get ahead, my different would require me to shift into a mode somewhat unfamiliar to me! Pam and her good friend Stormy Wellington had been introduced to an opportunity with a company called Total

Life Changes, How fitting is that name? My decision was not to take another contract; I needed to invest in Pam since she was passionate about the products. I thought, just like all of the other times, who knows, maybe this is the one. After all of the other Network Marketing companies and no success, what made this company any different? I didn't know, but I was a sucker for her level of belief and passion! I wasn't sure at that moment, but I knew that we both couldn't go all in on it, the kids would suffer even more, and they didn't deserve that. I believed that something would happen. I didn't know what or when, but I had nothing to lose at that moment. It was rarely in the cards financially for both of us to travel and attend events, since I was working most of the time. Pam would attend the events and bring the excitement back home. There were times that I didn't feel the excitement because an event is something that you have to feel in person, but I still believed in what the industry offered! One of us had to hold down the fort on this one. My investment would initially mean me understanding the statistic that Network Marketing is dominated 86% by women. My plan was to free Pam up to do whatever she needed to do to make the biggest impact in the shortest period possible. I realized that this was the short-term sacrifice for a long-term gain phase for me. I took on a lot of the household duties, anything that she didn't have the time to do, I made sure it was taken care of it. That following month the vacation rental skyrocketed and we found ourselves homeless, and having to move in with Stormy. She welcomed us with open arms, and she could identify with us because she was going through the same thing at that very moment in life as well. Here's where the rubber meets the road I thought. We are staying in one bedroom of the house with my entire family. Things were tight, but the atmosphere was right for a comeback! I felt like the movie 300. This is where we stand. This is where we fight! Take from them everything but give them nothing, lol. I started thinking about all of the people that said No to us, and all of the people that laughed and said what now! All of the people that said we were crazy! It is the moment of truth, and it was now or never, sink or swim! For the next six weeks Pam dug in with TLC, and I continued to job search. I also began to make small investments that could yield us some return. We were in quick money mode, and we were both scrambling to make whatever we could work. At the six-week point we were financially able to get a very small three-bedroom apartment. Humility made it hard to remember the seven-bedroom home that we left in Atlanta. At this point, the tiny apartment felt like a mansion! A few weeks later in Houston, TX Pam was recognized for earning 22k. I started to think to myself that something was working this time around, what was different? After that event it happened. Everything ramped up to 100 quickly; it was like suddenly turning the radio all the way up! People heard about the tea and they wanted it, they also wanted to sell it and build a team around it. Momentum was high, and marketing was constant. I noticed the income increasing significantly every week! Over the next 4 months, our lives changed, with a monthly income of 50k plus, but my job situation had not. I began to think about working the business full-time with Pam, so I asked her what she thought about it. She was all for it. It was what we had visualized for a very long time. We talked about how we would do it. We thought about the scripture that says if one can put a thousand to flight, then two could put ten thousand to flight. We received confirmation in Atlanta GA. The VP of sales Mr. Kenny Lloyd said it was time for me to plug in. I had an opportunity to speak on stage about our journey and how proud I was of my wife! She had earned $250,000 in 7 months! I wanted to let her know on that stage in front of everyone how amazing she was, and that I would be locking arms to help her build our legacy! I will always remember that day because, through the tears and smiles, our long-term dreams started to come true on that stage in Atlanta GA. We finally had the opportunity to build a business together. Our team continued to grow, and five months later we hit the $500,000 mark. The team expanded even more, and seven months after that we hit the $1,000,000 mark, a milestone that we had always dreamed and believed would one day happen. We were always confident enough to know that we would someday become millionaires, but never imagined it would happen in just 17 short months! We understood that it would not just take practicing some of Napoleon Hill's 17 Principles of Success, but it would require the application of all 17. I will leave you with my favorite Principle of Success. Applied Faith is an active state of mind. That belief in yourself is applied to achieve a definite major purpose in life. You can do it if you believe you can!

Nathan McCray | Bio

Nathan McCray is a family man, a husband, a Military Veteran, a retired corporate Engineer, and a seasoned Network Marketing leader. He is a Father of 4, and has one grandson. Nathan served his country during Operation Desert Storm. He is a decorated combat veteran with leadership, communication and combat skills. His contributions to his country were abundant, and he committed himself to serving. His contributions to his family are Loved and revered. His contributions to corporate America were respected and sought after. He has led teams of soldiers in domestic and foreign lands to protect and secure that which we hold dear. He has led teams of Engineers that have designed some of the most complex networks in the country. His mantra is "Leadership through Integrity and Humility creates sustainability" One of his passions is coaching individuals on what it takes to survive and thrive in each life lesson. He believes that if a person has the desire, self-motivation and drive, they can have everything that they are destined for Spiritually, Physically and Financially. His personal belief is that the first half of his life was preparation for a prosperous 2nd half. His philosophy is simple, If a person is to live life limitlessly, they must first believe in themselves enough to tap into the power within that propels them towards that opportunity!

Nathan can be reached at:

nathanmccray1@gmail.com

IG: nathanmccray1

FB: Nathan McCray

CHAPTER 22

An Open Letter To A Friend

By Jim Shorkey

How would you like to acquire more riches than you ever dreamed possible, way beyond your wildest expectations? How cool would that be?

I want you to think about that word — riches. When you do think about riches, what pops into your mind? Please give this much thought. Write down every single idea you have pertaining to riches. Do you see your dream home? Are you walking down the aisle toward the person you love? Have you achieved the body of your dreams? Describe what riches look like to you. This word means something different to each individual. What do you really, really, really want? Where do you really, really, really want to go? And, most importantly, why do you want this? What advantages will you enjoy as a result of achieving your goal? This is your process and your process only.

Please allow me to share with you what the word riches means to me. After giving this much thought, I have grown to realize that in order to be rich I must have great health, great wealth, great love, great happiness, and great spirit. I am a rich person when I live my life with each of these factors in balance. This is a top priority for me. My approach to every single day of my life includes placing equal emphasis on each one of these five desires:

1. Great Health – I choose my healthy lifestyle in terms of proper diet, regular exercise, and positive thinking. Each of these factors combine to help me choose the best possible strategies in order to age successfully. My worthwhile goal is to live 122 healthy years! A woman in France has done this, therefore, I can do this as well.

2. Great Wealth – I am creating abundance in my life so that I can always pay my way and do what I desire to do when I desire to do it. I have specific, definite and worthwhile goals in this area.

3. Great Love – This area of my life is my "why" for each one of my worthwhile goals. Family, friends and romance — if I fail here, I

fail everywhere. This will not happen! This desire is always front and center for me. Like my desire to create great wealth, I have specific, definite and worthwhile goals for family, friends and romance in my life.

4. Great Happiness – Fulfillment. That is the best and only way to describe this desire. I am doing something that is way bigger than me, and this brings me great happiness and joy. My desire is to coach people into identifying and achieving their worthwhile goals. When an individual follows my proven formula for successful living, amazing results always happen. How cool is that? And, believe me, anybody can do this. It is a formula! Like each area of my life, I have specific, definite and worthwhile goals for great happiness as well.

5. Great Spirit – Enthusiasm, zest and passion. This is my approach to every aspect of my life, every day, all day long. I choose to make each day a great day — no matter what. Consequently, I have great experiences every single day. This is amazing to me. Great spirit is my philosophy as opposed to being my goal. Maintaining my spirit has a direct impact on my health, wealth, love and happiness. This is the glue that holds these four together. No doubt about it!

I am certainly a work in progress. I make a conscious effort to improve myself step by step on an everyday basis within each of these five desires. My goal is progression, not perfection! I am paying the price. I have much work to do, but I am so happy and grateful for this opportunity. I will continue to improve myself for the next 63 years — I promise! This balanced philosophy makes me a rich person, and I will become even richer going forward. How exciting is that? You can do the same thing. I am no one special. I am simply following a proven formula for successful living. Obviously, you can do this as well. Do you believe you can? Are you ready? Let us get started.

We are about to embark on a journey where I will teach you my proven formula for successful living. I will do my part, but you must do your part and it is simple: be willing to learn! Are you coachable?

Please allow me to show you how I do this. My goal is to teach you how to be more successful, how to create great riches in your life. Remember, you must define what riches mean to you. Is it money? I will show you how to create a lot of money. What do you think about that? Is it passion for life? I will teach you how to ignite your spirit. Would you agree with me that it is way more challenging to live your life unsuccessfully versus living your life successfully? Living your life unsuccessfully has harsh consequences. These consequences are tough to live with. Living your life successfully has great rewards, and these rewards are fun — lots of fun! And, are pleasures to live with. Think about this for a moment. Do you think I am right?

Now, to be clear, successful living does require self-discipline and a great plan. You must pay the price — hard work. No free lunches here! This is not an entitlement program, nor is this a get rich quick scheme. The world does not owe you a thing. You must earn your riches! Here is the best news: You can learn the self-discipline required to take these steps because I am giving you my plan to do just that. Therefore, you can learn how to live your life successfully as well. Believe me; it is my personal experience that it is way easier for me to live my life successfully. Living my life unsuccessfully was dreadful. There is no way that I will ever go back to that. You must follow my proven formula for successful living. You can do this! Are you ready?

Please stop here, pause, take a break and think about this: Are you ready? Are you sick and tired of being sick and tired? Tired of your present lifestyle? Disgusted with your current results? Frustrated? Feeling overwhelmed by doom and gloom? If you are, then the answer is a resounding YES! You are ready to learn a much better way of living! When you implement my proven formula for successful living, you will be amazed at your new results. Results are always the name of the game. The rules are simple: good actions produce good results, and bad actions produce bad results. If you are not happy with your results, you must go back and study your actions. To change your results, you must change your actions. However, more importantly, in order to change your actions, you must change your thinking. Everything begins with your thinking!

You must implement my proven formula for successful living 100% and with zero deviations — every single detail! I am serious about this. This is how you are going to pay the price for everything that you want. You can have it all! You can become the person you desire to become. You really can! But you must want this really bad, even more than you want to breathe! Yougottawanna! (We will learn more about this later!) Now one more time: Are you ready?

Ralph Waldo Emerson said, "A man is what he thinks about all day long." What if this was true? I am here to tell you: This is true! This is a universal law. You must control your thinking. When you control your thinking, you will control your life. "You become what you think about all day long." When you think positive thoughts, you will create positive results in your life. When you think negative thoughts, you will create negative results in your life. It really is that simple. You become what you think about, so use caution! You and I are the creators of the results in our respective lives; you must believe this. Again, results are always the name of the game. Are you happy with your results? Are you ready to make the necessary changes on your part to create improved results? This is not easy, but it is doable, and you need to do this!

You must be inner-directed. In my early days, I was outer-directed. I was the king of playing the blame game — a real pro! Bad results were seldom my fault; mostly somebody or something other than myself was to blame. I was arrogant! Now I am primarily inner-directed. I take full responsibility for all results in my life, good or bad. No, I cannot control my grumpy next-door neighbor, but I can control how I respond to my grumpy neighbor. With this state of mind, I get great results. You can as well. When I experience a bad result, I always look for what part I played in creating it. If this bad result is outside of my control, then I do not concern myself with it. I simply dismiss it. I only control my response – I control the "controllables." Think about that. By the way, my state of mind is one of my controllables. I must control my thinking and you must control yours!

So, what can you do to create better results? Remember, when you are inner- directed, you are always in control of your life. When you are outer-directed, somebody or something else is in control of your life. I find this to be unacceptable. Your choice! I am in control of my life, and I love it that way. If you're not, you need to give it a try. You will appreciate it!

I want to share with you three of my favorite quotes. These quotes describe very well the idea of what I am writing here. I keep these three quotes in front of me at all times. I must continually remind myself of the importance of this message. I believe in these quotes with all my heart, and I live my life with the philosophy behind them. Please read these several times before moving on — they are powerful!

"People are always blaming their circumstances for what they are. I don't believe in circumstances. The people who get on in this world are the people who get up and look for the circumstances they want, and if they can't find them, make them."

— George Bernard Shaw

"The first and best victory is to conquer self. To be conquered by self is, of all things, the most shameful and vile."

— Plato

"Whether you think you can or think you can't – you are right."

— Henry Ford

I am in control of my thinking, and this is one method I utilize to accomplish this. I have each quote memorized, and I often repeat each one out loud. I also read and write them to help rewire my brain. Mind control! You must take possession of your own mind and direct it to ends of your own choice. You must! You must! You must! This is the secret of living a successful life. "You become what you think about all day long." Think about this! Now is the perfect time for you to form a new habit, assuming you really want to do so. Do you? I think you do. But you must be ready!

I want you to concentrate on the next 47 days. Your mind will think only the thoughts you allow it. You are in control for 47 days and it is time to form a new habit! You must maintain a healthy, optimistic state of mind. This requires willpower, which is self-mastery, self-control and self-discipline. Please go back and read the three quotes several more times, right now. Allow them to sink into your mind. 47 days to change your life! This will also require persistence, which is ceaselessness and tenacity. When you combine willpower and persistence toward the step-by-step achievement of your worthwhile goal, your results will shock you. This works for me every single time.

If I can do this, you can do this! "You become what you think about" is something to keep in mind, as you need to think positive thoughts exclusively for the next 47 days. NO STINKING THINKING! How simple is that? You cannot give in to negative thinking. Shut down all negative thoughts, one thought at a time. Step by step! You will improve one day at a time. Do we have a deal? Do you accept my 47-day challenge?

Next, let us discuss your worthwhile goals. People with worthwhile goals succeed because they know their final destination before they begin their journey. Think about the navigation system in a car. I used the one in my car today — I love it! I am amazed every time I use it and it leads me to my destination. What a cool system! What do you really, really, really want? Where do you really, really, really want to go? Type this information into your navigation system and it will guide you to your destination — every time!

Program your worthwhile goal into your mind (just like your navigation system). Visualize your worthwhile goal, including several pictures and reminders about your goals. You must keep your worthwhile goal in front of you as much as possible during the next 47 days. Make sure your goal is specific and clearly defined. This is really important! (Again, think navigation!) You are a successful person because you are achieving your worthwhile goal, step by step. One day at a time, one step at a time for 47 days. Your journey begins today — it always does!

So, what makes a goal worthwhile? Is it ethical? Is it beneficial to humanity? How will it impact the environment? Are you proud of your step-by-step actions in achieving your worthwhile goal? Put your goal through your own filters. You will know what feels right and what doesn't. Do not confuse this validity check with your comfort zone. Change of any kind is challenging, and you will not feel comfortable if your goals are worthwhile because they are found outside of your comfort zone. It may even be scary! If your goal feels right, you need to fight through your comfort zone. Just know that fear, worry, and anxiety will appear, but you must fight through this scariness to achieve your goals.

Your returns in life will be in direct proportion to the quality and quantity of your service and the spirit (enthusiasm, zest and passion) with which you deliver that service. This is another law: give, give, give! The more you give, the more you get back. You must give first AND with no thoughts about what you are going to receive. Focus on giving only — quality, quantity, and spirit — during the next 47 days. Do your very best, better than you have ever done in the past and watch what happens. Higher service yields higher returns; lower service yields lower returns. You cannot circumvent this law. When you provide excellent service, you will enjoy prosperity in all areas of your life — health, wealth, love, happiness and spirit. But do beware! The law works in both directions! Balance is essential. Go the extra mile and you will prosper!

Lastly, you must have a great plan. Napoleon Hill states, "You must have plans which are faultless." Please allow me to share my great plan with you. This is my step- by-step process that I use to achieve my worthwhile goals. This works for me every single time and in each of the five areas of my life. I have tested this formula for 23 years — it works! This is my proven formula for successful living:

1. Set a definite worthwhile goal for yourself.

You are the creator. Stop worrying about what others think, do or say. This is none of your business. Stop thinking of competition and think creation! Focus on what you really, really, really want and where you really, really, really want to go. Write your worthwhile goal down on a 3x5 index card. You must be specific and definite. This is essential!

2. Why do you want to achieve your worthwhile goal?

What is in it for you? What are the advantages that you will enjoy when you achieve this goal? Write your advantages down on the back of the 3x5 index card. These advantages are your reasons 'why.' Again, this is another essential part of achieving your goals.

3. Your goal card.

You now have a tool that you must carry with you at all times. On one side you have your worthwhile goals; on the other are your advantages, your reasons why. Carry this with you always and review it several times daily for the next 47 days. This is a must to turn the image of exactly what you want into reality! You can do this! I know you can!

4. Develop your plan.

What are the specific action steps you are going to take to achieve your goal? Seek expert counsel during this process. This is a shortcut to riches. Write down each of your action steps on a separate 3x5 index card, using both sides if necessary. Keep this second card with the first and review it often throughout the day. This will keep you accountable. You must stick with your plan and execute your action plan step by step!

5. Action.

Get into action now! Every day for 47 days and then even longer! You must take action. No procrastination! Your ideas are of no value until you act on them. This is the biggest hang-up for many people. You must get into action right now!

6. Persistence.

This is ceaselessness and tenacity. Og Mandino wrote an awesome book called The Greatest Salesman in the World. Please read the section titled, "The Scroll Marked III – I will persist until I succeed." You can find this on the Internet for free. Great stuff! I have repeated this affirmation out loud thousands of times over the years: "I will persist until I succeed!" Doing this has always been and continues to be most helpful to me. Form a new habit by repeating affirmations. You will be glad you did!

I also want to refer you to *Think and Grow Rich* by Napoleon Hill. This is my favorite book. This is such great advice about persistence by Hill:

From the section, "*How to Develop Persistence*" the necessary steps are:

1. A definite purpose backed by a burning desire for its fulfillment.
2. A definite plan, expressed in continuous action.
3. A mind closed tightly against all negative and discouraging influences, including negative suggestions by relatives, friends and acquaintances.
4. A friendly alliance with one or more persons who will encourage one to follow through with both plan and purpose.

These four steps are essential for success in all walks of life. The entire purpose of the thirteen principles of this philosophy is to enable one to take these four steps as a matter of habit. More from *Think and Grow Rich*:

These are the steps by which one may control one's economic destiny.

They are the steps that lead to freedom and independence of thought.

They are the steps that lead to riches, in small or great quantities. They lead the way to power, fame, and worldly recognition.

They are the four steps, which guarantee favorable 'breaks.'

They are the steps that convert dreams into physical realities.

They lead, also, to the mastery of fear, discouragement, and indifference.

There is a magnificent reward for all who learn to take these four steps. It is the privilege of writing one's own ticket, and of making life yield whatever price is asked. Wow! That is impressive. I have read *Think and Grow Rich* 110 times to date. I have implemented Napoleon Hill's philosophy within my business, and the business moved from bankruptcy imminent to incredible prosperity in 12 years. I continue to apply this same philosophy in all five areas of my life — health, wealth, love, happiness and spirit. This works every single time. These four steps are a formula!

For this reason, *Think and Grow Rich* is an essential step in my proven formula for successful living — step by step. I am particularly great at copying successful people. I am a copycat and I believe I am more successful because of it. I do not have any interest in reinventing the wheel. So, I invite you to copy me! Read Napoleon Hill's book and use it as a guide as I did. This will help you stay on track. Pay close attention to the part on "developing persistence." For me, this is the most important section of the entire book. Execute the four steps mentioned above. Trust me — it works!

7. Willpower.

This is self-mastery, self-discipline and self-control. Please read Plato's quote out loud three more times:

"The first and best victory is to conquer self. To be conquered by self is, of all things, the most shameful and vile."

Read it several times per day, each day during the next 47 days. You must control your thinking. You must take possession of your own mind and direct it to ends of your own choice. You must! You must! You must! You do this one thought at a time: self-mastery, self-discipline and self-control. You must form a new habit! This takes time and effort. This is difficult. There will be setbacks — bingeing on Ben & Jerry's ice cream kind of setbacks! The key is to get back on track as soon as possible and to stay on track as long as possible. Over time, you will form a new habit. This requires persistence. How bad do you want to achieve your goal? Stop all negative self-talk. Stop beating yourself up. No more of this! You must have willpower.

8. Desire: Yougottawanna!

Keep this in front of you at all times during the next 47 days. Print it out as a banner to keep in front of you and as a small card to carry with you. I keep one in my wallet, I have one in my car and I use one as a bookmark. Remember when we talked about wanting something even more than you want to breathe? That is desire! You must desire your worthwhile goal more than air. As I write this, I am looking at my Yougottawanna cards. This is so helpful to me and it can be very beneficial to you as well. Place yours someplace where you will see it multiple times each day. Pound this message into your head. Desire! Yougottawanna! Start now.

9. Faith: Yesican!

I have this message on the back of my small "Yougottawanna" cards. I love this message. I must believe in me. I must believe I can do this. Yesican! You must believe in you. If I can do it, then you can do it. All of it! This is another sign that you must keep in front of you for the next 47 days. I am looking at this sign right now as I write this. I believe in you! I know you can do this. You have to have faith. Say "Yes I can" out loud twenty times each day for the next 47 days and see what happens! This will change your life! Will you do it?

Napoleon Hill writes, "Desire backed by faith knows no such word as impossible." I love this quote! Desire (Yougottawanna) backed by faith (Yesican) knows no such word as impossible. I know this is true! The question is, do you?

10. Accountability.

You must know your numbers. You must track your numbers. You must keep score and measure everything. 47 days! This is how you know if you are achieving your worthwhile goal. You must be answerable to yourself. It is difficult, however, it is very doable. You can do this! Face all issues head on. Keep willpower (self-mastery, self- discipline and self-control) and persistence (ceaselessness and tenacity) in the forefront of your mind. You must look yourself in the mirror and hold yourself accountable.

11. Adaptability.

You must be ready for the possibility of modifying your plan based on your accountability. Are you happy with your progress toward your worthwhile goal? If so, then proceed with your present plans. No? Then you must modify your plan. This is a shortcut to riches, but it requires humility. Keep it very, very, very humble. Seek expert counsel! Find an expert and copy, copy, copy! This is what I did, and I became incredibly successful. This is what I continue doing today. It works! How simple is that?

12. Seek Expert Counsel. Always!

If you are the smartest person in the room, then you are in the wrong room. Find an expert who has already achieved your worthwhile goal and copy them. You must seek out experts; people who write books, make recordings, organize Think Tanks and so forth. They are out there and want to share with you! The Internet is a great resource too. YouTube and Google are great places to start. Success always leaves clues. Seek expert counsel and copy, copy, copy! Just now, I went on the Internet and purchased two books. The Strangest Secret and Think and Grow Rich for $12.38, including shipping! Are you kidding me? These books are worth riches beyond your wildest dreams. What an incredible opportunity you and I have!

Do not forget to ask for help. Do not attempt to do this all by yourself. Your results will improve dramatically when you find an expert and copy him or her. You will also hit your worthwhile goal much quicker. Remember: Successful people always leave clues. Copy successful people!

13. Read inspirational books.

It is essential that you maintain a high level of inspiration and motivation during the next 47 days. This will help you develop the habit of doing it every day. I am currently reading two books: Think and Grow Rich by Napoleon Hill and The Strangest Secret by Earl Nightingale. There are audio and video recordings for each if you prefer those formats. I exclusively listen to The Strangest Secret when I am in my car. This is a habit I have formed. You must create a new habit of reading or listening to inspirational material. Rewiring your brain is critical to change — this is how you do it! Commit to reading ten pages each day for 47 days, and you will eventually have read each book at least one time. If that's easy enough, then try twenty pages each day. Self-discipline! These two books will positively help you achieve your goal. You must be inspired! Read this chapter often. You must continuously remind yourself of how important it is that you form a new habit. Note: I do this every single day!

14. The Creative Cycle.

This is a process where everything we have discussed comes together to create a powerful cycle. In short, decide what you really, really, really want? Then, decide where you really, really, really want to go? Establish that both of your outcomes are worthy goals. Next, determine why you are seeking this goal. Remember: What's in it for you? After you have determined the advantages of your worthy goal, it is time to develop your plan. What are the specific action steps you will take to achieve your goal? When you have determined your specific plan, it is time for a steady combination of persistence and expert counsel, as well as willpower. These tools will lead you into action where you can then analyze your results and decide if your plan is working. If so, then continue executing your formula and analyzing your results. If not, then be willing to adapt and adjust. Stay in The Creative Cycle and you will achieve your worthwhile goal. This works every single time! Form the habit now.

15. Mind Control.

For the next 47 days, you must control your thinking. You must take possession of your own mind and direct it to ends of your own choice. You must! You must! You must! I wanted to write this one more time. I wanted to say this one more time. Mind Control! I am rewiring my brain every day! This is powerful and is my secret to successful living. This is now your secret for successful living! Stop criticizing yourself, stop the negative self-talk and thinking about the reasons why you cannot achieve your worthwhile goal. 47 days! You will form a new, life-long habit. Mind control! Think about all the reasons you can. This is great stuff!

You must be super-vigilant with the following seven actions for the next 47 days. This is how you control your thinking! This is mind control in action. Consider these questions to help shape your worthwhile goal:

1. What are you reading? (Think and Grow Rich is a great start!)
2. What are you listening to? ("The Strangest Secret")
3. What are you watching? (Motivational videos for free — YouTube!)
4. What are you saying to yourself? (Affirmations and positive self-talk)
5. What are you writing? (Write out a description of the person you want to become. Read this out loud, with a lot of emotion, in front of the mirror for 47 days.)
6. What are your actions? (Follow your plan. Take action every day towards your worthwhile goals.)
7. Who are you hanging out with? (You are the sum of the five people you associate with most. If you want to be healthy, then hang out with healthy people.)

I want to tie this whole thing together with two great quotes by Albert Einstein — ultimate expert counsel!

"We can't solve problems by using the same kind
of thinking we used when we created them."
"Insanity: Doing the same thing over and over
again and expecting a different outcome."

And so, I implore you to do the following:

1. Follow every detail of my letter for 47 days.
2. Then, do it again for another 47 days.
3. Then, do it one more time for 47 more days. This will put you at almost five months. This is how you form a new habit! Step by step.
4. Repeat the above three steps forever! It works, and you must stay vigilant.
5. Once you develop this new habit, you will continue doing this for the rest of your life. That's how habits work! You will be following a proven formula for success — a blueprint for success!

You will enjoy prosperity and abundance beyond your wildest dreams. Riches? Whatever you really, really, really want! Wherever you really, really, really want to go! You will have it all! Riches are yours for the asking. This is creation, not competition. Ask, then follow the details of this chapter and watch what happens! This is what I did to achieve incredible success in my life. This is what I continue to do every single day. Health, wealth, love, happiness and spirit. You can do this as well! You know you can. I know you can! Start now!

Successful people always leave clues. I have left you a treasure map. Start today! 47 days! I believe in you! I wish you the very best. Your journey begins today — it always does!

Your good friend,

Jim Shorkey

P.S.

I have two additional success principles that must be viewed separately from the main body of the letter. These two must stand all by themselves. Without these two, the whole letter falls apart. This isn't extra credit — these are required!

1. Integrity: The quality of being honest and having strong moral principles; moral uprightness. You must have integrity! There is no compromising with this one!
2. Courage: The ability to do something that frightens one. Strength in the face of pain or grief. The content in this chapter requires great courage to execute. However, I want to go much deeper. I want to draw your attention to two more words:
   A. Discourage: Cause someone to lose confidence or enthusiasm.
   B. Encourage: To give support, confidence, or hope to someone.

Are you encouraging yourself or are you discouraging yourself? Your choice! You must have integrity and courage to make this work. I believe you can!

P.S.S.

If you are interested in receiving a digital, formatted design of YOUGOTTAWANNA, YESICAN, or The Creative Cycle, to print for yourself, or would like to receive a copy of this chapter, please send an email to info@resultsfromthinking.com.

Jim Shorkey | Bio

Jim Shorkey is a successful businessman who, in just over a decade, expanded his western Pennsylvania automotive dealership into a six dealership conglomerate, recently adding a seventh, that is consistently among the top performing companies, in any industry, in the region. Jim attributes his success to the skills he has learned from studying the lessons of the most successful people the world has ever known. These principles have not only helped Jim in the business sector but have helped to improve his personal life as well. Jim created his newest venture, Results From Thinking, for the sole purpose of sharing the formula for success that Jim himself followed while building his automotive empire. Jim's belief is that this formula is transferrable to anyone and any business. His informative and inspiring talks will take you through exactly what he did to turn his business from "bankruptcy imminent" to the profitable company that it is today and, through his programs, he will teach you the skills needed to reach this level of success in any area of your life. If you can tell Jim what you want, he can show you how to get there!

To learn more, visit:

www.ResultsfromThinking.com or you can email Jim directly at JimShorkey1957@gmail.com

Napoleon Hill Bio

NAPOLEON HILL
(1883-1970)

"Whatever your mind can conceive and believe
it can achieve."

— Napoleon Hill

American born Napoleon Hill is considered to have influenced more people into success than any other person in history. He has been perhaps the most influential man in the area of personal success technique development, primarily through his classic book Think and Grow Rich which has helped million of the people and has been important in the life of many successful people such as W. Clement Stone and Og Mandino.

Napoleon Hill was born into poverty in 1883 in a one-room cabin on the Pound River in Wise County, Virginia. At the age of 10 his mother died, and two years later his father remarried. He became a very rebellious boy, but grew up to be an incredible man. He began his writing career at age 13 as a "mountain reporter" for small town newspapers and went on to become America's most beloved motivational author. Fighting against all class of great disadvantages and pressures, he dedicated more than 25 years of his life to define the reasons by which so many people fail to achieve true financial success and happiness in their life.

During this time he achieved great success as an attorney and journalist. His early career as a reporter helped finance his way through law school. He was given an assignment to write a series of success stories of famous men, and his big break came when he was asked to interview steel-magnate Andrew Carnegie. Mr. Carnegie commissioned Hill to interview over 500 millionaires to find a success formula that could be used by the average person. These included Thomas Edison, Alexander Graham Bell, Henry Ford, Elmer Gates, Charles M. Schwab, Theodore Roosevelt, William Wrigley Jr, John Wanamaker, William Jennings Bryan, George Eastman, Woodrow Wilson, William H. Taft, John D. Rockefeller, F. W. Woolworth, Jennings Randolph, among others.

He became an advisor to Andrew Carnegie, and with Carnegie's help he formulated a philosophy of success, drawing on the thoughts and experience of a multitude of rags-to-riches tycoons. It took Hill over 20 years to produce his book, a classic in the Personal Development field called Think and Grow Rich. This book has sold over 7 million copies and has helped thousands achieve success. The secret to success is very simple but you'll have to read the book to find out what it is!

Napoleon Hill passed away in November 1970 after a long and successful career writing, teaching, and lecturing about the principles of success. His work stands as a monument to individual achievement and is the cornerstone of modern motivation. His book, Think and Grow Rich, is the all-time best seller in the field.

The Seventeen Principles

1. **Definiteness of Purpose**
2. **Mastermind Alliance**
3. **Applied Faith**
4. **Going the Extra Mile**
5. **Pleasing Personality**
6. **Personal Initiative**
7. **Positive Mental Attitude**
8. **Enthusiasm**
9. **Self-Discipline**
10. **Accurate Thinking**
11. **Controlled Attention**
12. **Teamwork**
13. **Learning from Adversity & Defeat**
14. **Creative Vision**
15. **Maintenance of Sound Health**
16. **Budgeting Time and Money**
17. **Cosmic Habitforce**

About Tom "too tall" Cunningham

Tom "too tall" Cunningham's God-given life purpose is to encourage and inspire people to live positively with and through life's obstacles and adversities.

He does that as a Napoleon Hill Foundation Certified Instructor, Founder of Journey To Success Radio, and creator of the Amazon International #1 Bestselling series of books, Journeys To Success.

Tom has lived with Juvenile Rheumatoid Arthritis from his jaw to his toes since the age of 5, 48 years now.

During that time, he has had 4 hips, 4 knees, and 2 shoulders replaced and been hospitalized about 40 times.

Despite his physical challenges, Tom always answers AMAZING when asked how he is doing. He tells people that 80% of the time it is true and the other 20% of the time it is to remind himself that it is true.

About Brad Szollose

Brad Szollose

(pronounced zol-us)

> *"...No one knows Millennials or cross-generational management better than Brad, and it shows; our attendees are still talking about his work."*

— Robbins Research International, Inc., a Tony Robbins Company

TEDx Speaker, award-winning business author and Web Pioneer Brad Szollose helps businesses and organizations dominate their industry by tapping into the treasure of a cross-generational workforce. Brad has been called The Millennial Whisperer, and his Liquid Leadership workshops show attendees how to ignite the power of their workforce and their customer base.

Brad is also a global business adviser and the foremost expert on Generational Issues and Workforce Engagement. His bestselling book, *Liquid Leadership: From Woodstock to Wikipedia*, shares Brad's journey beginning as a bootstrapped business idea in a coffee shop to C-level executive of a publicly traded company worth $26 million in just 24 short months; becoming the FIRST Internet Agency to go public in an IPO!

As a C-Suite Executive Brad applied his unique management style to a young, tech-savvy Generation X & Y Workforce producing great results; The company experienced 425% hyper-growth for 5 straight years with only 6% turnover. Brad's management model won K2 the Arthur Andersen NY Enterprise Award for Best Practices in Fostering Innovation Among Employees.

Today the world's leading business publications seek out Brad's insights on Millennials, and he has been featured in Forbes, The Huffington Post, New York Magazine, Inc., Advertising Age, The International Business Times, The Hindu Business Line and Le Journal du Dimanche to name a few, along with television, radio and podcast appearances on CBS and other media outlets.

Today Brad's programs have transformed a new generation of business leaders, helping them maximize their corporate culture, expectations, productivity, and sales growth in The Information Age.